THE BEATLES: IMAGE AND THE MEDIA

THE
BEATLES

IMAGE AND THE MEDIA

MICHAEL R. FRONTANI

UNIVERSITY PRESS OF MISSISSIPPI   JACKSON

www.upress.state.ms.us

The University Press of Mississippi is a member of the Association
of American University Presses.

Copyright © 2007 by University Press of Mississippi
All rights reserved

Manufactured in the United States of America
First edition 2007
∞
Library of Congress Cataloging-in-Publication Data

Frontani, Michael R.
The Beatles : image and the media / Michael R. Frontani. — 1st ed.
p. cm.
Includes bibliographical references and index.
ISBN-13: 978-1-57806-965-1 (cloth : alk. paper)
ISBN-10: 1-57806-965-3 (cloth : alk. paper)
ISBN-13: 978-1-57806-966-8 (pbk. : alk. paper)
ISBN-10: 1-57806-966-1 (pbk. : alk. paper) 1. Beatles. I. Title.
ML421.B4 F76
782.42166092'2—dc22

2006029326

British Library Cataloging-in-Publication Data available

For my "Fab Four,"
Heidi, Dante, Thelma, and Roy
With Love

CONTENTS

PREFACE

ON THE NIGHT OF DECEMBER 8, 1980, as John Lennon and his wife Yoko Ono returned to their New York City home from a recording session, a voice from the shadows called, "Mr. Lennon." As Lennon turned to face the speaker, Mark David Chapman pumped four bullets from his Charter Arms .38 caliber revolver into the musician's back and shoulder. "I'm shot!" gasped Lennon as he stumbled into the doorman's office. Chapman dropped his gun, which was quickly kicked aside by the doorman. "Do you know what you just did?" asked the doorman. "I just shot John Lennon," replied Chapman. Lennon was pronounced dead upon his arrival at Roosevelt Hospital, located fifteen blocks from Lennon's Dakota apartment ("Death of a Beatle" 35–36).

The death of Lennon set in motion a month of activities and commentaries honoring and remembering the fallen ex-Beatle. The night of the murder, mourners began to gather outside the wrought-iron gates of the Dakota apartment building in which Lennon and Ono had lived since 1973. By 1 a.m. the crowd had grown to five hundred (Ledbetter B7).[1] News of his death spread quickly around the world. According to the *Times* of London, "Sorrow over the loss of a prodigally talented musician is mixed with horror that, once again in America, an assassin has found it a matter of absurd simplicity to destroy a life at whim. In the immediate aftermath, the killing is being compared with the murder of President Kennedy in 1963, immediately prior to the Beatles' greatest success" (Leapman 1).

Radio stations all over America devoted airtime to Lennon and Beatle retrospectives. In Los Angeles more than 2,000 people took part in a candlelight vigil. In Washington, D.C., several hundred mourners gathered at the Lincoln Memorial for a silent tribute. Record stores across the country reported that the Lennons' new album, *Double Fantasy*, their first in five years, had sold out, as had other Lennon and Beatle albums ("Last Day in a Life" 18). At 2 p.m. EST on December 14, at the request of Yoko Ono, a ten-minute period of silence was observed around the world. At least 100,000 people gathered in New York City's Central Park, within sight of the Dakota, to observe the period of silence; 600 people gathered in Los Angeles' Griffith Park; 2,000 in Boston's Copley Square; and 4,000 at Chicago's Cricket Hill (Haberman B8). In Sydney, Australia, an observance was held at 6 a.m. to coincide with the period of silence. In Liverpool, England, where Lennon was born and raised, a memorial concert and candlelight vigil were held. Many radio stations in the United States, Europe, and Australia went off the air at the appointed time, while others aired commercial-free Lennon tributes (McFadden 43). Major magazines, among them *Time* and *Newsweek*, offered cover stories on the killing and its aftermath. Many viewed Lennon's death as a cruel end to all that had seemed possible in the idealized 1960s. As Anthony Elliott notes in *The Mourning of John Lennon* (1999), the death "provided the impetus for cultural mourning on a worldwide scale—mourning for lost dreams, ideals, hopes, beliefs" (152–53).

Yet, in the wake of Lennon's brutal murder, some commentators, far from eulogizing the man, perceived an opportunity to advance their cultural agenda. Lennon—who once declared the Beatles "more popular than Jesus," promoted the use of recreational drugs, and actively opposed the Vietnam War—was far from a favorite of the American Right. This became readily apparent as the conservative press attempted to transform eulogy into condemnation. Dorothy Rabinowitz, writing in *Commentary*, observed that the "spectacle attending Lennon's memorializing served primarily as the occasion . . . for a collective self-portrait of a generation whose faith in its own special stature may well be its principal distinction and sole enduring accomplishment." She proceeded: "In the absence of those political certainties which had once defined them and served as their chief moral credentials—certainties which had been discredited by subsequent events—all that remained to distinguish this particular generation were the ineffable qualities of 'feeling,' 'sensitivity,' 'openness,' 'awareness,' and so forth" (Rabinowitz 59). The mourning rituals "reevoked for a moment the atmosphere of the 60's: the cowed silence that once prevailed in the face of the ludicrous claims and pretensions of the 60's activists, not to mention their assaults, violent and otherwise, on free speech, mounted in the name of idealism" (60). For Rabinowitz, much of the public mourning, including the ten-minute silent vigil held on December 14 in Central Park, was just another example of the 1960s generation's penchant for "expressions bespeaking self-approbation" (Rabinowitz 60). Richard Brookhiser, senior editor for the *National Review*, in "John Lennon, RIP," appearing in the December 31, 1980, issue, noted, "Lennon and his friends influenced other things besides music, *mostly for the worse* [italics added]. They were not leftists—the lyrics of 'Revolution' refer sarcastically to Chairman Mao—but then, who in the sixties was?" He continues, "It is hard to think of a zany idea zipping through the ether which the Beatles, as cultural lightning rods, did not conduct—psychedelia, Maharishi Mahesh Fakir, all we are saying is give peace a chance" (Brookhiser 1555). Emblematic of comment from the Right, Brookhiser dismissed much of the sociocultural movement of the 1960s.

In death memorialized and vilified, Lennon meant different things to different people. But why? What was it about Lennon and the Beatles that made them such "lightning rods" for comment—

both positive and negative—ten years after the breakup of the band? These questions mark the starting point for my work on this book.

On the Beatles' 1967 recording, "Baby You're a Rich Man," Lennon asks the musical question, "How does it feel to be one of the beautiful people?" By 1967 the Beatles truly were "beautiful people," the band's image was radically different from that which was first introduced to the American public in late 1963. The image was inextricably bound to the time, and America had changed radically over the previous four years. Careful examination of that image provides insight not only into the history of the band, but also into the culture in which it developed. This book is a cultural history of the Beatles' image in the 1960s, based upon a close reading of American media texts contemporaneous to the Beatles' career in America, from late 1963 until the breakup of the band in 1970. My focus is on the Beatles' image and those texts from which the image was, and is, composed. This book aims to explain the transformation of the Beatles' image from that of teen idols, as they were portrayed in the earliest print media coverage of "Beatlemania,"[2] to cultural agents and leaders of the youth movement, as they were increasingly presented from the middle of the decade.

Over the years of researching and writing this book I have called upon so many people for advice, courting and exploiting their limitless patience. Whatever strengths this book may have are, I am sure, owed to these people who gave so freely of their time and minds. I owe a debt of gratitude to the faculty of the graduate program in Mass Communications at Ohio University, and to Dr. Joseph Slade, a mentor and friend. I am also grateful to the faculty of the graduate program in Critical Studies at the University of Southern California's School of Cinema and Television, in particular Professor Rick Jewell, for his insights and for introducing me to the fields of star theory and reception studies, and Professor David James. I also wish to thank the staffs of the libraries of those universities;

time and again they were able to locate documents that were essential to my research. I would like to thank the Faculty Research and Development Committee of Elon University, which provided funds for research and completion of the book, in the form of a travel grant and research fellowship. That travel grant was used to visit the Museum of Radio and Television in Manhattan, where I spent numerous hours going through their impressive collection of video and audio recordings from the 1960s and 1970s. The museum's staff was courteous and helpful and saved me countless hours with their advice on accessing their collection—thank you. I am also indebted to *American Journalism* for use of materials first appearing in the article, "'Beatlepeople': Gramsci, The Beatles, and Rolling Stone Magazine" (*American Journalism* 19.3 [Summer 2002]: 39–61).

I would like to thank the University Press of Mississippi, in particular its director Seetha Srinivasan, who first approached me about the project and provided advice, information, and, at times, motivation—and abundant patience. To the degree that this book is successful in its intended task, Seetha is to thank. Also, thanks to Walter Biggins for his invaluable help in guiding the manuscript through to publication, managing editor Anne Stascavage, and copy editor Will Rigby, for his detailed and insightful edit. A special debt of gratitude is due Douglas Kellner, George F. Kneller Philosophy of Education Chair in the Graduate School of Education at UCLA, for his invaluable criticism and advice throughout the writing of this book. Numerous friends and colleagues read various versions of chapters for the book: Appreciation is also due my colleagues at Elon University, including Michael Strickland, Director of Writing Across the Campus, who provided invaluable editorial advice as the book neared completion. Dr. Yoram Lubling, of the Department of Philosophy, and Dr. Kevin Boyle, of the Department of English, offered advice on early versions of a number of chapters. I am also indebted to Dean Paul Parsons, of the School of Communications, for his support of this project. Thanks go to Professor Jacob Dorn and Professor Carter Findley. Also, Dr. Robert Hislope, of Union College, provided invaluable advice and hours of conversation, dating back to our days in the graduate school at The Ohio State University. A special debt of gratitude goes to Roy Frontani and Heidi Frontani, who reviewed numerous versions of the manuscript. For the Brothers. Thanks to Jack, Gary, and Stephanie Lyn. Last, but certainly not least, my greatest appreciation is saved for my family, for my parents, and for my wife and son, Heidi and Dante. It may be a cliché, but it is nevertheless true—I could not have written this book without them. And, of course, thank you, John, Paul, George, and Ringo.

Michael R. Frontani

THE BEATLES: IMAGE AND THE MEDIA

ONE

"The Twentieth Century's Greatest Romance"
Imagining the Beatles

MANY BABY BOOMERS COULD RECITE the facts of how a group of working class kids lived their own rags-to-riches story, rising from the tough northern English port city of Liverpool to enjoy the greatest commercial success ever witnessed in the history of popular music. They could tell how these four lads—John, Paul, George, and Ringo—affected everything from hairstyles to philosophies. In fact, many children (and grandchildren) of baby boomers could tell you the basic story. Many more could deliver a favorite lyric or two. The Beatles remain successful nearly four decades after their breakup, and they continue to send recordings to the top of the charts. Undoubtedly this can be partly explained by their celebrated songbook. But, surely, other bands and entertainers from the 1960s have well-thought-of music catalogs. With the Beatles, however, there is something extra. People continue to be fascinated by the four young men behind the music, and for many the Beatles resonate with those times as no other phenomenon or icon. Better, the Beatles' *image* resonates with a youthful and halcyon ideal of those times. This book concerns that image and its evolution from teen idol vacuity to countercultural ideal and takes a chronological approach in answering the following questions: How were the Beatles depicted over time in the mainstream press? How did their image evolve? How did the evolution of the Beatles' image interact with cultural and historical processes and events? Finally, how were the different

I

aspects of the Beatles' image incorporated into American culture with regard to lifestyle and world view?[1]

The Beatles arrived in an America in the midst of great change. It was an America on the verge of events that would highlight divisions of age, race, gender, and class. And it was an America on the brink of a conflict that would have repercussions upon America's foreign policy, international reputation, and national conscience for decades to come. How best, then, to capture these times and the place of the Beatles' image in contemporaneous American culture? For this study, American mainstream media are the primary sources, for it is through these media, these various industries and companies competing in the marketplace, that the image is defined for the public. I have focused my research on the most widely circulated presentations of the image, found in the mainstream press, on the national television networks, in film, and on sound recordings.

The *New York Times* was chosen for analysis because of its reputation and its position as a major media gatekeeper. For the years under consideration, 1963–70, few American newspapers were as renowned for their thoroughness and independence or as influential in defining what was newsworthy. More importantly, the *New York Times* was widely read by other journalists (*Whole World* 299); as such, the *Times'* detailed coverage of the Beatles was influential in shaping coverage by other media outlets, particularly during the band's first visit to the U.S. and throughout the touring years, 1964–66. Other sources, among them *Time, Life, Newsweek, Look,* and *Seventeen*, were analyzed as outlets for widely circulated images of the Beatles; before the advent of the rock press, these publications provided the most detailed and widely distributed representations of the image. For the period under consideration, these publications were among those magazines having the greatest number of readers (Daniel Starch 2–20). *Rolling Stone's* presentation of the Beatles is described in detail. It was the most successful and influential of the rock and roll publications founded in the 1960s, expanding beyond a dedicated countercultural readership to become a respected monitor of youth culture. While competitors such as *Crawdaddy!*, *Cheetah*, and *Eye* struggled and ultimately went out of business, *Rolling Stone*'s circulation continued to grow. It became the rock and roll publication with the most currency among the youth of the period and one of the most important vehicles for creation and transmission of the Beatles' and other performers' images. The sources for this study present a thorough time capsule of the evolving image; they also present a window on the zeitgeist of the culture for which the image had so much meaning.

For our purpose, *image* refers to the vehicle by which audiences know the Beatles. A complex media construct arising and evolving over the span of their career and beyond, the Beatles' image initially was framed along traditional notions of entertainment. The group's manager, Brian Epstein, so the story goes, made the band more presentable, more commercial. Hence, the Beatles' early image was promoted along a predictable path, one serving the requirements of the market. Consistent with industry practice, the Beatles were presented as a British variant of the then-popular teen idol. Further, the story of their rise to fame was framed within the context of the American myth of success, a ubiquitous foundation for the images of film stars, politicians, celebrity athletes, and music stars, and an ideologically loaded statement of the country's unique status as a land of opportunity for all, unburdened by the restrictions of class that still held sway in Europe.

The foundation for my use of the term *image*, here used interchangeably with *star-text* and *star image*, is Richard Dyer's *Stars* (1998), in which the author defined and elaborated a field of inquiry within film studies intended to evaluate the impact of the star on both the film industry and audience. In expanding this type of analysis into the realm of popular music, I understand image (as does Dyer) to be the product of four categories of media text: promotion, publicity, work product, and commentaries/criticism.[2] *Promotion* refs to materials created specifically to shape the Beatles' image, including items appearing in or derived from pressbooks and fan club magazines, fashion pictures, television appearances, and product endorsements. Additionally, the Beatles' physical appearance was an important part of their promotion and image, and aspects of their appearance, including their "moptop" haircuts and manifestations of manager Brian Epstein's early efforts to make the band more commercial (including putting band members in tailored suits), as well as their later adoption of countercultural fashions, had significant repercussions for the Beatles' image and its reception. Of the four media text categories, promotion is the most intentional in creation of the star image in that it is crafted specifically to define the star without external interference.

Image is also a product of information viewed by many to be more authentic than promotion. *Publicity*, or information gathered by the media through interviews and other journalistic practices, is not, or appears not to be, the product of an effort directed at starmaking. The scandal ignited in the United States on the eve of the band's 1966 summer tour by reports of Lennon's statement that the Beatles were "more popular than Jesus," and that flowing from McCartney's public admission in 1967 that he had used LSD, are examples where publicity transgressed the boundaries of the image created, cultivated, and promoted by Epstein. Of course, publicity may be just as coached or manufactured as promotion. For instance, in the months preceding the release of the album, *Sgt. Pepper's Lonely Hearts Club Band* (June 1967), the Beatles regularly contributed to speculation that they were breaking up, despite the fact that they were hard at work on recordings that would shortly help validate rock music as an art form among establishment intellectuals and solidify the band's status as cultural bellwethers and catalysts.

As important as promotion and publicity, the *work product* of the Beatles, including their recorded music, live performances, and film and video, was another foundation for the image. Lennon and McCartney's early songs were crafted to appeal to the opposite sex through their direct address of the young female audience; the Beatles' perceived availability, demonstrated in the lyrics of the songs (e.g., "P.S. I love you," "I'll get you," "Please please me," or "I want to hold your hand"), was incorporated into an image designed to promote the band as teen idols. As the Beatles matured, their music evolved and became more expansive in terms of themes and incorporation of other musical forms into the heretofore limited rock and roll palette. Their image evolved as well, to incorporate their status as artists.

Contemporary critics recognized the Beatles' broadening of the rock and roll idiom. By the time of the release of the album *Rubber Soul* in 1965, each new record was viewed as a progression in the band's artistic development and as an expansion of the parameters of popular music, and the image reflected and promoted notions of the Beatles' artistry and importance. Reference to the teen-idol Beatles was largely relegated to the fanzines following the release, in April 1967, of the single "Penny Lane"/"Strawberry Fields Forever," followed by the album *Sgt. Pepper's Lonely Hearts Club Band* (June 1967), for which critical acclaim was nearly unanimous. *Criticism and commentary* (the last group of media texts making up the image) of this nature was emblematic of the preeminent standing enjoyed by the band within the establishment and counterculture presses. This category comprises opinions and interpretations of critics evaluating the Beatles and their work product, and includes reviews of sound recordings and films as well as biographies and obituaries.

One final point—obvious though it may be—must be made about the image: the image itself is a foundational text for the image. That is, the image is self-reflexive, constantly referring to itself. Early promotion of the band highlighted the manic reaction of the fans, as well as the band members' working-class[3] backgrounds, vitality, irreverence, and youth. The same events and descriptions of the band were recounted over and over in the nation's press and became part of the "story" of the Beatles that became fixed in the public's imagination. The story was retold even as the image evolved to accommodate the Beatles' maturation and artistic development; these, too, became part of the Beatles' story, and important components of the image that continued to evolve.

The importance of the star to the music industry has long been acknowledged. In *On Record* (1990), Simon Frith and Andrew Goodwin note that the "most important commodities produced by the music industry . . . may not be songs or records but stars," performers who stand "for what we possess, how we are possessed" (425). Even within the ostensibly anti-consumerist counterculture, this point was well understood and even commented upon within the counterculture's most successful and influential publication, *Rolling Stone*. The magazine's respected critic, Jon Landau, bemoaned this imposition of the star system, the "crudest and most primitive form of escape," in which "we express our dissatisfaction with ourselves by endowing another with superhuman qualities," as a cornerstone for the counterculture (Anson 80–81). These commentators are lamenting the way in which the industry, audience, performers, text, and symbols interact, or "articulate," with one another, to the detriment of rock music's perceived revolutionary possibilities. Lawrence Grossberg, in *We Gotta Get Out of This Place: Popular Conservatism and Postmodern Culture* (1992), describes a process of *articulation* as "a continuous struggle" at definition of "the possibilities of life" (54). Specifically, as applied to popular music, Keith Negus (1995) notes that an artist is always articulating (through language and other cultural codes) through intermediaries (the music industry and its various apparatus of production and distribution, the press, and so on) to audiences who are part of the process of articulation (389). This book is concerned with the ways in which the Beatles' image interacted, or articulated, with established and emergent societal forces in postwar America, and how the image evolved to address and embody the values of the youth culture. The image existed in a web of relationships between historical, political, economic, artistic, technological, and popular forces. It not only presented a model to be emulated within the youth culture but also represented that culture to the establishment and "straight" society, as many counterculturalists and their sympathizers referred to what they viewed as a traditional, conservative, ruling elite enforcing puritanical restraints on expression and experimentation, particularly in the realms of drugs and sexuality.

To consider the Beatles' image is to contemplate an evolving and complex array of signs that carry with them cultural meanings. Based to a large degree around their unprecedented commercial success and adoring fans, the Beatles' image initially upheld the ideological underpinnings of the American myth of success, that America is a land of opportunity for all. Over time, however, the Beatles' positive manifestation of the myth gave way to a critique of that myth and its underlying assumptions. This critique, with the experimental and exploratory aspects of the counterculture, was embedded in the Beatles' image, an image that reflected a countercultural ideal. The Beatles' image, in comprising both a positive and oppositional aspect, is emblematic of the complexity of sign systems, a complexity embraced by semiotics, the study of these systems first proposed by Swiss linguist Ferdinand de Saussure (*Course in General Linguistics*, published in 1916) and redirected by French semiotician Roland Barthes in his analyses of postwar culture and mass culture.[4] For our purposes, Jean Baudrillard's injection of semiotics into the Marxist critique, and his introduction of a sign-value into Marx's theory of the commodity, is particularly informative. While accepting Marx's notion that a commodity possesses a use-value (i.e., utility of objects) and exchange-value (i.e., commercial value), Baudrillard maintains that it is produced, distributed, and consumed for its conspicuous social meaning and that, in fact, this "sign value" can eclipse its use and exchange values.

This was nowhere more evident than in the youth culture of the 1960s, where one's appearance and choice of music could carry with them all sorts of political and social meaning. Proposing the concept of a commodity's "enhanced use value," David Buxton, in "Rock Music, the Star System, and the Rise of Consumerism" (1990), rightly maintains that for products, such as rock and roll records, lacking any precise functional use (as opposed to, say, food and shelter) the ability of the commodity to absorb meaning is boundless. This book is, in a sense, about the enhanced use value of the Beatles' image. To emulate the Beatles, in dress, speech, or worldview was to place oneself at odds with the adult world and the establishment. The symbolic value of the image is displayed in the Beatles' centrality to much of the public dialogue of the 1960s on topics such as civil rights, religion, the drug culture, art, mass media, Vietnam, and other issues marking the boundary between the establishment and America's young.

It should be noted that while the 1960s were a period of great political and social upheaval, it was not political radicalism that had the most lasting impact upon society. Ian MacDonald argues convincingly that the Left found its victory not in politics but in the realm of lifestyle (24–25). The countercultural lifestyle of the pop star was emulated by many youths, and aspects of that lifestyle did indeed become assimilated into the values of the hegemonic class. This assimilation is readily apparent in the growing acceptance of countercultural style and fashion into the mainstream, including longer hair on men, bell-bottom pants, or tie-dyed shirts. For committed counterculturalists such as the hippies, as noted generally of postwar youth cultures by Dick Hebdige in *Subculture* (1983), dress was a way of declaring one's difference and of attesting to one's acceptance of a different lifestyle from that required and promoted by a capitalist system.

This was a losing battle. By its nature, hegemony changes over time, and the lifestyle and fashion choices of the young, exemplified in those of the Beatles and other pop celebrities, were quickly commodified and coopted into the hegemonic system as industries were reconfigured to cater to young people. George Lipsitz, in "Who'll Stop the Rain?" (1994), succinctly describes the situation with regard to the youth market: "In 1964 seventeen-year-olds became the largest age cohort in the United States, and their purchases of records by the Beatles and other rock groups demonstrated their potential as an economic and cultural force. In succeeding years, the taste preferences of this group displayed considerable power to reshape the economy" (212).

The Beatles' initial massive success obviously was tied to the buying power of this market. As described in chapter 2, it also appeared to some intellectuals to be further proof of the country's vulgar consumerism. In the postwar period, critics on the left decried the debasement of American cultural life through its crass commercialization. Among the most influential critiques of western capitalism were those of the Frankfurt School.[5] In *Dialectic of Enlightenment* (1944), their attempt to explain the general quiescence and complacency of the populations of the western capitalist democracies, Theodor Adorno and Max Horkheimer identified the "culture industries," including the film and broadcast industries, advertising, and the mass-market press, as the purveyors of mass culture created and distributed in the interests of organized capital. The resulting culture—homogenized, commodified, standardized, and produced for mass distribution—is produced not only to return maximum profit but also to provide ideological legitimization for the capitalist order, and to assimilate individuals into that system. Thus, with mercenary zeal, Hollywood film was largely standardized to incorporate happy endings, romantic entanglements, and narratives revealed in an easily followed chronological order and peopled with "stars" of known commercial potential. Popular music, too, manifested the characteristic standardization and pseudo-individualization of the culture industries. For Adorno, listening to popular music was "manipulated into a system of response mechanisms wholly antagonistic to the ideal of individuality in a free, liberal society" (Adorno 305).

The critique was echoed in Dwight Macdonald's influential essay, "Masscult and Midcult," appearing in the *Partisan Review* in 1960. Macdonald decried the rise of "masscult," crassly commercial work such as rock and roll, and "midcult," watered-down high culture for the masses, as exemplified by the Book-of-the-Month Club and the middle-class magazine the *Saturday Evening Post*. Macdonald wrote of a mass cult "fabricat(ed) by technicians hired by businessmen": "They try this and try that and if something clicks at the box-office, they try to cash in with similar products . . . like a Pavlovian biologist who has hit on a reflex he thinks can be conditioned" (214).

Adherents to the Frankfurt School's notion of the culture industry would have recognized immediately in the Beatles' early image the industrial footprints of standardization and pseudoindividualization. That is, the Beatles' image was developed along a predictable path in which they were presented as safe teen idols, very much like those then populating the record charts. They were differentiated from other teen idols only in the most superficial sense, by the length of their hair and their Britishness. Further, as noted, the Beatles' image incorporated the American myth of success, long a standard feature of the star image of actor and teen idol alike. The process of standardization, in fact, was part of their "story." As recorded in the nation's media, their manager and promoter, Brian Epstein, exerted great control over the image of the band throughout the touring years, particularly during the years of the band's rise first to national prominence in England and then to international stardom. He "cleaned them up," sanitizing the rougher, more rebellious image that had been developed in Liverpool's Cavern Club and on Hamburg's Reeperbahn. Gone were the leather jackets, swearing and smoking on stage, interactions with the audience, and other unprofessional behavior. Rather, Epstein marketed the Beatles as clean, wholesome entertainment. Well-coifed and donning suits and ties, the new Beatles were cheeky and at times irreverent, but never vulgar. In essence, Epstein brought a very traditional notion of entertainment to his management of the band, and it was this image, the subject of chapter 2, that debuted in the United States in late 1963 and that was exploited to great effect upon the band's first visit to the country in February 1964.

Chapter 3 describes the crystallization of the Beatles' image in the film *A Hard Day's Night*, and follows the evolution of the image as Beatlemania crested in 1965 and waned in 1966 (a year marred by scandal in the Philippines and the "more popular than Jesus" controversy). During this period, the image retained its "showbiz" cast, but traces of more "authentic" elements were introduced as the Beatles were called upon to discuss contemporary issues of importance to the burgeoning youth culture, and as they and the mainstream media took account of their status as artists. Much to Epstein's chagrin, the boys found it increasingly difficult to remain mum when asked by reporters about Vietnam, race relations, and a host of other issues. The Beatles' image was in flux, straddling the line between the old order, where entertainers were expected to entertain, and young people were expected to keep their opinions to themselves, and the new order, in which a youth culture with a growing awareness of itself was beginning to exercise a voice in the critical issues of the day. Further, well aware of the artistic currents of their time, the Beatles increasingly viewed themselves as artists and what they did as art, and their image began to reflect this as the touring years came to a close. While leaving their "lovable moptop" incarnation behind for a more consciously artistic and countercultural status, the Beatles remained extremely popular. It is a measure of the image's effectiveness in ameliorating apparent contradictions that the Beatles could at once continue to enjoy broad appeal and also model the values of an oppositional youth culture.

Of course, the Beatles' pronouncements joined an increasingly vocal and very public opposition by American youths to the establishment and its institutions. While the Beatles were the first youth-oriented entertainers to speak openly on a number of topics, many American youth had already begun to demand a voice in defining American culture. By the early 1960s, there was ample evidence that the country's social fabric was being altered by forces unleashed by America's unrivaled economic power and the arrival of the baby boomers as a political, social, and economic force. Greater activism was present on the nation's campuses with the establishment of the Student Nonviolent Coordinating Committee and Students for a Democratic Society (SNCC and SDS, respectively). The SDS inaugurated a decade of student radicalism with the publication of its Port Huron Statement (1962), which criticized the political system of the United States and the failure of the government to address the social ills plaguing the country, and advocated civil disobedience (such as the SNCC's sit-in at a Greensboro, North Carolina, Woolworth's) to create a "participatory democracy." Among the ills identified in the statement were the dehumanizing effects of capitalism, limits on expression, and, importantly, the racial inequality that continued to afflict American society. In part a reaction to the growing violence directed at the civil rights movement, the statement was the manifesto of America's New Left, which became more influential as the decade progressed. In fact, it would be the increased radicalism of the SDS and allied organizations at the end of the decade, as America's involvement in Vietnam escalated, that led to the schism within the youth culture, between those advocating abstinence from politics in favor of a new consciousness and lifestyle, and those advocating direct political action. This rupture, described in chapter 6, played out at *Rolling Stone* and was a defining moment in the image of the Beatles; against a growing chorus of critics, the band retained their countercultural disposition toward universal notions of love and peace and rejected the growing radicalism of the New Left.

The SDS and allied organizations bemoaned the failure of the country to desegregate in the years following the U.S. Supreme Court's 1954 decision in *Brown v. Board of Education*, which held state-sanctioned segregation of public schools to be a violation of the U.S. Constitution, the Fourteenth Amendment guaranteeing due process and equal protection and protecting rights against state infringement. With "separate but equal" at an end, blacks sought equality in all parts of American life but faced opposition. American media covered the subject in detail, and it was a momentous time for the assertion of black rights and federal authority. Robert Drew's documentary *Crisis: Behind a Presidential Commitment* detailed the Kennedy administration's deliberations and efforts to forcefully integrate the University of Alabama, efforts that culminated with the Alabama National Guard (federalized by Kennedy) facing down Governor George Wallace at the doors of the registrar. Its broadcast on ABC, just one month before the president's assassination, fueled public debate on the race issue in the months preceding the Beatles' first visit to the United States.

At the time of the Beatles' first full U.S. tour in the summer of 1964, the public's attention was riveted to news of the disappearance of three civil rights workers in Mississippi. Even before the discovery of their bodies, national media coverage of the investigation emboldened civil rights workers and helped to extend the influence of the movement. On August 4, two weeks before the kickoff of the American tour, efforts directed by the Federal Bureau of Investigation, including a much publicized visit by bureau director J. Edgar Hoover, led to the discovery of the bodies of James Earl Chaney, Andrew Goodman, and Michael H. Schwerner and the conviction three years later of seven Ku Klux Klansmen.[6] In August 1965, in the weeks preceding the start of the Beatles' second tour of the U.S., passage of the Voting Rights Act broke southern disenfranchisement efforts and led to a sharp increase in voter registration among African-Americans. The act was signed into law by

President Johnson on August 6; days later the Watts riots (August 11–16) in Los Angeles were ignited by a traffic squabble between a white motorcycle police officer and a black motorist and fueled by the state's efforts to circumvent parts of the act. The Beatles played the Hollywood Bowl on August 29.

Of course, I am not claiming any significance for the appearance of the Beatles on these momentous events of 1964 and 1965. Quite the contrary: The events' proximity to the Beatles' appearances had a very direct effect on the band's image. As Harrison said in the *Anthology*, "There were riots in every city. Students rioting, blacks rioting. . . . Every place we went, there seemed to be something going on" (Beatles 153). And the media was increasingly prone, amidst the vapid banter of the entertainment interview, to insert questions about current issues.

The Beatles' response to these questions—to these events—was an important integration of "authentic" qualities into the highly stylized and controlled early image. As described in chapter 3, the Beatles faced such questions at least as early as their first full-blown American tour in the summer of 1964, during which they caused a small stir when they said they would refuse to play shows at segregated venues, notably, Jacksonville, Florida's old Gator Bowl. Larry Kane, the only American reporter to be a part of the official press pool for the band's 1964 and 1965 American tours, asked about the band's position. Speaking for the band, McCartney replied, "We don't like it if there's any segregation or anything, because we're not used to it. . . . I don't think colored people are any different. . . . they're just the same as anyone else. . . . You can't treat other people like animals" (Kane 40–41). Over the next two years, in press conferences and interviews, the Beatles firmly established themselves as "fellow travelers" in the cause(s) of their young counterparts in America.

Also described in chapter 3 is the Beatles' public discourse on religion. In the 1960s, the role of religion in public life was among the great divisive issues of the time. In 1962 the U.S. Supreme Court ruled, in the case of *Engle v. Vitale*, that public schools in New York could not require students to recite a State Board of Regents–authored prayer in the classroom; the court held that the idea of state-sponsored or mandated prayer violated the establishment clause of the First Amendment. Further afield, but with huge repercussions for Roman Catholics, the Vatican Ecumenical Council authorized the use of the vernacular in Catholic mass, and acknowledged the necessity of the Church adapting to the modern world. Increasingly, Protestant and Roman Catholic churches in America were faced with declining attendance and the challenge of non-western religions and philosophies for the attention of the faithful, particularly among the nation's youth. The anxiety of traditionalists was on display in public debate about the role of religion in society and within the youth culture. The Beatles found themselves at the center of discussion about youth apathy toward the traditional faiths on more than one occasion, the most famous being the "more popular than Jesus" controversy of 1966—though Beatlemania had drawn the ire of religious groups from the start. The Beatles and other youth-oriented entertainers, with their generally unsympathetic view of what they saw as the hypocrisy of the established churches (and later with their investigations of Transcendental Meditation and other belief systems), further provoked traditionalists and strengthened ties to the counterculture.

The Beatles unprecedented commercial success allowed them unlimited time and effort in the studio and, in the post-touring years, artistry and opposition became essential elements of the image. Their music was viewed as revolutionary by establishment and alternative pundits alike. Chapter 4 describes the evolution of the image to one manifesting the Beatles' perceived artistic supremacy and, as a corollary, the legitimization of rock music as an art form. By the end of touring in 1966, Epstein's hold over the image, increasingly contested by the Beatles, was slipping. Mainstream coverage in the years following touring became more reflective of the "real" Beatles; that is, it presented an image more consistent with the Beatles' perceptions of themselves. By the summer of 1967, notions of the Beatles as artists and counterculturalists, and of their artistic supremacy, were central to the image and would remain so to the breakup of the band in 1970.

The concept of hegemony is useful for understanding the Beatles' roles as leaders of the youth culture. In developing his theory of hegemony in the first quarter of the twentieth century, Antonio Gramsci explained the same phenomenon as the Frankfurt School theorists, namely, the failure of Marxist revolutionary fervor to take hold in the capitalist West. Gramsci maintained that capitalism had retained its control not by force, but by assent. He contended that only weak states had to rely upon domination or the threat of force for legitimization. Strong states rule primarily through "hegemony," his term for a ruling ideology: The hegemonic class rules through a series of alliances in which its interests are universalized and "become the interests of the other subordinate groups" (Gramsci 181). In essence, consensus is drawn from the alignment of different groups at different times. Appropriated by Stuart Hall and his colleagues at the Centre for Contemporary Cultural Studies at Birmingham University in its critique of Margaret Thatcher's policies during her tenure as Prime Minister of Great Britain in the 1970s and 1980s, a "neo-hegemonic" theory was built atop Gramsci's "most distinguished contribution": "Hegemony is understood as accomplished, not without the due measure of legal and legitimate compulsion, but principally by means of winning the active consent of those classes and groups who were subordinated within it" (Hall 85).

Central to Gramsci's hegemonic theory is his concept of the intellectual. Gramsci dismisses the notion of intellectuals as a distinct social category. Rather, intellectuals are defined by their social function of definition and representation. In short, every social group produces intellectuals that give it cohesiveness and self-awareness of its position in the economic, social, and political realms (Gramsci 5). For Gramsci, intellectuals fall into two categories, the traditional and the organic. Traditional intellectuals are, as described by James Davison Hunter (1991), self-styled "heirs to the truths of the past," deriving their legitimacy from their appeal to historical continuity. Organic intellectuals, by contrast, promote "the new and dynamic sources of progressive social reform" (61). The effort to define the social order is carried on through these intellectuals, each vying for a dominant position. The terrain of this struggle is the location of popular culture, the area of both conflict and assimilation. The ultimate outcome of this ideological battle is either the restoration of the old hegemony or the establishment of a new one. The Beatles' image, as presented in *Rolling Stone*, was defined to a large extent in terms of its—and the counterculture's—opposition to tradition, the establishment, and its institutions. While the Beatles influenced culture at the level of the teen idol (that is, as models of style and consumption), they also evolved to be viewed as leaders of a grouping increasingly aware of its own status as a social, economic, and political force. As described in chapter 4, the Beatles were understood to be leaders of the youth culture and described as such in the mainstream press. They represented to young people and the establishment what it meant to be "one of the beautiful people," providing a lifestyle model for the former and, perhaps, for the latter a less worrisome alternative to the student radicals and their leaders.

Their presentation as organic intellectuals is described in chapter 5, which looks at the Beatles' image within *Rolling Stone*, a magazine catering to the interests of youth and the counterculture. It was here that the Beatles' image was most explicitly invoked in terms of their leadership of the youth culture. The Beatles are consistently depicted as model counterculturalists, the values and ideals of the culture in human form. As the magazine's standard-bearers for countercultural values, the Beatles were also a focus for founder Jann Wenner's assault on "straight" society and on the mainstream press, a press that had "distorted the picture of being a Beatlepeople [sic]"(Wenner, Review of *The Beatles* [book] 17–18). Wenner time and again called upon the Beatles, literally and otherwise, to fortify his countercultural claims and position his magazine as the dominant underground publication of the period. His exploitation of the Beatles ultimately contributed to *Rolling Stone*'s success beyond its initial counterculture audience and facilitated its transformation into a successful commercial publication. Within the pages of *Rolling Stone* the Beatles became countercultural beacons, calling youth toward a future based around counterculture values. In effect, Wenner proposed the Beatles, with their indisputable, lifestyle-centered counterculture credentials, to the mantle of leadership, but leadership largely outside of the political sphere, in opposition to New Left radicalism. Increasingly frequent draft calls and rising casualty rates led to growing hostility to the war, however, and New Left activism grew in influence (Patterson 631–32). Displaying a countercultural apathy towards politics, the members of the band ultimately rejected taking direct action at the head of the youth culture, which placed them at odds with radicals in the United States and abroad, and their political capital among the New Left quickly dissipated. Jean-Luc Godard, the French New Wave director and radical filmmaker, famously commented: "There are plenty of people in Britain with money and open minds. But alas, they don't use their minds, and they are usually corrupted by money. People could do things but won't. Look at the Beatles, for instance" (Giuliano 372). The Beatles' apoliticism and faithfulness to a countercultural ideal based on notions of universal love and enlightenment through intellectual, spiritual, and pharmacological experimentation contributed to their rejection of effective political leadership and militant opposition to the establishment that the radicals demanded. As the countercultural lifestyle came to be viewed increasingly as politically ineffectual in dealing with America's problems, particularly the escalation in Vietnam, the Beatles' refusal to engage the establishment directly led to their decline in influence among more radicalized quarters of the counterculture and the New Left. Nevertheless, their image retained its idyllic timbre. The band broke up 1970 while still a commercial and social force, and the Beatles' image continued to benefit from being forever frozen in time as a youthful ideal for an idealized time.

In 2006, two of the Beatles are dead, one the victim of an insane fan, the other falling to cancer; one surviving Beatle has been knighted and continues to tour and record; and the last continues to record and tour the nostalgia circuit with other rock stars and icons of the past. Nearly forty years after the breakup of the band "The Beatles," this memory whose life now approaches half a century, continues to fascinate. Derek Taylor, Brian Epstein's assistant and the Apple Corps press officer, once memorably called the relationship of the Beatles and their fans "the twentieth century's greatest romance."[7] This book is an attempt to shed some light on the function of image in that romance.

TWO

"Ladies and Gentlemen, The Beatles!" Introducing the Image

As JOHN LENNON, PAUL MCCARTNEY, George Harrison, and Ringo Starr crossed the Atlantic on Pan Am flight 101, there was a sense of excitement, for success in America would solidify the position of the Beatles as Britain's greatest exponents of pop music; yet the Beatles were apprehensive. McCartney confided to Phil Spector, the American record producer accompanying the group "across the pond," that "America has always had everything. . . . Why should we be over there making money? They've got their own groups. What are we going to give them that they don't already have?" (Giuliano 82). Unknown to McCartney and the other Beatles, Beatlemania had landed on American shores even before the Beatles themselves. The Beatles, scheduled to make their first appearance on *The Ed Sullivan Show* on February 9, 1964, were greeted by 3,000 screaming teenage fans when they arrived at Kennedy International Airport on February 7. Disc jockeys, who had a stake in popularizing the group, had urged young people to meet the Beatles at the airport. Joining them were two hundred reporters and photographers from newspapers, magazines, foreign publications, and radio and television stations, all looking to exploit the band's arrival.

In view of the Beatles' modest stature in the United States, manager Brian Epstein scored quite a coup in obtaining top billing for them on *The Ed Sullivan Show*. Despite their growing popularity in Europe and their established success in Great Britain, the top of the U.S. record charts had eluded the Beatles. Capitol, the American record company and a subsidiary of EMI, the company holding the Beatles' recording contract, was unwilling to release the Beatles' "Please Please Me" in America, even after its rise to number one on the British record sales charts in early 1963. George Martin, the Beatles' producer, sent the single to Alan Livingston, the senior Capitol executive in New York, who replied: "We don't think the Beatles will do anything in this market" (Martin 159). Martin was thus forced to shop the single around to other American record companies in competition with Capitol's parent company. Vee-Jay finally released it in February 1963 but, with little promotion, "Please Please Me" vanished from the charts. "From Me to You" met a similar fate, rising no higher than 116 on *Billboard*'s singles record chart. In August, "She Loves You" began its eight-week stay at the top of the British charts; Martin again appealed to Livingston to release the single on the Capitol label, and was again told that the Beatles were not considered suited to the American market. Swan, a small New York label, released the single instead. It failed to break *Billboard*'s "Hot 100."

At first glance, Capitol's hesitation to market the Beatles seems dumbfounding in light of the band's success in Great Britain, where advance orders for the next single was an unprecedented one million copies. Released on November 29, "I Want to Hold Your Hand" went straight to number one in the British sales charts, displacing the band's "She Loves You," which had sold over a million copies and had topped the British charts since August. By the end of 1963 the Beatles were dominating all aspects of British media and popular culture. Four consecutive singles and EPs[1] had gone to the top of the British charts, and their first two albums, *Please Please Me* and *With the Beatles*, had gone straight to number one on the album charts, setting sales records along the way. They had their own weekly radio showcase, the BBC Light Programme "Pop Go the Beatles." They made regular appearances on British television, including an appearance on the popular television program, *Val Parnell's Sunday Night at the London Palladium*. The band enjoyed successful, record-setting tours of the United Kingdom. They had even given a Royal Command Performance before the Queen Mother and Princess Margaret. One might think that Capitol would have little to lose in releasing a single. Yet a glance at the American charts in the months before the Beatles' release of "I Want to Hold Your Hand" offers some explanation for the American record company's hesitation to throw its commercial might behind promotion of the Beatles.

The label had in fact recently released singles by British acts Frank Ifield and Freddie and the Dreamers, and neither had attracted much attention. Further, Capitol's attempts in the late 1950s to promote one of Great Britain's biggest stars, teen idol Cliff Richard, had been a complete failure. But it was not simply that British acts, with rare exception, had failed to arouse interest among American record buyers.[2] Guitar-based rock and roll acts had also passed out of vogue. The charts in the early 1960s were populated by an eclectic assortment. In the weeks and months preceding the release of "I Want to Hold Your Hand" (December 26, 1963), top singles ranged from the Singing Nun's "Dominique" (number one for four weeks in December) to Allan Sherman's "Hello Muddah, Hello Fadduh!" (number two for three weeks in August–September); from crooner Bobby Vinton ("Blue Velvet," number one in September–October) to the Chiffons ("He's So Fine," number one in March–April); from the Four Seasons' "Walk Like a Man" (number one in March) to Kyu Sakamoto's "Sukiyaki" (number one, June); and, from Leslie Gore ("It's My Party," number one in June) to Peter, Paul and Mary ("Puff the Magic Dragon," number two in May) (Whitburn, *Billboard's Top 10* 89–108).

Further, in the past year, apart from Sakamoto's "Sukiyaki," Capitol had had only modest success at the top of the charts. Crooners Al Martino and Nat King Cole had top ten hits in June ("I Love You Because" and "Those Lazy-Hazy-Crazy Days of Summer," respectively). Bobby Darin broke into the top ten with "You're the Reason I'm Living" and "Yellow Roses," and the Kingston Trio had a number eight hit with "Reverend Mr. Black." Of Capitol's roster, only Darin and the Beach Boys had had success as youth-oriented acts. The record charts, with rare exception a blend of novelties, teen idols, folk singers, and girl group pop, gave Livingston little reason to believe that the Beatles would find an audience in the United States. With their aggressive beat and raw vocals and harmonies (by the industry norms of the time), as well as their reliance upon a growing but commercially unproven catalog of songs penned by Lennon and McCartney, the Beatles promised to be of little value to the company. Still, the band's momentum was undeniable and, by early November, promoting the band seemed less of a risk: They were at the top of the British entertainment business, gaining a following abroad, and their latest single was likely to sell in excess of one million units in advance of its British release (Lewisohn 128). On the basis of their British success, Epstein finally convinced Livingston to promote the Beatles and release their new single, "I Want to Hold Your Hand"/"I Saw Her Standing There" on December 26, 1963.

Estimates of Capitol's total expenditures promoting the band range from $40,000 (an amount demanded by Brian Epstein for promotion of "I Want to Hold Your Hand") to $100,000 (Spizer, *Beatles' Story, Pt. I* 8). Whatever the sum, it was an unheard-of amount for promotion of a single—and it worked. With the Beatles' arrival in America imminent, the single entered the *Billboard* charts at number forty-five, climbed to number three the following week, and reached number one on February 1, 1964, displacing Bobby Vinton's "There! I've Said It Again" (Whitburn, *Billboard Top 10* 107–8).

Prior to the Beatles' visit, media coverage was limited and mixed in its assessment of the band and its fans. *Time* warned that, while "irresistible" to the English, the Beatles "might be achingly familiar" to Americans ("New Madness" 64). Network news coverage was equally dismissive. NBC, ABC, and CBS filmed the Beatles' performance on November 16, 1963, at Winter Gardens Theatre in Bournemouth, UK. The footage was used in reports on November 18, 19, and 21 and on December 7. Of the group's fans CBS's Alexander Kendrick condescendingly noted, "Some of the girls can write," and opined that the Beatles "symbolize the 20th century non-hero, as they make non-music, wear non-haircuts and give none-mersey [i.e. a pun on the Beatles' Merseyside origins in Liverpool]" (Lewisohn 129).

On January 3, 1964, a month before "I Want to Hold Your Hand" reached number one on the *Billboard* and *Cashbox* charts and the Beatles' appearance on *The Ed Sullivan Show*, NBC aired footage of the band on *The Jack Paar Program*. Paar, an admired television personality, had followed Steve Allen as host of *The Tonight Show* in 1957. His highly popular run as the show's host ended in 1962, when he left after a dispute with NBC's censors.[3] Nevertheless, he returned to the network later that year to host a variety hour for NBC, *The Jack Paar Program*, aired on Friday evenings at 10 p.m. Paar's "live" debut of the Beatles on American television opened with footage from the Bournemouth Winter Gardens performance and contained material from the BBC documentary *The Mersey Sound*, which, due to problems filming and recording the Beatles in actual performance before hysterical fans, actually showed the Beatles on stage in an empty theater performing "She Loves You" (shots of screaming fans were edited into the performance footage to re-create a live performance). Paar's interest, as he told his audience that Friday night, was "in showing a more adult audience that usually follows my work what's going on in England."

Paar broke with the generally negative coverage the band had received thus far:

You know, everyone talks about the Beatles, but no one does anything about them. The Beatles are an extraordinary act in England, I think of the biggest thing in England in twenty-five
years. And actually, the music is rock and roll. Now we've never
in my seven years at NBC, ever, or on a *Tonight Show*, ever had
a rock and roll act, but I'm interested in the Beatles as a psychological, uh, sociological phenomenon. I want to show them to you
tonight. They're from the toughest part of England. It's Merseyside, near Liverpool in the dock area, and it's a very tough area
where these four nice kids come from. They're kind of witty—
one said, someone said, "What's so exciting about living on the
docks at Liverpool?" He says, "Just staying alive is exciting." But
they're nice kids and I'd like to show you now all for the first time
what it looks like in an audience in England when the Beatles
are about to perform. (*The Jack Paar Program*)

With that, footage of the Bournemouth fans screaming and fainting,
punctuated by a barely audible "From Me to You" emanating from
the stage, was shown to Paar's running commentary: "I understand
science is working on a cure for this. . . . These guys have these crazy
hairdos and when they wiggle their heads and the hair goes the girls
go out of their minds. . . . Does it bother you to realize that in a few
years these girls will vote, raise children, and drive cars?" The BBC
documentary performance of "She Loves You" followed. The segment ended with a final shot of a screaming audience, to which Paar
quipped, "I'm glad to see that the English have finally risen to our
cultural level," and the studio audience broke into applause.

Paar's observations did more than amuse his audience, however.
Interestingly, in addition to presenting a model for hysteria that would
be taken up by fans, Paar observed aspects of the Beatles' emerging
image, notably, their hair, their wit, and their working-class origins
in "the toughest part of England." These were core elements of Capitol's promotional campaign for the band. The broadcast contributed

to interest and brought the band much needed publicity, though the *New York Times*' critic, Jack Gould, dismissed the band in his re-cap of the broadcast the following day: "It would not seem quite so likely that the accompanying fever known as Beatlemania will also be successfully exported. On this side of the Atlantic it is dated stuff" (Gould, "TV: It's the Beatles").

The mainstream media, however, were far from unanimous in dismissing the band and the chaotic reaction of its fans as peculiarly British fads. In November, the *New York Times Magazine* reported on the disturbance of the "English peace" embodied in the Beatle-mania phenomenon. "To see a Beatle is joy, to touch one paradise on earth, and for just the slimmest opportunity of this privilege, people will fight like mad things and with the dedication normally reserved for a Great Cause, like national survival," wrote Frederick Lewis in December 1963. He elaborated: "For months now they have been the preoccupation of the British, eclipsing the Govern-ment, the prospects of a general election, Christine Keeler,[4] even football. One shake of the bushy fringe of their identical, moplike haircuts is enough to start a riot in any theater where they are ap-pearing and bring out the massed and augmented forces of order, ranging from the fire brigade to elderly auxiliary constables called up from retirement because there aren't sufficient ordinary coppers to cope" (124). Importantly, he noted their humble origins: "They are working-class and their roots and attitudes are firmly of the North of England," and are "part of a strong flowing reaction against the soft, middle-class South of England, which has controlled popular culture for so long" (126).[5]

Lewis's observations reappeared in the *National Record News*, a key element in what *Billboard* called, "one of the most efficient and effective promotional campaigns in recent memory" (Kittleson 4). The mass-distributed tabloid was accompanied by a memo in-structing the Capitol sales force to send copies in bulk to retailers for distribution to consumers, and to disc jockeys for on-air promotion and giveaways. The memo also suggested a more direct address of the potential teenage consumer: "But most important, make arrangements with local high schoolers to distribute them to fellow students after school. . . . The idea is to get as many copies of this tabloid as possible into the hands of potential Beatle buyers" (Spizer, *Beatles' Story, Pt. I* 10). The issue was compiled from British and American sources by Capitol publicity director Fred Martin, who moved quickly to establish an image for the Beatles (Spizer, *Beatles' Story, Pt. I* 9). A number of themes and elements emerge from the four-page tabloid: the Beatlemania of the fans; the Beatle hairstyle; the band's working class origins in Liverpool; the individuality of the members of the band; their universal appeal; and the importance of manager Brian Epstein to their meteoric rise. These aspects of the Beatle image would be parroted and further developed over the ensuing months and years.

At this early phase in selling the Beatles to the American public, before the band became the focus of the press, promotional texts were dominant in creating the image. Largely unfettered by contradictory publicity, Capitol's campaign followed a predictable path marked by a retelling of the standard star narrative, with the Beatles' meager backgrounds and meteoric rise to fame presenting a British version of the American myth of success at the core of the American star narrative. Following the Hollywood star-making practice of eliciting identification with the star through promotion of the star's similarity to his or her audience, the music industry marketed its stars along very similar lines. Sinatra, for instance, had emerged from the tough streets of Hoboken, or so his promotion would have had one believe. Virtually all of rock and roll's early pioneers had similar ordinary, if not impoverished, backgrounds. Elvis Presley was raised in a two-room shack near Memphis, before becoming the "King of Rock and Roll." More recently, teen idols had been sold along the lines of the "boy next door," a sweet and fairly innocent object of affection for teenage and pre-teen girls. The centrality of ordinariness to the star image was firmly established by the time Capitol built its promotion of the Beatles around the model.

It is instructive at this point to consider the promotion of the Beatles in terms of the "culture industries" theorized by Horkheimer and Adorno. In these industries, including, among others, the film industry, radio, television, and advertising, production of culture resembles that of the assembly line, and is marked by two processes—standardization and pseudo-individualization. One could view Capitol as applying standard industry practices to the promotion of a band, utilizing a standardized narrative to elicit identification so that teenagers would buy the standardized product, be it the music or the image itself. The Beatles' story was related in terms already known to be acceptable to the audience, their rise from obscurity to fame closely resembling that of countless stars. At the same time, the very fact of the Beatles' "Britishness," not to mention their hairstyle, allowed the audience to differentiate them from other standardized products of the music industry, to this point essentially American. The focus of Capitol's efforts was readily apparent on the front page of the *National Record News*—the headline of which boldly proclaimed, "'Beatlemania' Sweeps U. S."—which was concerned primarily with the group's Liverpool origins and the band's rise from obscurity to fame; that is, the image was crafted from elements of the standardized American star-text.

Also referenced on page one was a *Daily Mirror* (London) interview with a "well-known psychiatrist (unnamed because of medical ethics)," who commented, "A revolution is taking place. . . . It amounts to freedom with a sense of responsibility and honesty. The fans recognize the honesty that shines from the Beatles." Beatlemania, it was noted, had not "stopped with you," but had "touched virtually everybody, high and low, rich and poor, scholars and the less educated" (*National Record News* 1). Page two invited fans to "Be a Beatle Booster" and purchase "an official, reasonably authentic Beatle wig for $2.00," as well as "a 'Be a Beatle Booster' button . . . [and] an autographed photo . . . for $2.50" (*National Record News* 2). The Beatles' hairstyle also figured prominently on the page. A Beverly Hills hairstylist for "some of Hollywood's most famous and beautiful actresses," called the "Beatle-cut" the "biggest thing in women's hair styles in 1964" (*National Record News* 2).

Another important aspect of this early promotion was the focus upon the individual members of the band. Pages three and four contained items on each of the Beatles (and manager Brian Epstein), accompanied by headshots of the four Beatles with John, Paul, and George mislabeled. While the place of the American myth of success in the Beatles' image is taken up later in this chapter, it is worth noting that one of its central tenets—that anyone can find success in America, regardless of one's background—is already part of the image displayed in the descriptions of the ordinariness of band members. John, the "angry young man" and "chief Beatle," was a failure in school that had found his calling with the Beatles. Paul, son of a Liverpool cotton salesman, hoped to attend art school before joining the Beatles. George, a failed electrician's apprentice, joined the band as a schoolboy. Ringo hoped to make enough money from his stardom to do "something with me hands," like pottery or basketwork. Finally, there was manager Brian Epstein, "their guide, philosopher, and friend," and the "fifth Beatle" who "made the Beatles. He got them a recording contract and made their sound important enough to cause a revolution in the record business" (*National Record News* 3–4).

Very quickly, in anticipation of the Beatles' arrival in the U.S., the mass-market magazines expanded upon elements of the image promoted in the *National Record News*. For instance, *Life*, with its photographs of the band and their shrieking adolescent fans, provided American teenagers with an example of behavior that they would soon be emulating. The January 31, 1964, issue contained a description of Beatlemania and eight pages of pictures of teenage girls screaming, crying, and fainting. The magazine's Timothy Green reported: " 'If those girls caught those ruddy lads,' commented one officer, 'they'd tear them to pieces.' At one theater a hundred girls battled police for four hours outside when they couldn't buy tickets" (Green, "Here Come Those Beatles" 27). Green provided an early description of the chaos surrounding an appearance by the band, noting that the police of some English cities had required the Beatles to be safely inside theaters before schools let out, "Otherwise the police will not be responsible for the consequences." The trials of the constabulary were further detailed: " 'I nearly got my ruddy shoulder dislocated trying to stop three girls dashing under a bus,' grumbled one London police sergeant. 'These girls are like eels— through your legs and after the Beatles before you know where you are' " ("They Crown Their Country" 30).

Thus, importantly, even prior to their arrival in America certain ideas were being consistently connected with the Beatles and their image was already being established for the American audience. The mainstream media presented the band's distinctiveness in terms of their appearance, sense of humor, and the Beatlemania of their fans, and noted their irreverence and seemingly universal appeal. On the eve of their American debut performance on the Sullivan show, the public knew enough about the band and their hit single for both to be parodied by the Andre Tahon Puppets on the Saturday night broadcast of *The Hollywood Palace*, the American Broadcasting Company's new variety show, that night hosted by actor Gig Young (*Hollywood Palace* February 1964). Pushed by Epstein, Martin, and the fans, Capitol's publicity machine had at last cleared the path for the Beatles to take their best shot at success in America.

The importance of reports of the ecstatic reaction of young Beatle fans to the early image of the Beatles and Capitol's promotion of the band is impossible to overstate. Even the sleeve notes for the first Capitol album, *Meet the Beatles* (written by Tony Barrow, the Beatles' press agent), focused upon the mania of British fans. The young American audience was primed for a similar reaction.

The Beatles appeared on *The Ed Sullivan Show* for the first time on the evening of Sunday, February 9, 1964. Of the 50,000 requests for tickets to the show, only 728 could be granted. Before an audience packed to capacity and dotted by groups of girls and young women beside themselves in anticipation of the big event, Sullivan made his famous introduction: "Now, yesterday and today our theater's been jammed with newspapermen and hundreds of photographers from all over the nation, and these veterans agree with me that the city never has witnessed the excitement stirred by these youngsters from Liverpool who call themselves The Beatles. Now, tonight you're gonna twice be entertained by them—right now and again in the second half of our show. Ladies and Gentlemen . . . The Beatles!" (*Beatles: First U.S. Visit*). In the first half of the show the Beatles performed "All My Loving," "Till There Was You," and "She Loves You." There they were for the studio and television audience: Lennon on the right, Harrison at center, and McCartney on the left. Starr, though behind the band, was on a raised platform, thus according him a centrality, even an equality not seen since Jo Jo Jones, Gene Krupa, and Buddy Rich, during the heyday of big band and jazz, from the 1930s to the 1950s.[6]

The Beatles played "I Saw Her Standing There" and "I Want To Hold Your Hand" in the second half of the show, to the deafening screech of their hysterical, screaming fans. An estimated seventy-three million people, or nearly sixty percent of all American television viewers, easily the largest television audience assembled to that time, witnessed this first live appearance by the Beatles on American television. It was even reported that the crime rate was lower on that night than at any point in the previous half-century. (Lewisohn 145; Norman, *Shout* 224–25).[7]

This was not the reaction that had been expected when the Beatles were signed to perform on *The Ed Sullivan Show*. The American variety show host had become aware of the group as he and his wife awaited a departing flight from London's Heathrow

Airport. Sullivan, ending a talent-scouting trip to Europe, was taken aback by the pandemonium accompanying the Beatles' return from an October 1963 tour of Sweden. He was impressed enough to sign the group for an appearance on his television show, though his initial intent was to book the group as a novelty item on a show otherwise centered about an established American act. Brian Epstein, in New York City in November, 1963, promoting one of his other acts, insisted, however, that the group be given top billing. In exchange for a cut appearance fee, Sullivan agreed. The Beatles contracted to headline on February 9, again on February 16, and to tape a number of songs for a subsequent show. The fee for each appearance was $3,500, and $3,000 for the taping. The show's producer, Bob Precht, recalled, "Even for an unknown act, that was about the least we could pay" (Norman, *Shout* 204). With expectations initially so low for this "novelty" act, the reaction stirred by the appearance came as a welcome surprise.

Commentators on the phenomenon, journalists and others, were alternately bewildered and amused by the commotion accompanying the English singers' arrival and subsequent appearance on the Sullivan show. The program's musical director, reported the *New York Times*, said, "The only thing that's different is the hair, as far as I can see. I give them a year" (Buckley 70). The paper's Paul Gardner called them "glandular," but was perceptive enough to call their arrival a "dreamy American success story with a British accent" (Gardner, "British Boys" 19). The influential radio and television critic, Jack Gould, was dismissive of their appearance: "The pretext of a connection with the world of music . . . was perfunctorily sustained by the Beatles. But in the quick intelligence beneath their bangs, there appeared to be a bemused awareness that they might qualify as the world's highest-paid recreation directors." He continued: "In their sophisticated understanding that the life of a fad depends on the performance of the audience and not on the stage, the Beatles were decidedly effective." He termed their Sullivan show appearance a "sedate anticlimax" ("TV: The Beatles" 53).

Yet Beatlemania continued to pick up steam. "Wild-Eyed Mobs Pursue Beatles," read the headline of an article appearing in the February 13 edition of the *New York Times*. "The efforts of an army of energetic press agents," wrote Robert Alden, "particularly on radio, helped to whip up the youngsters and to send them into the streets in search of their idols." Dozens of girls were injured as they pursued the Beatles around Manhattan. Angered police claimed that press agents were bringing fans to the Plaza Hotel, where the Beatles were staying, though the unsubstantiated statement was later withdrawn (Alden 26).

Following a brief trip to Miami, Florida, where they again appeared on *The Ed Sullivan Show*, the Beatles returned to New York. Four thousand fans were at Kennedy International Airport to welcome them back, and to see them off as they departed for England. The *New York Times* reported that the crowd was so large "100 airline mechanics and baggage handlers were called upon to reinforce the already augmented police" ("Beatles Depart" 18). The Beatles' success in America enhanced their popularity at home, and between eight and twelve thousand screaming teenagers awaited the Beatles at London's Heathrow Airport. Several hundred "enthusiasts" had camped out all night on the observation deck, others in the terminal, giving it the appearance of a "refugee camp" ("Usual Sound and Fury" 87). The manic behavior of fans, a focus of the national media, was the norm throughout 1964 and 1965.

While the *New York Times* critics took a somewhat skeptical view of the Beatles and their fans, positive assessments filled the nation's mass-market periodicals, which had quickly identified their own stakes in promoting and publicizing the band and its exploits. In the February 24 issue, *Newsweek* called the Beatles "a band of evangelists" whose "gospel is fun," for whom "audiences respond in a way that makes an old-time revival meeting seem like a wake" ("George, Paul, . . ." 54). In recapping the band's visit, a *Time* commentator described the Beatles' progress "through scenes that might have been whimsically imagined by Dante." In New York and Miami, "massed thousands [of teenage girls] closed in as if to devour them." In Washington, D.C., they were greeted by "hundreds of grotesquely clawing hands reach[ing] toward them through the massive iron bars that partition Union Station." Finally, at Manhattan's Carnegie Hall, in words resonant with the country's martial culture, the Beatles "stood on stage in a hail of their beloved jelly beans" as "flashguns . . . lighted the great interior like night artillery, and they [the Beatles] boomed their electrified rock 'n' roll into the wildly screaming darkness." While impressed by the pandemonium, the critic was dismissive of the Beatles' talent. "All this seemed redolent of flackery, and the Beatles were certainly well publicized. . . . But part of the Beatles' peculiar charm is that they view it all with bemused detachment [and] they disarmingly concede that they have no real talent at all" ("Unbarbershopped Quartet" 46).

Talented or not, the Beatles were at the center of a phenomenon that begged explanation. A three-part series on the Beatles and Beatlemania in the *New York Times* described the social aspects of the phenomenon. Among the factors contributing to Beatlemania noted in "Peoplewise" were adolescent revolt against parental authority, the increased status of belonging to a group, the sexual attractiveness of the Beatles (and their appeal to the maternal instinct), the support of individuals seen as fellow teenagers and underdogs, and the "frenetically felt urgency for having a good time and living life fast in an uncertain world plagued with mortal dangers." Central to the article were comments by Barnard sociologist Renee Claire Fox, who theorized that the "wide range of the Beatles' appeal stems from their personification of many forms of duality that exist in our society." These dualities included the Beatles' male and female characteristics (with explicit reference to their hair), their positioning as both adults and children, and their appearance as "good boys who nevertheless dress and pose as bad ones—London's Teddy-boys."[8] The article continues, "In the Beatles, Dr. Fox believes, people see four basically nice young boys who project some of the same contradictions that exist in many Americans, who are having a wonderful time at the acceptable expense of both themselves and their audiences" (Osmundsen 20).

David Dempsey, in his article "Why the Girls Scream, Weep, Flip" in *The New York Times Magazine*, provided a number of different perspectives on the frenzied behavior accompanying appearances by the Beatles. His is among the first articles to explore the phenomenon of Beatlemania as a cultural event, and as such provides an interesting contemporary analysis. Dempsey presented four areas of inquiry into the phenomenon: the anthropological, the psychological, the socioeconomic, and the moral. Dempsey's description of Beatlemania as a "malady," however, underscored his generally critical view of the phenomenon. His observations were welcomed by many, but strongly objected to by Beatlemaniacs and others speaking on the teenagers' behalf. Dempsey's article and the response it engendered are worth reviewing.

Anthropologically, writes Dempsey, rock and roll is a "throwback, or tribal atavism. . . . It is probably no coincidence that the Beatles, who provoke the most violent response among teen-agers, resemble in manner the witch doctors who put their spell on hundreds of shuffling and stamping natives" (15). In terms of psychology, the deliberately induced outer frenzy of Beatlemania is "aimed at staving off the inner frenzy that threatens young people during a difficult period of adjustment." Such a view was propounded in 1941, with regard to jitterbugging, in an article by Theodor Adorno appearing in the scholarly journal *Studies in Philosophy and Social Science*. Dempsey, drawing upon Adorno's work, finds that the "vast, noisy and clamorous mob of adolescents . . . are expressing their desire to obey. They are products of a conformist, and sometimes authoritarian, society, and their obedience to the beat [as Adorno wrote] 'leads them to conceive themselves as agglutinized with untold millions of the meek who must be similarly overcome'" (69–70).

Dempsey's socioeconomic interpretation of Beatlemania holds that hero worship, "such as that conferred on Fabian, Johnny Mathis and the Beatles, is ultimately the product of an affluent society which, for the first time in history, has made possible a leisure class of professional teenagers." From this new class emerges an "enormous market of consumers" which insists that its heroes be approximately the same age as its constituents; hence, according to this view, teenagers find their idols among equally youthful singers, actors, and popular entertainers of all kinds. The youth of the personalities makes it easier for "female members of the cult to go berserk," and by "mobbing" their idols, they are "thus able to reverse the boy-girl roles" and act as the aggressors (70).

Finally, Dempsey notes the moral component of Beatlemania. Simply put, teenagers have "found a new, and perhaps a last remaining, excuse for being young." This so-called "last-fling" theory "proves again that rock 'n' rollers are rather desperate even in fun." Further, the "violent and spectacular diversions of the young are taking place in a moral vacuum caused by the abdication of their elders. If this vacuum is filled with tin gods, it is largely because the adult world has not offered them a valid religion." Dempsey likens the "hysteria of the Beatlebug" to the "compulsive shuffle of the aborigine, the rage of the Bacchante, [and] the frenzy of the tarantella dancer," concluding that there is "[n]o wonder the jumpers can seldom explain what makes them jump. And no wonder that they have such a miserably happy time doing it (Yeah! Yeah! Yeah!)" (70–71).

In the weeks that followed, the Dempsey article sparked a lively correspondence in the "Letters" section of *The New York Times*

Magazine. The March 8 edition contained two letters commenting on the piece. "Teen-agers like rock 'n' roll because its basic sound moves and excites them, or because its rhythm and beat make it enjoyable to dance to, or because a particular singer inspires wistful longing in the teen-age breast," wrote one observer; it is not because "the Beatle mopheads remind them of witch-doctor ancestors" (Chaikin 4). Another reader believed the Beatle-struck teenagers "are screaming and weeping and flipping only to call attention to themselves." They continued, "Anyone who loves music would not scream about it but would absorb it. Anyone who loves the Beatles should do likewise" (Bernstein 4). The following week, on March 15, a reader complained: "I don't see why people have to analyze things all the time. With all the stress and strain there is in our complicated society, I'm glad the Beatles arrived to take our minds off these problems" (Pollack 12). This prompted a response, in the April 5 edition, from an older reader who found that "people analyze things because their minds are more active than their emotions," and concluded that the Beatles "could not possibly have been a success without the cooperation of naive, unsophisticated audiences who lacked the shrewdness and the wit to see that they were being skillfully used" (Reusch 10). Later that month, on April 19, a reader countered that "a young person is immediately confronted with the shocking death of our President, mass extermination in Hochhuth's 'The Deputy,'[9] the possibility of nuclear holocaust, racial tension, brutality and daily reports of Americans being killed in an effort to stave off Communism in South Vietnam," and concluded, "The Beatles may not last for very long; the anxieties which contributed to their success will" (Zeitlin 46, 48). A final observer noted that, "Perhaps it is the four generous young men [i.e., the Beatles] who are being 'used'" (Carrighan 48). Beatlemania obviously sparked strong emotions among fans and detractors alike.

Interestingly, Dempsey refers to "female members of the cult" who "reverse the boy-girl roles" and act as the aggressors. Though there was no way he could have known it, he may have been witnessing the first stirrings of the women's movement. So claim Ehrenreich, Hess, and Jacobs (1992): "Beatlemania was the first mass outburst of the sixties to feature women. . . . To abandon control—to scream, faint, dash about in mobs—was, . . . to protest the sexual repressiveness, the rigid double standard of female teen culture. It was the first and most dramatic uprising of *women's* sexual revolution" (85). Drawing on the work of the German sociologist Theodor Adorno, Dempsey had argued that the girls were merely conforming. Ehrenreich and her coauthors agreed that Beatlemania exhibited conformity, but, importantly, it was conformity *against* the values and mores of adult society (89). For instance, part of the excitement for girls who participated in Beatlemania was sexual: "It was even more rebellious to lay claim to the *active*, desiring side of a sexual attraction: the Beatles were the objects; the girls were their pursuers. . . . To assert an active, powerful sexuality by the tens of thousands and to do so in a way calculated to attract maximum attention was more than rebellious. It was . . . revolutionary" (90).

Of course, this analysis has the advantage of hindsight. Closer to the event, Beatlemania was widely viewed as simply a temporary hysteria among the young (particularly young girls). Psychologist A. J. W. Taylor (1968), working from data collected shortly after the Beatles' 1964 tour of New Zealand, found that girls who were "keen" on the band were "younger, more gregarious, assertive, active, worrying, excitable, and inclined towards emotional instability than both the 'moderates' and the 'resisters.'" However, the relatively mild reaction of older adolescent girls encouraged the researchers that even the "keen" girls might "grow through their stage of immaturity and flagrant conformity to group pressures" (169). Interestingly, Taylor noted awareness on the part of adolescents that the Beatles would provide them with an "opportunity for conformity in exhibitionism," and "for which adults in authority expressed their resentment and apprehension in advance" (165). This seems to support Ehrenreich and others in their assertion that, in their conformity to Beatlemania, girls and young women were exhibiting a rebelliousness and rejection of the values of the adult world. It was a feminist awakening of sorts, and an important step in the development of the women's movement that crystallized later in the decade.

As we have seen, the Beatles' early image was consistent with the standard star image in that it was based around a rags-to-riches narrative and the teen idol example. Coupled to this process of standardization was Adorno and Horkheimer's pseudo-individualization, and great effort was expended on establishing the Beatles' uniqueness, as expressed in the length of their hair, their clothing, their manner, and their "Britishness" (most apparent in their accents and jargon). Even before their arrival in America, the Beatles' hairstyle had caught the attention of American media. It was something new, to be sure. The hairstyle had developed over time, first taking shape in Hamburg, Germany, during their second visit to the city, in 1961, and reaching its final shape during a visit later that year to Paris. The "Beatle-cut" had its origin in the hairstyle the boys first adopted from German art students. Soon, the long front of this "French" cut was combined with a long back, retaining a connection to the Beatles' "rocker"-inspired ducktail (also called a DA, for "duck's ass") (Miles 60–61; see also Spitz 244–45, 267). Hardly new to German and French youths, the hairstyle was a shock to America's sensibilities, where crew cuts and other short styles were the norm. The promotional value of the haircut was seized on by Capitol, which, in late December 1963 during the buildup to the Beatles' arrival, began placing advertisements featuring a silhouette of the "moptop" in *Billboard*.

Look published a two-page photo spread showing the Beatles' effect on hair length in England ("What the Beatles have done to Hair" 58–59). In November 1963, *Time* was impressed by neither the band's talent nor the reaction of their fans, but nevertheless noted the Beatles' unique appearance: ". . . [T]he boys are the very spirit of good clean fun. They look like shaggy Peter Pans, with their mush-room-haircuts and high white shirt collars" ("New Madness" 64). The January 31 issue of *Life* reported the uproar in Great Britain over the Beatles' hair. The executive officer of the aircraft carrier *Bulwark* snapped, "I note with alarm an increasing number of pe-culiar haircuts affected by teen-age members of the ship's company, attributable, I understand, to the Beatles. . . . Get deBeatled now." The headmaster of one boys' school was similarly unimpressed: "This ridiculous style brings out the worst in boys. . . . It makes them look like morons." Faced with the ultimatum to cut his hair or else, a Kent schoolboy declared, "I would rather leave than change my hair." And so he did ("They Crown Their Country" 30). Across the country—and shortly, in the U.S.—the "Beatle-cut" became a sign of rebellion and nonconformity among boys; hair length con-tinued to grow throughout the decade and became an important symbolic statement for the counterculture. In 1964, suddenly, there was an alternative to the DA for rebellious youths (". . . it's better than a duck's," said one Brooklyn youth who was drawn to the Bea-tle's "tough sound" [Cameron 34B]).

Accompanying the band on their limousine ride from Kennedy Airport to their motel after their arrival in the U.S., *Life*'s Gail Cam-eron had this exchange with Ringo Starr:

> While searching the car for my shoe I asked if this was just a routine day for the Beatles.
>
> "NO," he [Ringo] said emphatically. "We never expected anything like this—it was really GEAR."
>
> Gear?
>
> "Fab," he explained, translating quickly from his native

Beatle-ese, "you know—really great." (Cameron, "Yeah-Yeah-Yeah" 34B)

The Beatles were somewhat exotic, as Cameron learned: "They're just so sexy, also foreign," said one young female fan. "No, no," interrupted several disgusted boys. "It's the sound, it's a tough sound. . . . The American rock 'n' roll is getting to be a drag," said a boy with a Beatle haircut. "I don't know what the Beatles' beat is, but it's different" (34B).

Along with the length of their hair, their clothing, their manner, their sound and their "Britishness," the Beatles' image also focused on their obvious sense of humor, another aspect adding to their uniqueness. This sense of humor was most often exhibited in the Beatles' irreverence before the press, fans, even the royal family. In November 1963 *Newsweek* reported Lennon's now-famous remarks at the Royal Command Performance. The Beatles were "unawed," with Lennon quipping, "People in the cheaper seats, please clap, . . . The rest of you just rattle your jewelry" ("Beatlemania" 104). The audience may have found the "boys" somewhat cheeky, but they also found them entertaining. The Beatles' often-noted irreverence was an important aspect of the Beatles' image that helped extend their appeal across generational and class lines. In January 1964 *Life* described life as a Beatle, recounting the Command Performance anecdote and adding to the mounting evidence of the band's sense of humor: "Asked to explain their funny haircuts, John replied, 'What funny haircuts, old man? What exactly do you mean, funny?' When Ringo Starr was asked why he wore four rings on his fingers, he responded innocently, 'Because I can't fit them all through my nose'" (Green, "They Crown" 30).

Shortly after the Beatles' departure from the U.S., *Newsweek* succinctly described the madcap world of the Beatles. Walter Shenson, the producer for the Beatles' proposed film for United Artists,[10] said of his first meeting with the band, "I thought I was in a Marx Brothers picture. They have a marvelous quality of disrespect." The article continued: "At the British Embassy party last week, the Beatles had a twenty-minute private session with British Ambassador Sir David Ormsby-Gore and his wife. At one point, Sir David, confused about the names, asked John if he was John. No, John said, he was Fred. Then, pointing to George, he said: '*He's* John.' Sir David started to address George as John. 'No,' George said, 'I'm Charlie,' and, pointing to Ringo, said '*He's* John.' . . . As the Beatles were leaving, Ringo turned to the unsettled ambassador and inquired: 'And what do you do?'" ("George, Paul, . . ." 57).

As with *Life* and *Newsweek*, *Time* pegged the Beatles' irreverence as one of their most appealing qualities and noted their proclivity for skewering culture, the establishment and its media, and themselves:

> What recommends the Beatles more than anything else is their bright and highly irreverent attitude toward themselves and their international magnitude. Reporters toss ticking questions at them, but it is generally the replies that explode. . . .
> "What do you think of Beethoven, Ringo?"
> "I love his poems."
> What did the Beatles think of the unfavorable reviews they got in the *New York Times* and the *Herald Tribune*?
> "It's people like that who put us on the map."
> How do they rate themselves musically?
> "Average. We're kidding you, we're kidding ourselves, we're kidding everything. We don't take anything seriously, except the money." ("Unbarbershopped Quartet" 47)

The band's sense of humor, about themselves and about their reception by critics and young fans alike, created a path for a more general reception: one could be amused by the Beatles' behavior without being a fan of their music.

The Beatle wit did far more than merely amuse, however, though this was hardly apparent at the time. The band's vaunted irreverence would open up a space for the Beatles to comment on society and issues of particular relevance to their generation. It provided an important avenue to test the limits of that generation's insertion of itself into the discussion on topics as varied as fashion and politics. Youth, for the first time in the country's history, would assume a separate and distinct identity from that of the adult/establishment world with which it increasingly found itself at odds. The first big controversy, the "more popular than Jesus" furor (discussed in the next chapter), would demonstrate the growing freedom of the postwar generation to assert itself. That was still more than two years in the future, however. For now, the band's irreverent sense of humor offered a bridge to an audience well beyond their fanatical teenage following.

With regard to this teenage fan base, promotion and publicity proceeded along a predictable path. As with the teen idols that had preceded them on the charts, the Beatles were depicted as "safe." In January *Life*'s Green noted that England's Princess Margaret was "a devoted Beatle fan," as was the Queen Mother (Green, "Here Come" 25). His article was accompanied by Terence Spencer's photographs detailing the widespread acceptance of the Beatles; those counted among "fans" included billionaire J. Paul Getty, the "world's richest man," who was shown donning a Beatle wig at his Scottish castle, and the Salvation Army's Joystrings combo, which "rocks gospel tunes Beatle-style to 'keep up'" (Green, "Here Come" 30).

Ed Sullivan was instrumental in publicizing the Beatles' widespread appeal. The Beatles quickly won the approval of other entertainers and artists. Elvis Presley and Colonel Tom Parker (Presley's manager) sent their congratulations to the Beatles on their first appearance on *The Ed Sullivan Show*—a fact announced by Sullivan to his studio and TV audience. During their second appearance, a week later, Ed Sullivan announced to the audience that Richard Rodgers, the acclaimed American composer of popular music, had sent along his congratulations to the band, and that he was one of their "most rabid fans" (*Beatles: First U.S. Visit*). In the days that followed, other noteworthy people fell to the "contagion," a malady from which "[n]o one seemed wholly exempt," as *Time* called it. The magazine reported on the "infected," including the difficulties encountered by painter Andrew Wyeth when he tried to get his son a ticket to the Sullivan's show ("he would have gone himself if he could have found a pair"). New York Governor Nelson Rockefeller's wife Happy and two of her children from a previous marriage attended one of the Beatles' Carnegie Hall shows. The appearance of the liberal Republican's governor's wife caused a stir in the society pages—it was the "first time she has been photographed with her children since her divorce and remarriage." In Washington, the British Ambassador, Sir David Ormsby-Gore, hosted the "non-U foursome"[11] at a reception at the embassy, with his wife, Lady Ormsby-Gore, introducing the band to the gathered dignitaries ("Unbarbershopped Quartet" 46). *Life* caught the reaction of one young fan at the first Sullivan appearance: "Well," explained Kathy Cronkite, thirteen (daughter of the *CBS Evening News* anchor Walter Cronkite), who was there with her sister Nancy, fifteen, "their accents are so heavenly and their hair is so adorable. Our father doesn't really like our reaction very much, but we can't help it" (Cameron 34). The much-admired CBS news anchor was not condoning his daughters' behavior; nor, apparently, was he stopping it. The *New York Times* reported that famed conductor Leopold Stokowski, directing the American Symphony Orchestra at Carnegie Hall before 2,700 junior high school students, had turned his attention to the Beatles. Amidst the intermittent laughs and screams, he noted that the Beatles "give the teen-agers something that thrills them, a vision. . . . The boys and girls of this age are young men and women looking for something in life that can't always be found, a joie de vivre." He even indulged their hysteria: "I like anything that makes for self-expression. Life is changing all the time. We are all looking for the vision of ecstasy of life. I am too. . . . Whatever you enjoy doing, do it" (Shepard 13).

The Beatles were even introduced into the political rhetoric. The *New York Times* reported that British Prime Minister Sir Alec Douglas-Home, after visiting Washington, D.C., to discuss Britain's nuclear deterrent with President Johnson, returned to London and told a group of young Conservatives that his "secret weapon" [the Beatles] were "making sure there would be no dollar crisis for Britain this year" ("Home Says Safety" 3). "It seems to me that these blokes [the Beatles] are helping people to enjoy themselves," commented Prince Philip. In his estimation, they were a "helpful" influence ("Beatles Are 'Helpful'" 5).[12]

Adults, and especially parents, could take comfort from the fact that the Beatles were so widely accepted. Parents might even consider them preferable to previous heartthrobs. As noted in *Time*, Elvis Presley's pelvis had invited a reaction from his admirers that was "straight from the raunch." As for Frank Sinatra, "no lass misread the message" bobbed out on his Adam's apple. The Beatles, on the other hand, were "really Teddy bears" and "as wholesome as choir boys. They only stand and sing. In a mass of misses, they only bring out the mother" ("Unbarbershopped Quartet" 46). *Newsweek* similarly stressed the unthreatening nature of the foursome. "[T]he Beatles' appeal is positive, not negative. . . . They have even evolved a peculiar sort of sexless appeal: cute and safe." As one thirteen-year-old New Yorker had it, "The Beatles are just so funny and nice and, well, cool" ("George, Paul, . . ." 54). "The thing is . . . ," explained one fifteen-year-old girl to *Life*'s Gail Cameron, "they sing decent songs, they're not dirty or anything like a lot of the rock 'n' roll groups here." A seventeen-year-old observed, "You know, . . . this is the first time I've gone nuts over a singer that my parents didn't tell me it was disgusting" (34).

Not nearly so prevalent as descriptions of the Beatles' "safe" qualities, but certainly important to the band's image, was the

Beatles' "toughness": "They're tough. . . . Tough is like when you don't conform. It's not hoodlum. A leather jacket that's tailored— that's tough. Jimmy Dean was in the same class as the Beatles because he was tough. You're tumultuous when you're young, and each generation has to have its idols" ("George, Paul, . . ." 54). And recall the response *Life's* Gail Cameron elicited from teenage boys asked what set the Beatles apart: "It's the sound, it's a tough sound. . . ." For some of their fans, then, the appeal sprang not from perceptions of their being safe, but rather from perceptions of their rebelliousness.

The Beatles promised something that had largely disappeared from teen culture. It is important to remember that their arrival came only years after the teenage "problem" had been solved in America. Though undergoing no discernible increase, juvenile delinquency had emerged in the early 1950s as a cause célèbre for traditionalists, a point not lost on the mass media. The film industry was successful at both criticizing the perceived youth threat and exploiting the youth market, releasing films like *The Wild One* (Columbia, 1953), *The Blackboard Jungle* (MGM, 1955), and *Rebel Without a Cause* (Warner Bros., 1955). Hollywood offered teenagers role models like Marlon Brando who, as the biker gang leader Johnny in *The Wild One*, presented an iconic image of delinquency and rebellion. James Dean's portrayal of Jim Stark in *Rebel Without a Cause* seemed to capture the societal fear of the aimlessness of contemporary youth.

But Hollywood's exploitation of the youth audience was not traditionalists' only interest. Spurred on by the controversy sparked by publication of Frederic Wertham's *Seduction of the Innocent*, the Senate held hearings on the comic book industry. In the book, the New York psychiatrist argued that comic books, specifically "crime comic books" (such as *Superman* and *Detective* comics and various horror and suspense comics), in presenting environments full of cruelty and deceit, and suggesting criminal and sexually abnormal ideas, could negatively affect children. Perhaps exceeding Wertham's own views, at the time all too many people were willing to believe in a cause-and-effect relationship between comic books and delinquency. In 1954, hoping to short-circuit any efforts to have a government-imposed censorship regime put into place, the comic book industry followed in the footsteps of Hollywood, which in the early 1930s had imposed a Production Code. The Comics Code made it all but impossible to distribute any comics not in compliance with the Code's proscriptions, which focused upon the perceived preoccupations of delinquents, sex, and crime (Goulart 212–17).

Perhaps no force was more emblematic of the generational change lamented by traditionalists than the advent of a new musical form targeted specifically at teenagers. Rock and roll erupted in the United States in the mid-1950s. Arising from the social interaction of blacks and whites in the South, rock and roll was heavily influenced by black rhythm and blues (and white country and western music).[13] Numerous small recording studios, including Chess Records in Chicago and L&M in New Orleans, specialized in black, or "race," music. While rhythm and blues was growing in popularity in white clubs and venues, there was very little crossover between white-owned and black-owned radio stations. This began to change in the early 1950s. At Cleveland's WJW, disc jockey Alan Freed was hyping "rock and roll" as early as 1950; he was the first to program rhythm and blues (with the less racially charged label of rock and roll) for a white audience. Rock and roll did not come into its own, however, until the arrival of Elvis Presley. Presley's "black" sound and suggestive body movements found a large and devoted audience among the country's youth. Presley's popularity and the frenzy accompanying his early appearances were not surpassed until the Beatlemania of 1964 and 1965. In spite of its devoted following, rock and roll's first rush of popularity, led by singers such as Fats Domino, Chuck Berry, Little Richard, Bo Diddley, Elvis Presley, and Buddy Holly, was short-lived. By 1960, rock and roll had lost much of its rebellious aura due to the disappearance from the scene of its most visible practitioners: Elvis Presley was inducted into the U.S. Army in 1958; Jerry Lee Lewis's career foundered after his marriage to his thirteen-year-old cousin was publicized in 1958; Chuck Berry was imprisoned in 1959 after being found guilty of violating the Mann Act;[14] Buddy Holly, along with Richie Valens and J. P. Richardson (the Big Bopper), died in a plane crash in early 1959; in 1957 Little Richard found God and left the music business; and in 1959 the first rumblings were heard of what would become the payola scandal.[15] With these threats removed, the youth music of the early 1960s was safer, sanitized; into the void left by the passing of the first generation of rock and rollers stepped the teen idols, Brill Building pop, and the girl groups. In this context, the Beatles harkened back to a time, not so long ago, when rock and roll symbolized rebellion.

The Beatles' image included apparently contradictory qualities. They are described as "safe" and "tough," "choirboys" and "sexy." As noted of the film star image by Richard Dyer, the Beatles' image appears to have been effecting a "reconciliation of . . . apparently incompatible terms" (Dyer 26). To the audience at the turn of this century, it is perhaps unexpected to see the Beatles discussed in terms of their toughness. Yet this aspect of the band was pronounced in their early promotion. Their toughness was an indispensable component of their *ordinariness*—an essential element of the star image covered in greater depth, below. It is useful to recall that Jack Paar, in introducing the Beatles (and their image) to his prime-time audience, noted that the Beatles were from "the toughest part of England. . . . Merseyside, near Liverpool . . . in the dock area" (*The Jack Paar Program*). Toughness certainly was part of the band's image prior to their being "cleaned up" by Brian Epstein. Epstein himself, in his autobiography *A Cellarful of Noise* (1964), recalled his first glimpse of the Beatles at a lunchtime performance of the band at Liverpool's Cavern Club, on November 9, 1961: "They were not very tidy and not very clean. . . . I had never seen anything like the Beatles on any stage. They smoked as they played and they ate and talked and pretended to hit each other. They turned their backs on the audience and shouted at them and laughed at private jokes" (Epstein 98). Meeting them after the performance, and beginning a courtship that would culminate in Epstein becoming the band's manager in January 1962, Epstein noted, "There was some indefinable charm there. They were extremely amusing and in a rough 'take it or leave way,' very attractive" (Epstein 99). George Martin, meeting the band for the first time in April 1962, was intrigued by the Beatles' sound, which showed "a certain roughness I hadn't encountered before" (Martin 122). Despite the sanitizing influence of Brian Epstein, the Beatles' early image possessed an aura of wildness, one brought to life in much of their music.

The Beatles were utterly unlike anything heard in the United States since the end of rock and roll's golden era of the mid- to late 1950s. Their harder edge was a resounding rejection of contemporary pop slickness, a fact that was quickly discerned by many of their young fans, and that was obvious on their first U.S. single for Capitol, "I Want to Hold Your Hand"/"I Saw Her Standing There," and on the album *Meet the Beatles!* The single introduced the American audience to the sound created in Hamburg's Star Club and Liverpool's Cavern: a tough, guitar-driven sound anchored to a heavy beat. On the A-side, the vocals exhibit more than anything else the youthful impatience of the song's protagonist. Lennon and McCartney push their vocals to the breaking point: "I can't hide, I can't hide, I can't hide!" they sing, as the guitars, bass, and drums crescendo into the next verse. "I Saw Her Standing There" exhibits, one suspects, the "certain roughness" that first interested George Martin in meeting the band. The recording sounds as if it could have been captured at a live performance of the band, McCartney shouting out across the Cavern crowd. Raw, exuberant, aggressive— the single was unlike anything to hit the charts in years.

While drawing attention to their uniqueness (for example, their hairstyle and the fact that they came from England), Capitol promoted the Beatles in much the same way any teen idol or teen-oriented group would be marketed. Greg Shaw (1992) succinctly describes the standardized world of the male teen idol: "The songs were aimed primarily at teenage girls, the ones in the suburbs who wanted big fluffy candy-colored images of male niceness on which to focus their pubescent dreams. Charming, wholesome dreamboats, the singers were safe and well mannered, perhaps with a teasing tendency toward wildness" (108). Indeed, the Beatles' songs were directed at teenage girls, and Capitol, in the sleeve notes for *Meet the Beatles!* as well as in the *National Record News* that was distributed as part of the promotional campaign, called attention to the ardor of young female fans and urged its sales staff to do likewise. As reported in the mainstream press, the band apparently enjoyed universal appeal across generational and class lines, which seemed to confirm that the Beatles were "nice" and "safe"—and "tough."

Thus the Beatles' early image was, in many respects, consistent with that of the teen idol. Despite the band's resemblance to, and marketing as, teen idols, however, the Beatles were more formidable than their predecessors for one essential reason: they wrote their own music and, in so doing, were in a unique position to exploit fully their core teenage, female market. By design, a significant portion of their songs dealt with relationships between the sexes, and most involved direct address of their young female audience. Though pursuing a grueling schedule of concerts and other appearances, Lennon and McCartney nonetheless set time aside for writing. Working diligently at their craft, they eventually settled on a "little trick," as McCartney later called it (Miles 148–49): personalizing lyrics through the use of first-person pronouns and direct address of their young female audience. In fact, the track listing devised by Capitol for *Meet the Beatles!* features *only* relationship songs: "I Want to Hold Your Hand," "This Boy" ("would be happy just to love you"), "It Won't Be Long" ("till I belong to you"), "All I've Got to Do" ("is whisper in your ear the words you long to hear, and I'll be kissing you"), "All My Loving" ("I will give to you"), "Little Child" ("won't you dance with me"), "Hold Me Tight" ("let me go on loving you"), "I Wanna Be Your Man" (". . . love you like no other baby, like no other can"), "Not A Second Time" ("You hurt me then, you're back again").

A generally positive and innocent view of relationships permeates the music of the Beatles throughout the touring years, and is most pronounced in 1963–65.[16] While many of their early compositions were "filler" written "to appease the mob," as McCartney later referred to the songs and the female fans for whom they were written (Miles 149), the fact that the Beatles were singing their own songs made them unique and different from the standard teen idols. One can imagine teenage girls across the country listening to *Meet the Beatles!* or the latest single and fantasizing that they were the objects of the Beatles' affections.

"I Want to Hold Your Hand" is a perfect distillation of the strengths and preoccupations of the album. Lyrically, the song approaches its intended female audience by means of Lennon and McCartney's finely tuned formula; musically, it displays more energy than any recording since the heyday of Little Richard and Jerry Lee Lewis. The verse is a direct and personal appeal for the girl to "let me be your man," which she can demonstrate if only she will "let me hold your hand." The bridge declares that intense kind of love most pronounced among the young: inescapable, uncontainable, and often agonizingly unrealized except in the fantasies of the smitten, "such a feeling that my love, I can't hide, I can't hide, I can't hide," as the opening musical phrase of the song is repeated by two guitars, bass, and drums. The direct and personal address to young female fans is heightened by the recording's driving beat, with opening chords that mirror the barely restrained energy of the lyrics. The Beatles' toughness is on display on a recording that is louder, more raucous, and more passionate than anything that had appeared in years, if ever.

The beat was infectious and inescapable, and the single quickly became a jukebox and dance favorite. In a sense, this was a very liberating recording: Above all else, perhaps, it demanded that one *move*. Coinciding with the advent of Beatlemania the song presented an opportunity for young girls and women to act out their own awakening sexuality, whether through the physical release of Beatlemania, or within the somewhat more controlled setting of the dance. The recording's effect was heightened by another feature separating the band from the standard teen idol: there were four Beatles upon whom to shower one's affections.

The urgency of the opening chords of "I Want to Hold Your Hand" signaled a change of epic proportions, and forces only hinted at in the 1950s were about to redefine the cultural landscape. The single, according to *Billboard* the "fastest-breaking disk in the label's history,"[17] ushered in an era of chart domination by the Beatles and other youth-oriented acts. More generally, it marked the beginning of youth domination of mass culture in America. America's baby-boom generation, for the first time exercising its economic power largely without adult interference, was a market of such size that its exploitation was guaranteed. And the youth-oriented acts did not simply produce music for the market; they provided models of behavior for their young fans, who donned similar apparel, adopted similar mannerisms of speech, and increasingly organized their lives around rock and roll music. To be sure, the seemingly inexhaustible appetite of the youth market resulted in the realignment around a youthful ideal not only of those industries catering to the young but, ultimately, of culture itself. It is tempting to view the evolution of youth culture solely within the context of its exploitation within the marketplace; however, this is not the whole story. Young people did not simply consume but began to *produce* mass culture in a way never before experienced. The baby-boom generation came into its own as an economic and cultural force.

As with the single,[18] market forces pushed Capitol's album campaign ahead of schedule. Faced with growing demand for Beatle product and aware that Vee-Jay intended to release *Introducing the Beatles*, Capitol pushed forward the release date of *Meet the Beatles!* from mid-February to January 20, 1964 (Spizer, *Beatles' Story, Pt. II* 4). Capitol, consistent with industry practices, chose to include both sides of the single, with the remainder of the album culled primarily from the Lennon-McCartney songs on the second British album, *With the Beatles*: "I Want to Hold Your Hand" and "I Saw Her Standing There" were joined by "It Won't Be Long," "All I've Got to Do," "All My Loving," "Little Child," "Hold Me Tight," "I Wanna Be Your Man," and "Not A Second Time." Also included were Harrison's "Don't Bother Me," the band's rendition of "Till There Was You" (from the Broadway show *The Music Man*), and Lennon and McCartney's "This Boy." For Capitol, there were financial reasons to rearrange the British releases, a practice that would continue with every American album until the release of *Sgt. Pepper's Lonely Hearts Club Band* in 1967. British albums typically contained fourteen tracks, and royalties were paid as a percentage on total albums sold. In the U.S., publishers were (and are) paid a mechanical licensing fee for each song that appeared on the album. As a result, more songs would mean more publishing fees that would have to be paid.

Interestingly, Capitol's shuffling of the Beatle catalog for this first album helped to foster notions of the Beatles' artistic and commercial command: On each of the first two British albums, *Please Please Me* and *With the Beatles*, nearly half of the tracks were by composers other than the Beatles. In contrast, *Meet the Beatles!* contained only one track not composed by Lennon and McCartney or Harrison. Prior to the Beatles' arrival, composing and performance were viewed as separate talents and activities, and songwriters rarely performed their own compositions. Even in Britain, the Beatles' self-reliance was rare in the pop idiom. Their ability to dominate the charts in terms of recordings *and* compositions placed them in a unique position and provided a model for many of the bands that followed.

From 1959 to 1963, music companies like Motown and Aldon Music had their own composers providing songs to their own producers and performers; Brill Building pop, Motown, teen idols, and girl groups dominated the charts. As Jon Fitzgerald (1997) describes in his article, "Songwriters in the U.S. Top Forty, 1963–1966," songwriters associated with girl groups and female soloists dominated the top forty singles charts of the early 1960s. In 1963–64, the songwriting teams of Barry Mann–Cynthia Weil, Kal Mann–Dave Appell, Gerry Goffin–Carole King, Jeff Barry–Ellie Greenwich, together with Ben Raleigh and Howard Greenfield, combined for forty-nine top forty singles. They wrote only seven in 1965–66, however, as their fortunes followed those of the acts with which they were associated (Fitzgerald "Songwriters," 107). During this period, the charts experienced a swing in dominance away from girl groups (such as the Marvelettes, the Ronettes, Martha and the Vandellas, the Shirelles, and the Shangri-Las) and soloists and toward male groups. While the nonperforming composer remained an integral part of the industry's production apparatus, the arrival of the Beatles inaugurated a period during which male groups recording their own compositions were on the rise. Lennon and McCartney's success as composers, quite apart from their status as entertainers, was also on the rise; in addition to the fourteen U.S. top forty hits penned for the Beatles in 1964, the pair also wrote six top forty hits for other performers, including Peter and Gordon and another act managed by Brian Epstein, Billy J. Kramer and the Dakotas (Fitzgerald 92–108).

Capitol's reliance on the compositions of Lennon and McCartney in structuring both the first single and *Meet the Beatles!* undoubtedly contributed to perceptions of the band's talent and uniqueness. Had Capitol simply reissued the Beatles' current British release, *With the Beatles*, an album brimming with recordings of songs by American composers, perceptions of the American influence on the music of the Beatles would have been more pronounced. In addition to covers of Meredith Willson's "Till There Was You," Chuck Berry's "Roll Over Beethoven," and "Devil in Her Heart" by the Donays, a Detroit girl group, the Beatles drew upon the songwriting talent of Motown for renditions of the Marvelettes' "Please Mr. Postman" (the first number one hit for Motown), the Miracles' "You've Really Got A Hold On Me" (written by Smokey Robinson), and Barrett Strong's top forty hit, "Money," co-written by Janie Bradford and Motown founder Berry Gordy, Jr. With the exception of "Till There Was You," these tracks and a cover of Little Richard's "Long Tall Sally"[19] joined a number of Lennon-McCartney originals for *The Beatles' Second Album*, released by Capitol on April 10, 1964.

Additional evidence of the Beatles' debt to American music was to be found on the Vee-Jay release *Introducing the Beatles*. Containing essentially the same track listing as the Beatles' first British album *Please Please Me* (with the title number and "Ask Me Why" excised), the album was released on July 22, 1963, to little fanfare, and again in January of the following year. To capitalize on the group's popularity on the eve of their first visit to the United States, the album was rereleased one week after *Meet the Beatles!*. Along with Lennon and McCartney's "I Saw Her Standing There," "Misery," "Love Me Do," "P.S. I Love You," "Do You Want To Know A Secret," and "There's A Place," the album contained American favorites from the Beatles' huge repertoire, including Arthur Alexander's "Anna (Go to Him)," Goffin and King's "Chains," Dixon and Farrell's "Boys," "Baby It's You" (David, Williams, and Bacharach), "A Taste of Honey" (Scott and Marlow), and the Isley Brothers' top twenty hit from June 1962, "Twist and Shout."[20] As this list demonstrates, the Beatles' musical influences were not limited to the first generation of rock and rollers like Chuck Berry, Little Richard, the Everly Brothers, and Elvis Presley. Their musical identity also resided in their eclectic taste and mastery of other genres of British and American popular music, including Tin Pan Alley and Brill Building pop, a point remarked upon by numerous commentators.[21] While American music had been formative in the band's development and a core element of its repertoire, one can see that Capitol's selections in compiling the single and first albums presented the Beatles as an independent and self-reliant music act fortunate to have a seemingly endless supply of hits provided by their two young songwriters.

Within the context of their image, it is possible to see other advantages rising out of the ashes of the Beatles' early failures in the U.S. market. In promotion first impressions are important, and the cover for *Meet the Beatles!* was a striking introduction of the Beatles to the American audience. At the Beatles' instigation, Robert Freeman shot the cover for *Meet the Beatles!* in the style of photographs of them taken in Hamburg by Astrid Kircherr (Spitz 447–48). The cover featured a headshot of the four Beatles, their faces half lit and emerging from the darkness. That cover broke with the conventions of the time, displacing the teen idol vacuity common to the idiom with the black and white austerity of an arthouse photograph, thus promoting the Beatles in a startling and unique way, and in the process creating a mold for promotion of the youth-centered acts that were about to explode onto the market.

It is also noteworthy that Beatles releases that had once failed to establish themselves in the charts upon their original debuts were a substantial portion of the singles and albums that flooded the charts during the six months following the band's first visit and preceding their first full tour of the United States, in August–September 1964. The *Billboard* "Hot 100" singles listing for April 4, 1964, showed the Beatles holding the top five positions: 1. "Can't Buy Me Love"; 2. "Twist and Shout"; 3. "She Loves You"; 4. "I Want to Hold Your Hand"; and 5. "Please Please Me." "Can't Buy Me Love" was released on March 16, 1964; there had been advance orders of over two million in the U.S. alone—an unprecedented feat. In addition to the top five positions held on the April 4 "Hot 100" charts, the Beatles also occupied positions 31, 41, 46, 58, 65, 68, and 79 (Whitburn, *Top 10 Charts* 111; Whitburn, *Top Pop Singles* 38; Lewisohn 138). Of the top five songs, only the first and fourth were released by Capitol; number two, number three, and number five were released by Tollie, Swan, and Vee-Jay, respectively, all of which briefly retained the rights to the Beatles' masters for those songs. Well into the summer of 1964, in addition to the Capitol releases, the singles charts were full of Beatle product released by smaller labels trying to exploit fully their limited (and expiring) interests in the Beatles.

The album charts were similarly awash with Beatle music as Capitol releases and those of other companies vied for chart position. *Meet the Beatles!* spent eleven weeks at the top of the album charts and was followed by *The Beatles' Second Album*, which spent five weeks at number one. *A Hard Day's Night*, the United Artists soundtrack album for the first Beatles film, hit record bins on June 26, 1964, just prior to the U.S. tour, and reached number one on July 25, staying there for fourteen weeks. In total, Beatles albums spent thirty weeks atop the charts in 1964 (Whitburn, *Top 40 Albums* 390). In addition to the aforementioned albums, Capitol released *Something New* (number two in August 1964) to claim some of the market United Artists had staked out with the hugely successful feature film and soundtrack album. *The Beatles' Story*, a biography of the band including narration, snippets of dialogue with the band, and parts of hit recordings, was released in December and reached number seven. RadioPulsebeat released a collection of interviews with the Beatles in June 1964; *The American Tour with*

Ed Rudy reached number twenty. Vee-Jay's *Introducing the Beatles* reached number two in the week following their first appearance on *The Ed Sullivan Show* (Whitburn, *Top 40 Albums* 28–29).

The effect (on their later success) of the Beatles' earlier failure to break into the U.S. market is worth restating: In 1964, in the interests of exploiting whatever rights one had over Beatles product, the market was flooded with recordings from no less than six separate labels (Capitol, United Artists, Swan, Tollie, Vee-Jay, and RadioPulsebeat). The Beatles' domination of the charts was such that *Billboard* noted a growing dissatisfaction within the industry: "Record manufacturers are asking when will it end? One man's Beatle is another man's poison, according to disk makers. With the wide variety of Beatle product on four labels, and the unprecedented air play this one act has been getting over the past month, disk sales on other than Beatles product has gone soft as a grape" (Maher "Beatlemania . . ." 3). Capitol's early rejection of the band had led predictably to a string of failed releases by lesser labels that possessed neither the incentive nor the resources to fully promote the band. As a result, the band had caused little stir among America's teens. Thus, once the decision was made to promote the band, Capitol was free to define the band as it saw fit. In the wake of that promotional campaign, the overwhelming reception and the public's voracious appetite for Beatles product meant the market was flooded with records from numerous companies, fueling the band's unparalleled dominance of the charts.

While most Americans remained largely unaware of Britain's class system, the Beatles' humble beginnings were nevertheless exploited in furtherance of their star image, their modest backgrounds providing the requisite element of identification for their fans.. Their defeat of the class system closely tracked the American myth of success, a ubiquitous feature of the star image. Richard Weiss, in his study *The American Myth of Success* (1969), defines this "most enduring expression[s] of American popular ideals," the notion "that

ours is an open society, where birth, family, and class do not sig-
nificantly circumscribe individual possibilities": "The belief that
all men, in accordance with certain rules, but exclusively by their
own efforts, can make of their lives what they will has been widely
popularized for well over a century. The cluster of ideas surrounding this conviction makes up the American myth of success" (Weiss
3). With roots in American Puritanism, the myth of success evolved
into its modern understanding through post–Civil War "rags-to-
riches" literature, of which Horatio Alger's stories are emblematic,
and the success literature of the late nineteenth and early twentieth centuries.

Dyer suggests that the American myth of success, particularly
as developed in the star system, orchestrates a number of contradictory elements: "That ordinariness is the hallmark of the star;
that the system rewards talent and 'specialness'; that luck, 'breaks,'
which may happen to anyone typify the career of the star; and that
hard work and professionalism are necessary for stardom" (Dyer 42).
Within this system, not only do most star images tout the humble
background of the star, they also demonstrate success through conspicuous consumption. In a sense, this conservative rendering of the
American myth of success offers a capitalist ideal, a kind of morality
play in which anyone, no matter how ordinary, who is willing to
work, can (with a little luck) find success, that is, the ability to purchase anything and everything one's heart desires.

The quality of "ordinariness" is a necessary prod to audience
identification in the United States and, hence, nearly universally
present in American star narratives. In Great Britain, it exemplifies
the ascendance of the working class within British culture. British television personality and journalist Kenneth Allsop, writing in
1967, noted, "Today's British pop entertainers are consanguineous.
The Beatles and the Rolling Stones, the Pretty Things and the Animals, the Who and the Kinks, Georgie Fame and Wayne Fontana—
and onward through the charts—are working-class boys. . . ." He

continues: "The interesting and quite emphatic change is that the predecessors of these entertainers traded on their 'commonness' and exploited it into a cheerily vulgar style." The Beatles, however, "have not put their sludgy Liverpool through any refining filter, but nor do they use it as a comic prop" (128–29). In the 1960s the British working class and provincials declared their presence as never before. From the "angry young men" of the stage to the rise to prominence of a new generation of authors, artists, film actors, and pop stars,[22] the working class of the industrial north helped to define British culture in the 1960s. To be working class, and from the north of England, suddenly carried with it a certain cultural capital, a change marked by Allsop:

> One of the deluge of surveys of teenagery recently gave this tape-recorded snippet of a very contemporary anxiety neurosis: "Being middle-class is the most degrading thing in youth. You'd do anything rather than be thought conventional. . . . One despises convention and yet has a sneaking fear of it." So a middle-class girl I know, and her 16-year-old friends in a £500-a-year Home Counties school, talk the Lancashire and Yorkshire of their disc idols all the time among themselves, and change with polyglot dexterity into orthodox county only within earshot of their parents (130).

The London establishment was far from welcoming. As one member of London's fashion community commented: "To be quite honest with you . . . in those days the Beatles were regarded—fashion wise, particularly, and quite generally, amongst our sort of set if you like—as hicks. I mean they were these guys with silly suits and hairdos out from Liverpool of all places!" (Lobenthal 200). In Britain, the Beatles pursued a grueling schedule of performances, television and radio appearances, and recording sessions before finally transcending the traditional limits of their origins. On the other side of the Atlantic, their commonness, along with their youth, offered an immediate point of identification between the band and their young fans.

Following a tried and true scheme perfected in Hollywood, the Beatles' ordinariness was a cornerstone of their image. *Time* provided readers with this description of the Beatles' backgrounds: "All from Liverpool, all in their early 20s, they come from similar working-class backgrounds. George Harrison's father is a bus driver. Paul McCartney's sells cotton. Ringo Starr, the somewhat corvine drummer, is the son of a house painter" ("Unbarbershopped Quartet" 46). *Newsweek* also noted their "lower middle-class origin," in Liverpool, which was described as "a gritty town where unemployment runs high." As Bill Harry, then the twenty-five-year-old publisher of Liverpool's *Mersey Beat* magazine, said: "A beat career is the equivalent of becoming a boxer in the beginning of the century— the only way into the luxury world" ("George, Paul, . . ." 55).

Two seemingly contradictory elements negotiated within the Beatles' image are the Beatles' luck in getting their big break, and the notion that they had earned their success through hard work. One of the first U.S. articles to profile the Beatles, appearing in *Newsweek* in November 1963, alluded to the role of luck in the Beatles' success: "Somehow—and no one can explain exactly how— the Beatles, rather than 200 similar [Mersey] groups, clicked. 'Everybody's trying to figure what suddenly makes a group go,' says drummer Starr. 'Sometimes I try to figure it out, too'" ("Beatlemania" 104). Luck may have brought them celebrity, but, consistent with the American myth of success, the Beatles' fortunes were also depicted as resulting from their hard work. One of "countless" Liverpool bands, the Beatles started their rise to stardom with "a long line of one-night stands. They actually went off to the beer cellars of Hamburg to become fully professional" ("Unbarbershopped Quartet"

47). *Seventeen*'s Edwin Miller provided even more details about the Beatles' time in Hamburg, where they "crystallized their power-driven style" playing "seven-hour sessions. . . . They took turns singing to save their throats" (Miller, "Bit" 83).

One lucky break came in the form of Brian Epstein's becoming aware of the band. Epstein's parents owned one of England's largest and most successful retail firms and numerous outlets, including the Liverpool appliance store in which their son Brian had created a successful record department. It was there that, in 1961, he got a request for a new single by the city's own Beatles, "My Bonnie," on which they back Tony Sheridan. Intrigued, he ordered the single, which promptly sold out. *Newsweek* recorded Epstein's recollection of the event: "I decided to sort them out . . . and found they were working 100 yards down the street. They were dead scruffy and untidy in those days, and actually it was an environment I wasn't used to, because I was always more interested in classical music. But I liked them enormously" ("George, Paul, . . ." 55). In much the same way that the press had portrayed Colonel Tom Parker as the man behind Elvis Presley's success, Brian Epstein was touted as the genius behind the Beatles. *Newsweek* provided a laundry list of his accomplishments just a week after the Beatles' return to England. Having first made "minor alterations" in their image, he first "got them into trousers and sweaters," before finally putting them in suits. He also teamed them with established British acts and in the process got them top or near-top billing. He advertised heavily and "posed them exotically, in junk and ruins, after the style of fashion layouts. And he made them wash." Above all else, the young entrepreneur believed in his charges. Epstein "confidently expected" their unprecedented success, coming to the States to "stir up interest" when the band failed to catch the attention of the American public. Epstein signed them with Ed Sullivan, who had already "been impressed" by the sight of 15,000 Beatlemaniacs at London airport

("George, Paul, . . ." 56). Thus, as presented in *Seventeen*, *Time*, and *Newsweek*, the Beatles' unparalleled success arose from hard work and good luck: they mastered their craft through long hours in the clubs and constant touring; they had the good fortune to have been spotted first by Brian Epstein and then by Ed Sullivan.

In years to come, as their recordings and music increasingly were viewed as innovative, the Beatles' uniqueness would be more securely tied to their talent. This was expressed in terms of their chart domination, their innovation, their artistry, and in terms of their singular position as leaders and models for the youth culture. In early 1964, however, notions of their specialness distributed through the mass media were limited primarily to the reaction of their fans, and to the novelty of the Beatles' physical appearance.

Even before their arrival in the United States, American media took note of success that was phenomenal even by the standards of the much larger American market. *Newsweek* reported in November 1963:

> They are the Beatles, and the sound of their music is one of the most persistent noises heard over England since the air-raid sirens were dismantled. This year they have sold 2.5 million recordings of their own compositions, songs like "She Loves You," "Love Me Do," and "Please, Please Me." Their theater appearances drew 5,000 screaming fans and a police riot squad in Manchester; 4,000 began queueing up at 3 a.m. in Newcastle-upon-Tyne; and 2,000 teen-age girls squealed their hearts out as they besieged bobbies outside the sold-out London Palladium. "This is Beatlemania," said the *Daily Mail*, and added plaintively: "Where will it all lead?" ("Beatlemania" 104)

Also that month, *Time*, while dismissing the Beatles as "achingly familiar," nevertheless acknowledged the Beatles' startling rise to the top, from the "din of the tough Merseyside pubs" to an earning capacity of $5,000 a week and record sales reaching 2,500,000 copies ("New Madness" 64).

Following their successful first visit to the U.S., *Newsweek* dissected the Beatles' commercial viability in greater detail: "In 1963 record sales alone around the world brought in $18 million (of which Beatles, Ltd.—the four Beatles only—received about $450,000). Another $500,000 was earned from sheet-music sales and personal appearances." The biggest business, however, was coming from the "fringe," from which 200,000 "official Beatle sweatshirts" were shipped to U.S. stores, and in which "Beatle wigmakers" were already 500,000 orders behind. Expected gross on official Beatle items was expected to reach $50 million in the U.S. alone in 1964. A spokesman for Remco, one of the involved companies, called the Beatles "the most promotional item since the flapper era" ("George, Paul, . . ." 56[insert]).

In the *New York Times* on February 17, Martin Arnold's "Moneywise" article detailed the fortunes of the one American company licensed to manufacture Beatle clothing, the Reliance Manufacturing Company, calling its Beatle-oriented business the "biggest promotion in [the company's] sixty years." The company reported that their sales of Beatle merchandise had already totaled $1.4 million wholesale, or more than $2.5 million retail. Another enterprise, the Lowell Toy Company, the only American company licensed to produce Beatle wigs, was turning out 15,000 a day (Arnold 20). Success, whether in terms of touring receipts, record and merchandise sales, or critical acclaim, remained an important part of the Beatles' image throughout the 1960s.

Arnold's analysis was part of a series of articles the *New York Times* ran that day that attempted to explain the Beatles phenomenon in terms of publicity, business, and as a social event. McCandlish Phillips, whom author and journalist Gay Talese called "one of the best reporters on the paper,"[23] observed that the Beatles could not have made it in America had they not first been successful in Great Britain, for the American market was already saturated with rock and roll acts; thus it was difficult for one act to distinguish itself from the "mass and stand forth in bold relief." It was easier for an act to differentiate itself in the "far less glutted British market." As Phillips noted, news accounts of Beatlemania's emergence in Britain appearing in the *New York Times Magazine*, *Variety*, and elsewhere spawned such demand for Beatle records that Capitol Records rushed its Beatles releases ahead of schedule and distributed a "million copies of a four-page tabloid full of publicity on the Beatles [the *National Record News*] to disk jockeys, buyers and the press," in order to further increase demand throughout the United States. In addition, Capitol also supplied a "seven-inch long-playing record to disk jockeys at hundreds of independent stations. The disk featured three Beatles songs and an 'open-end interview with the Beatles.'" Phillips further noted the "genial conspiracy to promote the Beatles" among disk jockeys, "so that Beatlemania would in turn promote them" ("4 Beatles and How They Grew: Publicitywise" 1+).

This mutually beneficial relationship would continue throughout the Beatlemania period and was essential to the group's first success in the U.S. and their unprecedented success in the months that followed. Radio's complicity in popularizing the Beatles— including record play, but also special promotionals, extensive news coverage, and giveaways—was such that by October *Billboard*, in an article titled "Beatles: Plague or Boon for Radio?," could note a certain level of dissatisfaction within the industry. Many radio programmers attributed the mania of the fans to complicit deejays—the "'Monster' was of their own making" (Faggen 16). Dissatisfaction with Beatle domination had earlier been expressed by labels competing with Capitol who found it nearly impossible to get airplay for their releases due to the unprecedented airtime being devoted to the Beatles (Maher "Beatles . . ." 1).

While top forty programming was eclipsing the era of the deejay personality, there were those who clung to the old ways. Within the New York market the disk jockey who became most associated with the Beatles was Murray "The K" Kaufman, who had inherited Allan Freed's evening spot at 1010 WINS in the competitive and nationally influential New York City market. WINS, faced with the problem of creating an ambience that would draw and maintain the attention of teenagers, had given Kaufman Freed's old time slot. Kaufman, with his nickname and rapid-fire delivery, emulated African American disk jockeys, as had Freed (Passman 246). If anything, however, he was more frantic than Freed and was, according to Tom Wolfe, the "first big hysterical disk jockey" (*Kandy-Colored* 40). For a time, his style allowed him to dominate the competition of the New York market. In response, the other stations employed their own "hysterical disk jockeys." WABC called its team of deejays the All Americans; WMCA called theirs the Good Guys. Eventually WABC's Bruce Morrow, known on the air as "Cousin Brucie," displaced Murray "The K" from the top, as did the Good Guys. That, however, was before the Beatles arrived.

By the time of the Beatles' arrival at Kennedy Airport, on February 7, 1964, the promotional campaign that Capitol had finally undertaken had begun to pay off. Every newspaper, television station, network, magazine, and radio station had someone there to cover the event. WINS, unable to think of a suitable news reporter to send to the airport for a live broadcast, sent Kaufman. Kaufman masterfully insinuated himself into the proceedings, placing himself at the feet of the band, which was seated behind a small table atop a temporary stage. The photographers were supposed to have first access to the Beatles, but while they snapped their pictures, Kaufman poked a microphone up at the band and proceeded to interview them, to the consternation of the gathered reporters and photographers. The next night Kaufman escorted the Beatles to the Peppermint Lounge, and acted as their unofficial tour guide for the remainder of this first American tour, even sharing a room with George Harrison in Miami (Wolfe, *Kandy-Colored* 43–46). The Beatles, a little awestruck by their reception in America, were only too willing to accommodate Kaufman's requests for plugs, not only for WINS but also for "Swinging Soiree," his nightly show. Thus the Beatles played an instrumental role in the promotion of Kaufman's station and of Murray "The K" as a radio personality. The self-proclaimed "fifth Beatle" (briefly) regained his position as New York's most popular radio personality.

Having appeared twice on *The Ed Sullivan Show* and played two shows at Carnegie Hall and one at the Washington Coliseum, the Beatles returned to England on February 22. Even in the Beatles' absence, however, American audiences were kept abreast of the mania accompanying the group's appearances. The first Australian concert, in Adelaide on June 12, 1964, "ended in a near-riot" as "tear-stained girls" stormed the stage. Earlier, the *New York Times* reported, "a hysterical crowd of 25,000 broke through barriers and formed a screaming mob around the Beatles' car when they arrived [in Adelaide] by plane from Sydney." It was further reported, "Two girls were trampled and a 60-year-old woman collapsed" ("Police Halt Beatles' Show" 14). In Melbourne, an estimated 250,000 people saw the Beatles on their six-mile drive from the airport, reportedly nearly twice as many as turned out to see Queen Elizabeth II and Prince Philip the previous year. The *New York Times* reported that "teen-agers swept away barricades and broke through police lines re-inforced by soldiers and sailors. . . . More than 300—mostly girls—were treated [for minor injuries] at emergency Red Cross stations. Fifty others were taken to hospitals" ("250,000 Australians" 35). The following week, in Wellington, New Zealand, "police battled thousands of screaming teen-agers" ("Beatles Fans Fight Police" 20). Shortly, these scenes would be repeated throughout the U.S. as the Beatles mounted their first full-blown tour of the country, in August and September 1964.

A number of factors contributed to the unprecedented success the Beatles enjoyed in the American market. The band possessed a highly developed star image before arriving in the U.S. Capitol defined the Beatles' image according to proven models and practices, and it was developed along the standardized path of the teen idol. The image was differentiated from other teen idols by the band's newness and uniqueness, their irreverence, their success, and the Beatlemania of their young fans. The group's "joie de vivre" (as Stokowski put it) was welcomed by their young fans, perhaps, in part, as a hopeful response to the national tragedy of President Kennedy's assassination. In a culture inundated with images of the star, permeating society by means of magazines, radio, television, movies, sound recordings, and newspapers, the Beatles' image had a distinctly American ring to it: modest backgrounds, success through hard work, talent, perseverance, and luck. Thus their early image validated the core value of the American myth of success—"the belief that all men, in accordance with certain rules, but exclusively by their own efforts, can make of their lives what they will" (Weiss 3).

Capitol spared no effort in promoting the Beatles once it became apparent that their music was indeed a viable product in the American market. This promotion, at an unprecedented cost, was instrumental in raising expectations upon the Beatles' arrival, and in enlisting the support of New York radio stations and disk jockeys. The Beatles' appearance on *The Ed Sullivan Show* and coverage in the national print media guaranteed them a national audience, not only for their music but also for the mania that they stirred. The vagaries of the market also contributed to the band's success: Once unable to secure a major label release, with the release of "I Want to Hold Your Hand," the Beatles' found themselves enjoying unprecedented success as (much to the chagrin of those promoting other bands and soloists) the charts flooded with Beatle product from record labels exploiting their limited and lapsing interests in the band.

At this early date, the image was in its most controlled and pristine state, an anglicized teen-idol ideal unblemished by the ravages of time or independent reportage. Promotional materials from Capitol were the foundation for much of the mass media's descriptions of the band in early 1964, and reveal the machinations of mass consumerism: a sketchily defined object becomes the repository of meaning for audience members who, in effect, declare their individuality by participation in the mass. A mass message eliciting an individual response on a mass scale, the Beatles' image was defined only enough to elicit identification. Their young fans filled in the details with product-fueled fantasies of romance and adventure.

Their unparalleled accomplishments, and the phenomenon of Beatlemania, ensured that the Beatles would retain a public presence throughout 1964. Their image, marked by their irreverence, newness, uniqueness, success, toughness, universal appeal, and the mania that their appearances aroused, was promoted in the months following their first visit to the United States. It was most prominently displayed in *A Hard Day's Night*, a film that both crystallized the image that would dominate throughout the touring years, and helped to bring the Beatles success and acceptance among a wider audience.

THREE

"Preparing Our Teenagers for Riot and Ultimate Revolution" The Touring Years, 1964–66

ON FEBRUARY 18, 1964, a week prior to the Beatles' departure from the United States, the *New York Times* noted that the Beatles had signed with United Artists Corporation to star in a movie ("Beatles Signed" 28). Riding high on their success in Great Britain, the Beatles inked a three-picture deal with United Artists even before actively testing the U.S. market. United Artists felt Beatlemania would peak by the summer, so they required the film be completed by June 1964. Hence, the film's preproduction was under way prior to the Beatles' first visit to the United States.

In October 1963, producer Walter Shenson enlisted Liverpudlian Alun Owen to write a script. To direct, Shenson recommended Richard Lester to the Beatles. Though they had never heard of him, once they learned that he had worked with Peter Sellers and the Goons, their favorite comic entertainers, they were anxious to work with him, and in January 1964 he was signed to direct what ultimately became *A Hard Day's Night*, a film that was wildly successful with fans and well received by the critics. The film helped to solidify aspects of the Beatles' image that emerged with the band's first visit to the United States. This incarnation of the Beatles—as witty, irreverent, young, and lovable moptops—retained its popularity with young fans throughout the touring years. During this period, the Beatles collected more accolades, gained greater recognition for their music, continued to dominate the record charts, and mounted numerous successful tours, including three circuits of the United States during the summers of 1964–66.

The Beatles followed *A Hard Day's Night* with *Help!* (1965), another hit at the box office. The commercial success of the Beatles, on record, on tour, and in the movie theater, allowed them freedom to experiment with their music, and by 1966, the progression from *Help!* to *Rubber Soul* and then *Revolver*, had culminated with compositions that were stretching the limits of sound recording and technical complexity, and that were increasingly difficult, even impossible, to bring to the stage. The Beatles tired of touring and performing before screaming crowds that could not even hear their performance. They were weary of playing cute, safe, pop stars, and were increasingly vocal on a whole range of topics including the conflict in Vietnam, civil rights, and religion. In effect, the Beatles transgressed Epstein's carefully cultivated image, the one promoted since late 1963, and actively presented a more authentic version of themselves to the public, one often radically different from that of the Beatlemania years.

This chapter looks at the development of the Beatles' image during the chaotic years of touring and Beatlemania. It begins with a discussion of *A Hard Day's Night*, the film that crystallized the Beatles' image of the Beatlemania period, and continues with an examination of the image's evolution up to the end of touring in 1966, a period during which the realities of America's changing society were reflected and responded to within the image.

In November 1963, Alun Owen accompanied the Beatles on tour to get an insight into both the Beatlemania phenomenon and the Beatle sense of humor. Owen, as noted above a Liverpool playwright, was well known for his depictions of northern England. He was handpicked by the Beatles to write the script for their first movie, which was to be structured around a day in the life of the Beatles. In creating the story, producer Shenson and writer Owen observed a number of rules crafted to be consistent with the promotion of the Beatles and their image. First, there was to be no evidence of romantic relationships. As Shenson said, "I'd be torn apart by those fans, probably deported, if one of the boys got mixed up with a girl." Second, no Beatle was to go unrecognized in the story, for it would strike English fans as absurd. Third, each Beatle had to have a solo scene—fans had their favorites, and Shenson also wanted to bring across the clearly defined personalities of the band members (Watts, "The Beatles'" 13).

Consistent with the image of the Beatles promoted on their first visit to America, Beatlemania figured prominently in the film. This was by design, noted Shenson to *Seventeen*'s Edwin Miller: "My idea was to begin the film with a shot of the Beatles running down a street followed by a mob of their fans. That way, even in Japan—where they didn't know the Beatles then—you would see that opening shot and know that they were successful performers of some kind" (Miller, "What Are the Beatles" 176). Their irreverence was also put to the fore, showing itself as cheekiness before the representatives of the establishment. For instance, in one scene the Beatles share a train cabin with "Mister Johnson," a stuffy establishment man. He is taken aback by their appearance, notably their hair, and even more so by their behavior. At one point, Ringo turns on his transistor radio:

> Johnson: And we'll have that thing off as well, thank you. [He rises and turns off the radio.]
>
> Paul: Yeah, but we want to hear it and there's more of us then you. We're in a community, like a majority vote. Up the workers and all that stuff! . . . Look Mister, we've paid for our seats too, you know.
>
> Johnson: I travel on this train regularly, twice a week.
>
> John: Knock it off, Paul, y'can't win with his sort. After all, it's his train, isn't it, Mister?

Johnson: And don't take that tone with me, young man! . . . I
fought the war for your sort.

Ringo: Bet you're sorry you won!

Johnson: I'll call the guard!

Paul: Aye . . . but what? They don't take kindly to insults.
Ah, come on, you lot. Let's have a cup of coffee and leave the
kennel to Lassie. ("Script")

This irreverence and rebelliousness appeals to the young women
in the train's restaurant car with whom the boys flirt (among them
the future Mrs. Harrison, Patti Boyd), in effect stand-ins for female
Beatle fans all over the world. The type of "wildness" the Beatles
exhibit is, of course, thrilling but safe, consistent with that of the
teen idol. At this point in the band's career, their status as teen idols
was still being cultivated within the image.

To fully grasp the film's role in solidifying the image in the public consciousness, it is important to place the film within its historical
context. The Beatles were associated with the newest trends and artistic movements in and out of popular music throughout the 1960s.
An early example is *A Hard Day's Night*, which is widely considered
a groundbreaking film. Because this film firmly places the Beatles
in the realm of the new and different, it is worthwhile to examine
its place within contemporary British filmmaking.

Having started his career directing commercials for television,
Richard Lester began making films in the beginning of the 1960s,
and made one short film and nine features during that decade. He
directed the Goons' *The Running, Jumping and Standing Film*, a film
with which the Beatles were familiar and which seemed, to film historian Roy Armes, "like a breath of fresh air after the committed so-
lemnities of Free Cinema" (258). Free Cinema was a documentary
movement within the British cinema of the 1950s. Led by Karel
Reisz and Lindsay Anderson, the movement was dedicated to the
notion that film should be a medium of personal expression dedi-

cated to illuminating the problems of contemporary life. In particular, films such as Anderson's *O Dreamland* (1954) and Reisz and Tony Richardson's *Momma Don't Allow* (1956) depicted the disillusionment and frustration of British working-class life. A product of its time, the emergence of Free Cinema coincided with the rise of social realism in British literature and theater, and was an influence on that movement's expression in British cinema in the early 1960s. Drawing inspiration and much of its source material from the "angry young man"[1] authors and playwrights, these films depicted the futility of working-class life. Generally set in the industrial Midlands and shot on location, the films featured working-class protagonists. The focus on working-class culture was unheard-of in British cinema, and marked a new level of realism in British narrative cinema. The environment inhabited by the hard-drinking, brawling miners and factory workers was shown in grainy black and white, the better to capture the gloom of the northern cities in which the stories took place. The genre's popularity was short-lived, however, and production of these "kitchen sink" films rapidly declined after 1963.[2] Its bleak images and subject matter fostered a reaction in the mid-1960s, one centered on "Swinging London" and exemplified by films such as *Alfie* (Lewis Gilbert, 1966), *Georgy Girl* (Silvio Narizzano, 1966), and those of Richard Lester.

Indeed, Lester's films stand in stark contrast to those of the Free Cinema movement and the social realist cinema that followed. While seeking to capture the real, the earlier film directors turned the camera's eye toward the dreary smokestacks of the north and sought immersion in the most oppressive settings they could find. In contrast, Lester's approach was detached, focused on the absurd and surreal. While the early part of the decade was marked by the bleakness of British social realism, that movement soon gave way to a British cinema dominated by expatriates, such as Lester, Stanley Kubrick, Joseph Losey, and Michelangelo Antonioni, whose films lack the obvious affinity for the working-class seen in the work of many of their British contemporaries.

As David Cook (1990) notes, in *A Hard Day's Night* (and *Help!*) Lester employs the "full cinematic arsenal of the New Wave, telephoto zooms and swoops, flashbacks, jump cuts, and every conceivable device of narrative displacement, to create a dazzling new kind of audiovisual comedy" (599). Lester's achievement in bringing the techniques of the art cinema to the popular film strengthened the Beatles' association with the new and different—and initiated a radical change in British cinema. Lester's highly acclaimed experimental technique, frantic pacing, and absurdist proclivities soon became de rigueur in mid-1960s British film. *A Hard Day's Night* shares numerous qualities with French New Wave cinema: It was shot on location. Many of the actors, including the Beatles, were new to acting or only slightly experienced (though some, such as Victor Spinetti, who plays the anxious television director, were professional actors). Lester makes use of a fast editing style, handheld 35 mm cameras, and natural lighting. This is apparent in the fan sequences; in the opening credits the camera operator runs alongside the screaming teenagers as they chase the Beatles through the train station. Perhaps most notably, Lester, like the French New Wave directors, utilized a great many jump cuts and other means to destroy the temporal and spatial continuity of the viewing experience. For instance, at one point the band is holed up in the baggage car. Lennon pulls out a deck of cards and they begin a game. Suddenly, the card players are transformed into musicians as the strains of "I Should Have Known Better" are heard and, in the place of cards, McCartney and Harrison hold a bass guitar and guitar, respectively, Starr taps drumsticks, and Lennon plays his harmonica. Another example is found in the sequence mentioned earlier, in which the Beatles are joined in their cabin by an establishment man, Mister Johnson, who demands that they abide by his rules for the cabin. The Beatles have had enough of Mister Johnson and, after some snide quips, exit the cabin. As Mister Johnson settles back to enjoy his solitude, they suddenly appear outside the cabin's window, running alongside the train, banging on the glass and taunting its stuffy occupant. This is absurd, but it works within the context of the environment Lester is creating. Throughout the film scarcely any attempt is made to utilize the seamless narrative and cutting style associated with Hollywood. Lester focuses on the specific qualities of film and editing, and employs them to create an unreal film environment that not only captures the Beatles' (and the director's) sense of humor, but also continuously reminds the audience that they are watching a film.

Noted historian of French cinema Susan Hayward (1993) said of the French New Wave, "This cinema . . . was as much about the process of film-making as it was about desanitising the sacred cows of the bourgeoisie. Film-making practice (the technology of media) exposed social practice (consumption)" (209). Similarly, A Hard Day's Night actively exposes filmmaking practice. At one point the boys, bored and constrained by the drudgery of their star-making lifestyle, break out of the television studio to gambol in a nearby field. The handheld camera shakes wildly, McCartney at one point lunging at the camera as if to wrestle it away from the operator; an aerial shot is used to look down on the momentarily emancipated Fab Four as they cavort in the field, as are varispeed techniques—all transgressing the classical Hollywood formula and pushing the audience's attention back to the process of filmmaking. The reflexivity of Lester's approach is also on display in the ever-present instruments of mass communication. One example is the Beatles' performance in the television studio at the end of the film. Lester is careful to show not only the band but the control room technicians and apparatus. In the final segment the director's assistant twists the knobs of her monitor, bringing the Beatles in and out of focus, blacking and whiting them out.

Though far from a cinephile, Lester favored the films of Buster Keaton, early Federico Fellini, Ingmar Bergman, and Jean Renoir (Yule 54). Keaton's influence, in particular, is evident in the slapstick nature of much of the film's comedy. The climactic chase scene, in which the Beatles flee the police in an attempt to make it back to the studio for their broadcast, could have come right out of a Keaton film, notably *Cops* (1922). Francois Truffaut is another director that comes to mind when viewing *A Hard Day's Night*. In particular, while Lester employed many of the techniques associated with the French New Wave, in *A Hard Day's Night* he also seems to borrow structure from Truffaut's *Les Quatres-cents coups* (*The 400 Blows*, 1959). The two films share a similar quality of space. As Gillain notes in *French Film: Texts and Contexts* (1990): "Visually *Les 400 coups* is built on an elegant binary opposition which is maintained throughout the film. Inside, at home or at school, the narration is dominated by static shots and close-ups, while outside, long and mobile shots prevail. These alterations give the film its powerful rhythm of tension and release" (Gillain 189). Similarly, Lester fashions a world in which tightly framed interiors become metaphors for the stifling aspects of his protagonists' lives, and in which camera movement and technique in exterior shots create a metaphor for a life unencumbered by stardom or the rules and institutions of the establishment. Interior scenes and the use of close-ups and medium shots dominate the first half of *A Hard Day's Night*. The settings (a train cabin, a hotel room) lend themselves to these kinds of tight shots; but there is more at work here. When the band escapes the confines of the television studio to cavort in a nearby field, they are filmed primarily in long and full shots. Symbolically, the Beatles have broken through the confines of their fame to the seemingly boundless freedom of the outside world, a sense accentuated by the camera's extravagant movements and the use of fast- and slow-motion.

A Hard Day's Night opened in New York City on August 11, one week prior to the start of the Beatles' American tour, to both critical and popular acclaim. Bosley Crowther, the *New York Times'* influential film critic, called it "a whale of a comedy," and "a fine conglomeration of madcap clowning in the old Marx Brothers' style." Crowther also lauded director Lester's inventive use of the medium. He concluded, "It is good to know there are people in this world, up to and including the major parties, who don't take the Beatles seriously" ("Screen: The Four Beatles" 41). He subsequently noted that the Beatles (and starlet Rita Tushingham, also of Liverpool) "are not synthetic creatures from hot-house dramatic schools or music conservatories that teach the refinements of Art. They are alive and true exponents of the feelings and the meanings of the mass." *A Hard Day's Night*, opined Crowther, "bids fair to be the most sensational commercial screen success of the year" ("Prides of Liverpool" 1). In fact, in its first week of release, total rentals for the film in the United States and abroad were the highest ever for a United Artists picture in a comparable period of time ("Beatles' Set Hot B.O." 4).

From a business standpoint, the release of a Beatles film one week prior to the start of their first full-scale American tour could not have been planned to better advantage, with the tour and the film generating interest in one another. Capitol once again had a competing label promoting its biggest property: United Artists, distributor of the film, also released the soundtrack album for *A Hard Day's Night* on July 18. On that same day, in a bid to cash in on the heightened sense of excitement with the tour and debut of the film looming, Capitol released "A Hard Day's Night"/"I Should Have Known Better," followed a week later by "And I Love Her"/"If I Fell," and "I'll Cry Instead"/"I'm Happy Just to Dance With You" on August 1 (all six songs appear in the film and on the United Artists album). In the first week of September, "Matchbox"/"Slow Down" debuted. Hence, in the weeks leading up to and from the tour's San Francisco opening on August 19 to the New York finale on September 20, the Beatles had four Capitol singles on the charts (including the number one hit "A Hard Day's Night"), as well as the top two albums, the United Artists soundtrack album and Capitol's *Something New* (which shared many of the same tracks).

The Beatles' sound, now propelled by Harrison's newly acquired Rickenbacker electric twelve-string guitar, proved influential in the direction that American rock and roll would take, particularly as adapted to the newly emerging folk rock. Among other young musicians sitting in dark movie theaters with other Beatle fans to see *A Hard Day's Night*, the members of the Byrds would be moved to electrify their folk sound, with leader Roger McGuinn taking up the twelve-string that would provide the "jingle-jangle" guitar playing so essential to the Byrds' distinctive sound. But there was also an "edge" to the Beatles' sound, and during the summer of 1964, from the opening chord of "A Hard Day's Night" to the climactic howl of "Slow Down," the Beatles were again exhibiting the "toughness" that was so distinctive and attractive to their young fans when the band first visited the U.S. in early 1964. This toughness was as much a function of the vocal delivery of Lennon as it was of the Beatles' big beat. In fact, it is difficult to identify another white singer of the period who even remotely approached Lennon's ferocity at the mike.

Of the Beatles, Lennon's rebellious nature was the most palpable. Harrison might occasionally be petulant, as with "Don't Bother Me" ("I've got no time for you right now, don't bother me"), and McCartney was second to none in his facility with Little Richard material, as with "Long Tall Sally" (on *The Beatles' Second Album*), a recording propelled along by McCartney's Little Richard–esque whoops and screams. No vocalist, however, presented as pure an encapsulation of rock and roll rebellion as did Lennon, and this was an attractive model of rebellion for teenage males. While McCartney impressed because of his technical mastery of the rock and roll shout, Lennon's attraction resided elsewhere: he seemed to *mean* it. Lennon had a harder edge. Whether covering the work of another or taking the lead vocal on one of his own compositions, Lennon was engaged in self-definition of himself as a rebel, and a working-class rebel to boot. In covering Bradford and Gordy's "Money," Lennon sings, "Money don't get everything it's true—what it don't get, I can't use. Now give me money, that's what I want," before his raw scream leads the song back to the opening riff. On their cover of Larry

Williams's "Slow Down," Lennon warns a wayward girlfriend that she "better slow down," before screaming, "You gotta gimme little lovin', gimme little lovin', *Owwww*—if you want our love to last!" His own compositions, or his contributions to songs composed with McCartney, tended to be tougher than his partner's. On "You Can't Do That," for instance, Lennon reveals the dark side of relationships as his jealousy boils over. Not one to stand idly by as he is cuckolded, Lennon cautions his girl that if he catches her "talking to that boy again, I'm gonna let you down and leave you flat." Emoting feelings far removed from the land of the teen idol, it is not so much love that Lennon fears losing as it is face, because everybody, "green" with envy over his apparent conquest, would change their tune: "But if they'd seen you talkin' that way, they laugh in my face."

Lennon revives in rock and roll something that had disappeared: a sense of rebellion and danger, even menace. Emerging from a British popular culture increasingly influenced by the working class, Lennon's voice struck out from its northern English working-class origins just as surely as any exclamation of the "angry young men." While McCartney's technical prowess and songwriting craft would be praised in the coming years and decades (or pilloried as the source of what some view as relatively facile solo work), Lennon from the start was raising the pop performance beyond presentation to revelation, an expression of authenticity that would be central to the mass media's presentation of Lennon as artist in the coming years. What could be characterized as mere youthful rebellion in the early years led naturally both to Lennon's growing self-awareness of his status as an oppositional artist and celebrity and to the evolution of his music and image toward more revelatory expression in the middle and late 1960s.

Lennon's delivery—harkening back to that of Little Richard and Jerry Lee Lewis, married to the big beat of the Starr/McCartney rhythm section and to Harrison's rock and roll and rockabilly–inspired guitar playing—placed the Beatles in a unique position.

A glance at the charts provides ample proof of the Beatles' relative "toughness": Joining "A Hard Day's Night," which reached number one on the Billboard singles charts for the week of August 1, 1964, were the Four Seasons' "Rag Doll," surf music stars Jan and Dean's "The Little Old Lady (from Pasadena)," crooner Dean Martin's "Everybody Loves Somebody," and recordings by artists including British singer Dusty Springfield, country singer and humorist Roger Miller, rock and roll singer and guitarist Johnny Rivers, and legendary jazz saxophonist Stan Getz. Unrivaled in terms of chart success, the Beatles were also marking out territory at the top of the charts for the guitar-driven big beat vocal groups that became characteristic of youth-oriented music, from then right up to the ascendance of rap and hip hop beginning in the late 1980s. American bands at first failed to meet the Beatles' challenge in kind. The first wave of British Invasion bands, marketed in the wake of the Beatles' phenomenal success as, essentially, more of the same—young, British, cheeky—including the Dave Clark Five, Peter and Gordon, and Gerry and the Pacemakers, were followed by the harder-edged Animals, Rolling Stones, Yardbirds, Kinks, and the Who.

"Toughness," for all its importance to the Beatles' early appeal, was only one feature of the band's music that contributed to their image. Another would have an even more significant impact on its later development. The ballads being written and performed with such mastery by the Beatles were not simply a foundation for the full cooptation of rock music into the profit-making apparatus of the music industry; they also pointed toward a more introspective approach. As is discussed in the following chapters, this introspection prepared the way for presentation of the Beatles as artists and intellectuals, functions necessary for the operation and legitimization of the youth culture. Included with the tough recordings on *A Hard Day's Night* and *Something New* were the Lennon-McCartney ballads "And I Love Her" and "If I Fell," and the Beatles continued to demonstrate their facility with the ballad. McCartney, in particular, proved adept at rendering ballads with commercial appeal. "Yesterday," released in September 1965, would go from a number one hit to an omnipresent pop standard, with over 2,500 recordings of cover versions by the mid-1990s (Whitburn, *Top Pop Singles* 39), surely a sign of rock and roll's cooptation by the music industry. Lennon's self-examination eventually would lead him in another direction, toward development of an image incorporating aspects of the artist and intellectual. The quick mind and trenchant wit obvious in Lennon's lyrics and other creative work would lead others, including Bob Dylan and Kenneth Allsop, to push him to say something with his music. He would respond with increasingly personal music, wending a path through the Dylanesque "You've Got to Hide Your Love Away," the autobiographical "Help!," "In My Life," "Nowhere Man," and "A Day in the Life," among others, and continuing with the starkly revealing pieces of his solo career. Making this possible was the emotion demonstrated by Lennon on songs such as "If I Fell" and, even earlier, "Ask Me Why."

The Beatles were greeted by 9,000 fans upon their arrival at San Francisco International Airport ("Beatles on Coast" 28), an event covered by *Life*'s Gail Cameron. Of the "tears and fainting fits," she wrote, "The cause of it all was the return of the Beatles and how can anyone describe what it means to a girl of 14 to *see* them, to *hear* them (as if anybody could above the screams), to breathe the very air they breathe, and maybe even to scoop up a blade of grass their boots trod upon? . . ." The Beatles played San Francisco's Cow Palace before a sold-out crowd of 17,000. In the photo essay accompanying Cameron's comments is a full-page picture of a teary-eyed teenage girl clasping a handful of grass. The caption reads: "Ringo! Ringo walked on this grass!" (Cameron, "A Disaster?" 61). Not everyone was so enamored, however. Local promoters were obligated to provide a special contingent of at least one hundred policemen to protect the "Loved Ones." Cameron also reported that authorities at Los Angeles' Lockheed Airport were so fearful that a fan might run out on the tarmac that they had forbade the Beatles to arrive during daylight hours. The band arrived in the dead of night, " like a troop movement in wartime or a shipment of gold to Fort Knox" (Cameron, "A Disaster?" 59).

From San Francisco the Beatles went to Las Vegas, where they were met by 2,000 chanting fans as they arrived at the Sahara Hotel. They played before "7,000 yelping, sometimes sweltering teen-agers" at Las Vegas Convention Center ("Beatles Gambling" 15). Other cities where the Beatles performed on that tour included Chicago, Minneapolis, Detroit, Philadelphia, and Pittsburgh. The Beatles were offered, and accepted, $150,000 from the Kansas City Athletics' extravagant owner, Charles O. Finley, to appear at Kansas City's Municipal Stadium on September 17 ("Beatles to Get $150,000" 22).

The "psychological phenomenon," as McCandlish Phillips called them, gave two concerts at the Forest Hills Tennis Stadium, in Queens, New York. Almost 2,000 squealing teenagers were kept at bay by one hundred policemen, including eighteen on horseback, as the Beatles arrived at Delmonico's Hotel, prior to their concerts. The *New York Times'* Phillips reported the ensuing "battle": "The teen-age backlash to adult authority threatened twice to get out of control, but swift decisive police action intervened. At 1:10 P.M., 40 girls rushed the revolving doors under the leopard-skin marquee. A mounted patrolman moved his horse onto the sidewalk and sent them fleeing. A few minutes earlier, 18 girls had pushed a guard at the service entrance and flattened him against a door in a flank attack, but the police came instantly to his aid" (Phillips, "Concentration" 9). A hotel spokesperson commented on the pandemonium: "We welcome the Beatles. We used to be dowdy, . . . But now we swing" (Phillips, "Concentration" 9). The "siege" of Delmonico's (the "Beatles' Fortress") entered a second day and, as recounted in the *Times*, more than 1,000 teenage girls stood behind police barricades while "clumps of girls in tight pants" made their "dark strategy" to gain an audience with the Beatles, the "objects of their hysterical affection" (Montgomery 95).

One of the more chaotic stops on the tour was in Cleveland, Ohio. The visit started as would be expected: 2,500 fans awaited the Beatles at Cleveland Hopkins Airport, an indication of the strength of Beatlemania in "middle America." The concert, at Cleveland's Public Hall, however, was anything but normal. The *Times* reported that police stopped the performance for about fifteen minutes in order to repel a "center-aisle rush" of teen-age girls ("Ohio Girls" 36). In the aftermath, Cleveland barred the Beatles and "similar singing groups" from the use of city facilities and the city's mayor opined, "Such groups do not add to the community's culture or entertainment." In the future, the Beatles and other groups would be limited to the use of private concert halls and facilities[3] ("Cleveland to Bar Beatles" 46).

Under the circumstances, the Beatles were relieved to leave Cleveland and proceed with the tour, ultimately returning to New York City for a $75,000 benefit concert for Retarded Infants Service, Inc., and United Cerebral Palsy of New York. In the midst of the pandemonium and disruption that had thus far characterized the tour, the Beatles' image nonetheless retained its universality. Indicating the wide sweep of their appeal, *Times* reporter Gay Talese, covering the benefit, reported the mingling of "chic and shriek": "Coolly elegant women in mink coats and pearls, together with men in black tie and in no need of a haircut, found themselves in the Paramount Theater . . . sitting amid 3,600 hysterical teenagers" (Talese, "Beatles and Fans" 44). This event capped off a successful, if chaotic, tour.

In 1965, back in England, the Beatles were named, individually, by the Queen, Members (of the Most Excellent Order) of the British Empire,[4] a fascinating episode in that it exhibits the simultaneous acceptance and rejection of the Beatles by the establishment and older generation (not to mention their fans). With bestowal of this honor by the British Crown, each Beatle was entitled to include the letters "M.B.E." after his name, and, when clothed in formal attire, to wear the medal identifying himself as a member of the Order. Though not the first entertainers to be so honored, they were the first pop singers to make the honors list.

As reported in the *New York Times*, the bestowal of the honor upon the Beatles prompted a wave of protest, with many previous honorees returning their medals. One prominent member of the Canadian Parliament, Hector Dupuis, returned his medal, complaining, "English royalty places me on the same level as vulgar nincompoops." Colonel Frederick Wagg, a veteran of two world wars and the Afghan campaign, returned twelve medals, stating, "I have written to the Prime Minister and I have resigned from the Labor party." In addition, he had ordered his lawyers to "write the Labor party out of his will which he said contained a bequest to the party of . . . ($30,800)." The letter displays the strong feelings that the event engendered among opponents—and fans.[5] "They've become respectable," moaned one sixteen-year-old girl, "and I don't want anything more to do with them" (A. Lewis, "Queen's Honors" 1). She wasn't alone in her consternation; many of the Beatles' young fans rejected the band as a result of their becoming "respectable." Nevertheless, 4,000 Beatles fans stood outside the gates of Buckingham Palace during the investiture ceremony. "Their squeals and chants of 'Yeah, Yeah, Yeah'," reported the *New York Times*, "downed [sic] out the pipes of the Scots Guards and the band of the Grenadier Guard Policemen linked arms to hold them back" (Schmidt 49). Beatlemania continued unabated.

Following the success of their first film, *A Hard Day's Night*, it was reasonable that the Beatles should quickly make another; at any rate, their contract with United Artists committed them to three films.[6] Part of a strategy of media saturation, the release of the film *Help!* coincided with the 1965 American tour, much as *A Hard Day's*

Night had prepared the way for the 1964 tour. Again directed by Richard Lester, this spoof of secret agent films, such as the James Bond and Harry Palmer stories (starring working-class actors Sean Connery and Michael Caine, respectively) then in vogue, involves the attempts of a murderous Thugee cult to take back at all costs from Ringo the ring necessary to their "filthy Eastern ways" (specifically, human sacrifice to the Hindu mother goddess Kali).

The film is a cinematic comic book more obviously and intentionally located within British pop art than was *A Hard Day's Night*. British pop art is traced to the work of the Independent Group[7] in the 1950s. Among its members were Richard Hamilton, Edouardo Paolozzi, Peter and Alison Smithson, and Lawrence Alloway. The group's aesthetic viewpoint was nonhierarchical and rejected teleological, universal explanations of the universe; its lineage could be traced back to Dada and Marcel Duchamp. Their embrace of machines, mechanisms, and ready-made artifacts represented a rejection of the high art/low art dichotomy. As Alloway observed: "The idea was of a fine art–Pop Art continuum, in which the enduring and the expendable, the timeless and the timely, coexisted, but without damage either to the senses of the spectator or to the standards of society" (Alloway, "Development" 36–38). Among the group's concerns was American mass culture, including films, advertisements, music, magazines, comic books, and celebrity.

Richard Hamilton is commonly attributed with coining the term "pop art." Prompted by Peter and Allison Smithson's suggestion that an exhibition be assembled centering upon an as yet unnamed new art form beginning to draw attention from critics in England, Hamilton described pop art as: "Popular (designed for a mass audience) . . . Transient (short-term solution) . . . Expendable (easily forgotten) . . . Low cost . . . Mass produced . . . Young (aimed at youth) . . . Witty . . . Sexy . . . Gimmicky . . . Glamorous, [and] Big business" (Hamilton, *Collected Words* 28). Through the work and exhibitions of the Independent Group and, in particular, their often lower-class students and former students in the 1960s, mass culture was reintegrated into a fine art that stood as a rejection of the high/low art dichotomy, and as a rejection of the social hierarchy of British society.[8]

While *A Hard Day's Night* arose out of the general pop milieu of 1960s London, *Help!* is patently a pop statement. Present is the fascination with all things "mass" and American: the running joke throughout is that the mad scientist Foot (played by Victor Spinetti), in attempting to steal the ring, cannot get any of his British gizmos to work properly, and so depends upon American goods. Paul, holed up with the other Beatles in Buckingham Palace and under the protection of Scotland Yard, passes time with "America's pastime," bouncing a baseball off of a wall and catching it. The Beatles' apartment is strewn with American comics and other "expendable" products, as well as automated dispensers of sandwiches and soft drinks (all emblematic of American mass production). In an interview with *Seventeen*'s Edwin Miller, the director pointed out the pop sensibilities of the film: "We're curious to see whether there isn't a correlation between pop music, pop art, and a pop movie." The film was "surrealistic, with sudden cuts, unexplained happenings." For instance, "Ringo may be fighting with a tiger in one scene, doing something completely different in the next. We want to keep the audience off balance, in a state where they cannot anticipate what will be seen next" (Miller, "On the Scene" 280).

Lester also told Miller that the costumes for the picture were "as extravagant as they would be in a comic strip." The trappings of a comic book are everywhere. An early sequence in the film details the murderous cult's first attempts to take back the sacrificial ring. An intertitle, which both harkens back to cinema's silent past and calls to mind a descriptive panel in a comic book, declares: "In the weeks that followed five more attempts were made to steal the ring." A parody of the methods employed by the evil masterminds of the Bond films and novels, these attempts include a magnetized elevator that nearly robs John and Ringo of their valuables, a Thugee-concealing mailbox, a guillotine-rigged public scale intended to sever Ringo's finger as he reaches for the slip of paper containing his weight, and a restroom with electric hand dryers tooled to suck up everything in the room (even the Beatles). The sequence culminates with another nod to the comic book: Harrison and Lennon, shot from the waist up, laugh at their predicament while text describes exactly what is shown—"Everyone laughs at Ringo's sudden apprehension."

Many scenes are introduced with on-screen text, as are the various attempts of the Beatles to solve the mystery of the ring, which, unfortunately for Ringo, is impossible to remove: "SEEKING ENLIGHTENMENT AS TO RINGS, THEY APPROACHED THE NEAREST ORIENTAL"; "NEXT. THE NEAREST RING SPECIALIST." Of course, all attempts to remove the ring fail, and the Beatles find themselves in harm's way. In one scene, Paul is shrunken to miniature when the somewhat starstruck Thug, Ahme, played by Eleanor Bron, accidentally injects him with a shrinking serum intended for Ringo. The very premise of the film, loveable moptops pursued by murderous Thugs, could have come out of a comic book. Throughout, the impossible is married to the improbable, but all is wholly acceptable within the confines of Lester's comic-book universe.

Pop art values are displayed in other ways. Classical music is frequently utilized in the most preposterous situations, which seems to be the point. The high art/low art dichotomy is collapsed as pop stars and football fans join in singing Beethoven's *Ode To Joy* in order to save Ringo from Roger, the "famous Bengal man-eating tiger" that recently escaped from the "famous London Zoo," in the words of the Scotland Yard superintendent (played by Patrick Cargill) protecting the Beatles. Similarly, Wagner's Prelude to Act III of *Lohengrin* is the musical accompaniment to the siege of the Beatles' apartment by Foot, his assistant, Algernon (Roy Kinnear), and the bloodthirsty Thugs, led by high priest Clang (Leo McKern). Tchai-kovsky's *1812 Overture* attends the destruction by the Thugs of the tank in which the band had sought refuge during the "Battle for the Salisbury Plain." (Unknown to the Thugs, the Beatles had already evacuated the tank.) At the Indian restaurant the Beatles visit in search of information about the ring, their own status as pop objects is reflected upon: a quartet playing classical Hindu instruments and music is replaced by a group of Thugs, who play the Beatles' song "A Hard Day's Night." *Help!* is full of these sorts of flourishes that play on the fragmentation and displacement of culture in postwar Europe and America, and at the same time evince the aforementioned "fine art–Pop Art continuum" envisioned by Alloway.

As with *A Hard Day's Night*, Lester impresses with his use of the camera and incorporation of the techniques of the French New Wave—for instance, direct address of the audience by the characters, use of varispeed techniques, and various absurd twists which draw the spectator's attention to the filmic process. At one point, Foot unleashes his secret weapon, a "Relativity Cadenza," upon the band, and the film footage drops into slow motion, as the voices deepen to unintelligibility. With *Help!* Lester consciously explores new territory, and the film brings into relief the values underlying contemporary British art culture. Plus, of course, it starred the Beatles. This fact alone made the film a hit with fans, and left United Artists reporting its highest earnings in its forty-eight-year history[9] ("United Artists Sets" 65).

Reception was mixed among establishment commentators. The *Washington Post*'s Leo Sullivan placed Richard Lester at the forefront of cinema's vanguard for his extravagant use of camera movement and editing (Leo Sullivan D11). The *New York Times* reported mixed reviews from the British press ("Critics Scorn Beatle . . ." 19). "Some of it is surprising," noted its film critic, Bosley Crowther, in his tepid review. He found that Lester had "played some witty pranks with his camera." There were "fetching title and color gags, and . . . amusing tricks." As for the Beatles, they were "exuberant and uninhibited in their own genial way," but had "become awfully redundant and—dare I say it?—dull." Perhaps trying to deflect the inevitable response to criticism of the Beatles, Crowther's review was delivered "with malice toward none and charity for all," and labeled the film, "90 crowded minutes of good, clean insanity." He continued, "there's nothing to compare with the wild ballet of the Beatles . . . in 'A Hard Day's Night.' . . . This one, without sense or pattern is wham, wham, wham all the way" ("Screen: Beatles Star in 'Help!'" 25).[10] Some Beatle fans were not mollified. The negative response to his review was such that he devoted an entire article to the topic, concluding, somewhat apologetically, "In the face of such dedication, how can a critic persist in protesting the limitations of the Beatles to their adoring fans? . . . Let's be patient fond parents, and hopeful. There are worse ways to begin than as a Beatlemane" ("Other Cheek" 1).

In addition to the film, in 1965 much of the media attention focused upon the Beatles' second U.S. tour and the band's financial standing. Initially, there was some question as to whether or not the Beatles would tour the United States again. "Under the Anglo-American tax treaty," reported the *New York Times*, "British and American artists are supposed to pay taxes on all their earnings in both countries only to their own governments. The Beatles' dollar earnings were so vast, Mr. Epstein [i.e., the Beatles' manager, Brian Epstein] said, that the United States apparently is having second thoughts" ("U.S. and British Taxes" 84). The impasse was such that, two days later, it was confirmed that the Beatles would not visit the U.S. Reportedly, Treasury officials were blocking the Beatles' receipt of the portion of $2.8 million earned during their tour of the United States and Canada ("Beatles to Shun U.S." 24).[11]

The Beatles did tour the United States for two weeks in August 1965, to the relief of their fans and various interested parties.

They arrived on August 13 and were greeted by 1,500 teenagers, who spent the day outside of New York City's Warwick Hotel battling one hundred police officers in an attempt to get into the building. "By noon," reported the *New York Times*, "they were behind wooden barricades, alternating between happy Beatle songfests and dour denunciations of the police. A few tried to spray the police with flour or squirt whipped cream at them" (Schumach, "Teen-Agers [Mostly Female]" 11).

On August 15, the Beatles staged their historic Shea Stadium concert before a sold-out crowd of more than 55,000—at the time the largest audience ever assembled for a concert. Hundreds of police officers were brought in to keep the shrieking fans in order. The concert was filmed in color by Ed Sullivan's company, Sullivan Productions, in association with Subafilms and NEMS Enterprises (both of which were part of Brian Epstein's growing media and entertainment empire). Ed Sullivan was on hand to introduce the band before the shrieking audience. The Beatles had to walk across the field to second base, where the stage had been set. Several fans, reported the *New York Times*, "called to the special police on the field: 'Please, please. Give us some blades of the grass. They walked on the grass.'" "They are psychos," commented a passing policewoman. "Their mothers ought to see them now" (Schumach, "Shrieks" 29). Footage of the event shows a band somewhat awed by the size of the audience, and giddy with success. Lennon goes temporarily "mad" (as described by Starr in the *Anthology* documentary) from the adulation. In time stadium shows would become a central venue for the rock tour; in 1965, they were solely the domain of the Beatles.

Commercial success was translated into various endeavors intended to exploit fully the band's profit-producing potential. Among these efforts were the 1965 public offering on the London Stock Exchange of stock in Northern Songs, the company set to collect the royalties of songs written by Lennon and McCartney, and the exploitation of the Beatles' image for the purpose of reaching the young Saturday morning cartoon audience.

Northern Songs had been created two years earlier with assets consisting solely of the copyrights to songs written by Lennon and McCartney. The offering was covered in the *New York Times*, *Time* ("Buying the Beatles" 94), and *Newsweek*, with the latter reporting, "Demand for the stock outran supply by four to one. Solomon[12] . . . had to postpone trading . . . so that it could work out some fair allotment of the limited shares and also clear all the checks it received." A Solomon official was unable to provide an estimate of the number of "youngsters [who], in their enthusiasm, have let their desire surpass their bank accounts" ("I Wanna Hold Your Stock" 71). *Newsweek* also reported EMI's profits from record sales to be $13.6 million, up from $11.6 million the previous year (Blue-Chip Beatles" 82). This success facilitated the offering, despite reservations expressed by many involved with the London stock market. Optimism carried the day, and Dick James, the president of Northern Songs Ltd., crowed that Lennon and McCartney were going to be the "Rodgers and Hammerstein of the future" ("Buying the Beatles" 94).

Evidence of the Beatles' universal appeal (and commercial power) was put on display with *The Beatles*, an animated Saturday morning children's show that debuted on ABC in September 1965.[13] The weekly program included two vignettes in which the animated Beatles traveled the globe singing and enjoying various adventures, and was intended to extend the Beatles' vast appeal into yet another audience (children) and to fully exploit the band's advertising potential within that market. The series was sponsored in large part by the A. C. Gilbert Company, whose representative termed the Beatles "the most powerful salesmen in the world today." According to the *New York Times*, the company was sponsoring the show to promote its line of toys, including "a Ride-Em Erector set, an auto-race set, a Chem Lab and an American Flyer train layout" (Carlson 58). The show also generated a number of specifically cartoon-inspired products, including a Colorform set, inflatable Beatle dolls, and finger puppets. Nestle's "Beatles' Yeah, Yeah, Yeah Candy" and Lux Beauty Soap were marketed with special cartoon-inspired giveaways (Axelrod 112–21). Apparently successful in its purpose, the show was broadcast for four years, completing its run in April 1969.

From the beginning, rock and roll music had been a symbol of freedom among youth in numerous countries, and thus had drawn the critical attention of society's watchdogs. Well known are the stories of riots breaking out at theaters and of young people mimicking the antisocial behavior of screen teens in MGM's *Blackboard Jungle* (directed by Richard Brooks, 1955), the theme song of which was Bill Haley and the Comets' recording of " (We're Gonna) Rock Around the Clock." That recording became a number one hit in the United States and abroad, and set the stage for Columbia Pictures' *Rock Around the Clock* (directed by Fred Sears, 1956), which featured the band, radio deejay Alan Freed, and the Platters. As a result of delinquent-led disruptions sometimes accompanying the film's exhibition (and that of *Blackboard Jungle*) in the U.S. and abroad (notably in England), the prevailing public association of rock and roll music with hooliganism and delinquency was strengthened.

Elsewhere, authorities were not pleased with the arrival of rock and roll and the youth culture it helped to define. Egypt was jolted in 1957 by an influx of American rock and roll films and recordings, and the emergence of rock and roll dance clubs frequented by high school and college students. Pushed by conservatives who opposed this further incursion of Western imperialism and decadence, the problem eventually reached cabinet level in President Gamal Abdel Nasser's government, where it was decided that it was best ignored rather than risk driving the youth culture underground. That same year, the *New York Times*'s Pulitzer Prize–winning journalist and historian, Harrison Salisbury, noted the rock and roll fad in Bulgaria, which had Sophians chanting "Rock and Roll!" as a show of solidarity with protesters they were shielding from the police. In East Germany numerous Elvis Presley fans were given prison terms of up to four and a half years for shouting unflattering comments about East German music and Communist party boss Walter Ulbricht, the future head of state. They also reportedly chanted "Long live Elvis Presley." Among the most Stalinist regimes of the Soviet Bloc, East Germany turned to increasingly drastic measures to "protect" and socialize its youth. An effort was undertaken to instill a "deadly hatred" of the West and a willingness "to fight for the Socialist way of life." In 1960 the Soviet press reported the smashing of a teenage black-market ring specializing in producing and selling recordings (cut into discarded hospital X-ray plates) of Elvis Presley and other rock and roll singers.[14]

Given this history, and the fanatical following the band was attracting, it is not surprising that the Beatles were not welcome in a number of countries. Dating back to early 1964, Israel, finding "no reason why Israeli youth should be exposed to attacks of mass hysteria," declined to allow the group to perform in the country ("Israel Bars Beatles" 47). In August 1965 the *New York Times* reported the Indonesian government's seizure of records and tapes from shops, announcing that, in order to "preserve the national identity in the field of culture," Indonesia would burn tapes and records of "Beatle-type songs and music" as part of the celebration of Indonesia's 20th Independence Day ("Jakarta" 8). In East Germany the Beatles became a symbol of a "cultural crisis," as young artists and intellectuals demanded more freedom; after long deliberation, however, it was decided that there were worse things than Beatles. In April 1966 the *Times* reported, "The [East German] Government has decided that the Beatles are okay because they are more like folksingers. . . . But the Rolling Stones are out. Too animalistic" (Shabecoff 64). In the age of mass communication, the Beatles (and rock and roll) became emblematic of Western cultural imperialism.

More important to understanding the Beatles' status in the United States in 1965, and to understanding the transformation of their image, was the increasing criticism that the Beatles were receiving from the religious right. Rock and roll, and the Beatles in particular, became the targets of criticism from numerous Christian conservatives—most notably fundamentalist preachers David Noebel and Bob Larson, both of whom viewed the Beatles as dupes of the international communist conspiracy. In February 1965 *News-week* offered this summary of one of Reverend Noebel's sermons: "'You listen to this, Christians,' shouted the Rev. David Noebel, speaking recently in a Claremont, Calif., Baptist church. 'These Beatles are completely anti-Christ. They are preparing our teenagers for riot and ultimate revolution against our Christian Republic.' It's all a part of the 'Communist Master Music Plan,' argued Noebel." According to Noebel, the beat was the instrument of Bolshevik subversion: "The drum is the key—little Ringo. . . . In the excitatory state that the Beatles place these youngsters into, these young people will do anything they are told to do. . . . One day when the revolution is ripe . . . they [the Communists] could put the Beatles on TV and could mass hypnotize the American youth. . . . This scares the wits out of me," worried Noebel ("Beware" 89A).

The view of the Beatles propounded by Noebel, however, was not widely shared among mainstream Protestants. *Christian Century*, an influential, liberal, nondenominational Protestant publication, commented upon both the Jakarta ban and the conservative Christian opposition to the Beatles in the U.S.:

Leftist President Sukarno of Indonesia has banned them from his domain, contending that Beatlism is a "mental disease." Rightist David Noebel, a Baptist minister and a stalwart in Billy

James Hargis' "Christian Crusade," insists that there is Marxist method in the madness of Beatle music, that the Beatles are part of the "Communist Master Music Plan" designed to soften up American youth for a communist takeover by means of mass hypnosis. Somehow Noebel's line of reasoning strikes us as less than persuasive, and if Sukarno's accusation has certain plausibility, we must say that as mental diseases go, Beatlism isn't so bad. Semihysterical hero worship is nothing new among subteen-agers and we refuse to believe that Beatlemania is a particularly pernicious variety. Surely the Beatles are at least an improvement over Elvis Presley. ("Beatlemania and the Fast Buck" 230)

Yet, as noted by Sullivan (1987), criticizing Presley was not an option for Noebel. Presley, a southerner and God-fearing, was a hero to much of Noebel's constituency. The Beatles, on the other hand, were British. As young foreigners, they were an easy target (Sullivan 316).

In addition to criticism from the religious right, the Beatles had to contend with a Beatlemania that was increasingly exhibiting a less benign side. The *New York Times* reported on the melee that followed a show in Paris on June 20, before 5,500 fans. As the Beatles departed the stage of the Sports Palace, a "free-for-all" erupted in which "hundreds of youths surged from the rear of the hall," and the police "moved in, seized the most violent fans and ejected them." Fighting continued in the streets before police were finally able to disperse the crowd ("Beatles Greeted by Riot" 17). Similar violence broke out in Barcelona, Spain. Among those arrested following a performance were two American students charged with assaulting two Spanish policemen who had ordered them to stop dancing on the tops of cars ("2 U.S. Students Held in Spain" 5). Behavior of this kind was increasingly commonplace, and prompted the Pope to warn against "frenzied agitation over some foolish entertainment" ("Pope Warns Youth" 2).

This type of ugliness would increasingly become part of the character of Beatlemania in 1966, a year marred by scandal, most notably a disastrous stop in the Philippines, and the tempest caused by John Lennon's claim that the Beatles were "more popular than Jesus." During that year's world tour, in between shows at Tokyo's Budokan Arena, which had been greeted with protests by Japanese incensed at a western pop group's appearance at a site of martial arts (considered by some to be sacred), and an uneventful but successful concert appearance in New Delhi, the Beatles had the most disastrous tour stop of their careers. They performed in Manila where, on July 4th, they drew 75,000 fans to two performances. They enraged their hosts, however, when they failed to appear for a private performance at the presidential palace. The Beatles claimed they were unaware of an invitation, but this did nothing to pacify many incensed Filipinos. At the airport, a mob hurled insults and manhandled the band as they prepared to leave the country. President Marcos released a statement expressing regret over the incident at the airport, which he called a "breach of Filipino hospitality" ("Beatles Are Booed" 39).[15] Rancor was such that the *London Times* reported that a British Embassy official in Manila had received a death threat "because of what he [the perpetrator] called a snub by the Beatles against the family of the Philippines President" ("Death threat" 9). The Beatles were lucky to have escaped the Philippines relatively unscathed, but they were increasingly dissatisfied with the life of a touring band. Their experiences in the United States would do nothing to counter their disenchantment with life on the road.

Early indications were that the summer 1966 tour would be as frenzied and successful as their previous American expeditions. On May 1, 1966, four months before the Beatles were to return to Shea Stadium, the *New York Times* reported that 2,000 screaming fans had stormed the box office while waiting to purchase tickets for the show, and it was an hour before the police could restore order (Clark

80). In other words, Beatlemania was proceeding just as one would expect, based on the experience of the previous two years.

Things were changing, however. The Beatles, contrary to manager Brian Epstein's wishes, had become more vocal in their opinions on a myriad of issues, including the assassination of John Kennedy, civil rights, the conflict in Vietnam, and the growing generation gap. The foursome's opinions had occasionally surfaced during the previous two tours, but the Beatles' press office had proven itself quite adept at controlling the image, and had parlayed the band's popularity and commercial appeal into a favorable position vis-à-vis the press. Press officer Tony Barrow negotiated editorial control over features written about the band, exercising veto power in exchange for exclusives that were then syndicated, thus ensuring continuity of the image as a safe, "clean-cut group of smart youngsters" (Barrow 134–35, 150). Occasionally, publicity overtook promotion as the Beatles, no longer content to play the role of cheerful pop stars, asserted themselves and in so doing often aligned themselves squarely within the youth culture. Larry Kane, a radio journalist on the 1964 and 1965 North American tours, recounted his experiences with the Beatles in *Ticket to Ride* (2003), including this exchange with Starr, late in the 1965 tour:

> Kane: Are you angry about the war drums beating now? What would be your method or way to go about ending war?
>
> Ringo: I think it's unfair that you get a leader of a country— then they force so many people to fight each other, and they don't get touched hardly. It is all the young men of the world who get shot, and bombed, and blown to bits. It's unfair. I know it sounds silly but they should let *them* fight it out, instead of fetching all those innocent bystanders. (177)

Kane also tapped the Beatles' opinions on racism in the United States, and notes that they had reportedly refused to play the old Gator Bowl, in Jacksonville, Florida, in September, 1964, if it remained segregated. When they arrived, the venue had acquiesced. Kane recalls that the Beatles were questioned about the topic throughout the 1965 tour, and openly criticized the prejudice that they witnessed throughout their travels in the country, particularly in the South.

But in 1966, it would not be anything said on that year's North American tour that would cause the greatest controversy; nor would it be the band's views on race or Vietnam that would preoccupy journalists on the tour. The offending statement occurred months before the planned American tour was to begin, in an interview intended for British audiences and given to the *London Evening Standard*'s Maureen Cleave. Lennon had stated: "Christianity will go. . . . It will vanish and shrink. I needn't argue about that; I'm right and I will be proved right. We're more popular than Jesus now; I don't know which will go first — rock 'n' roll or Christianity. Jesus was all right but his disciples were thick and ordinary. It's them twisting it that ruins it for me" (Cleave, "How Does a Beatle Live" 72).[16]

These comments drew little response from the British public. In fact, the Beatles had been quite open with the American press in criticizing Christianity, as this exchange with *Playboy*'s Jean Shepherd, from February 1965, makes clear:

> Playboy: You guys seem to be pretty irreverent characters. Are any of you churchgoers?
> John: No
> George: No.
> Paul: Not particularly. But we're not antireligious. We probably seem to be antireligious because of the fact that none of us believe in God.
> John: If you say you don't believe in God, everybody assumes you're antireligious, and you probably think that's what we mean by that. We're not quite sure *what* we are, but I know that we're more agnostic than atheistic. . . .

Paul: We all feel roughly the same. We're all agnostics.

John: Most people are, anyway.

Ringo: It's better to admit it than to be a hypocrite.

John: The only thing we've got against religion is the hypocritical side of it, which I can't stand. Like the clergy is always moaning about people being poor, while they themselves are all going around with millions of quid worth of robes on. That's the stuff I can't stand.

Paul: A new bronze door stuck on the Vatican. . . . But believe it or not, we're not anti-Christ.

Ringo: Just anti-Pope and anti-Christian.

Paul: But you know, in America . . .

George: They were more shocked by us saying we were agnostics.

John: They went potty; they couldn't take it. Same as in Australia, where they couldn't stand us not liking sports.

Paul: In America they're fanatical about God. I know somebody over there who said he was an atheist. The papers nearly refused to print it because it was such shocking news that somebody could actually be an atheist. Yeah, and admit it. (Shepherd 58)

Christian Century noted Lennon's comment about the clergy and their "millions of quid worth of robes" that same month, and had declared: "We're not even especially bothered by the fact that the Beatles say they are 'anti-Christian' (though not anti-Christ), for some of their reasons make pretty good, if naïve, sense" ("Beatlemania and the Fast Buck" 230). The *Playboy* interview had otherwise caused little stir among the public. Eighteen months later, however, as the Beatles set out on what was to be their last American tour, Lennon's comments to the *Evening Standard*'s Cleave appeared in the teen-oriented magazine *Dateline*, and public consternation reached a fever pitch. Interestingly, the comments had failed to cause a stir when carried in the *New York Times Magazine* in July 1966 (Cleave, "Old Beatles" 30). Yet, a month later, with their arrival imminent, a wave of anti-Beatle demonstrations spread across the Bible Belt and the South. The Ku Klux Klan marched. There were bonfires of Beatles records, and numerous radio stations banned Beatles records from their playlists.

The *New York Times* reported that a radio station in Birmingham, Alabama, had initiated the drive to ban the Beatles from the airwaves. As the station manager said, "We just felt it was so absurd and sacrilegious that something ought to be done to show them they cannot get away with this sort of thing" ("Comments on Jesus" 20). The newspaper also noted Brian Epstein's trip to America, one week before the start of the American tour, to quell the furor. Even Maureen Cleave, the reporter to whom the offending statement had been made, came to Lennon's defense: "He was certainly not comparing the Beatles with Christ. He was simply observing that so weak was the state of Christianity that the Beatles were, to many people, better-known" ("Beatles Manager" 13). Meanwhile, the *New York Times* reported the banning of Beatle records by numerous radio stations, as well as the South African Broadcasting Corporation. In the United States, radio boycotts were announced throughout the Bible Belt and beyond. Yet public hostility was not unanimous. The article further reported that "Station WSAC in Fort Know, Ky., began playing Beatles records for the first time 'to show our contempt for hypocrisy personified'," and that "Rev. Richard Pritchard of the Westminster Presbyterian Church in Madison, Wis., said that those outraged by the remarks should start blaming themselves and stop blaming the Beatles" ("Beatles Manager" 13).[17]

Lennon's comment revealed an important difference between his own English culture and that of the United States. His comparison of the band to Jesus Christ raised little concern in England where, according to a study conducted in 1968, only an estimated ten to fifteen percent of the population attended church regularly; by comparison, in the United States, forty-three percent of the population was believed to attend services on a regular basis (Patterson 456). The response to the comments was not simply a function of relative religiosity, however; it also reflected the anxiety spawned by the dashed expectations of many religious Americans. In the period following World War II, there had been widespread confidence that religion would become even more central to American culture than it had been. In Will Herberg's *Protestant Catholic Jew: An Essay in American Religious Sociology* (1955), the prominent theologian envisioned a quickly approaching future in which ethnic consciousness would matter less than it had in the past decades, and in which a "civic religion" of "Americanism" would arise wherein traditional expressions of faith would become mere reflections of American values and interests. Even more so than in the past, polls suggested, Americans openly identified themselves as adherents to one of the three faiths of the title (Patterson 328). Poll results from 1957 indicated that only fourteen percent of Americans believed that religion was losing its influence (Hudson 415).

Yet, in the 1950s traditional notions of faith increasingly came into question. Dietrich Bonhoeffer's call for a "secular interpretation" of biblical language (*Letters and Papers from Prison* [New York: Macmillan, 1953]) was among the first of a number of efforts aimed at transforming Judeo-Christian–based doctrine into one more readily meeting the needs of post–World War II Western society. In the United States, Richard Niebuhr's seminal essay *Radical Monotheism* (1960) initiated the secularizing movement among American theologians and philosophers. The development was apparent in Gabriel Vahanian's book, *The Death of God: The Culture of Our Post-Christian Era* (1961). Among those carrying forth the program of secularization were the "Death of God" theologians and thinkers, including Thomas J. Altizer, William Hamilton, and Paul Van Buren—"Christian atheists," as *Time* referred to them in April 1965, advocating a "theology without *theos*" ("Toward a Hidden God" 82).

Assailed by traditionalists for reducing Christianity to just another secular humanism, the "Death of God" thinkers were the most controversial voices to be heard on the topic but were far from alone. The problems of defining God and faith were taken up in popular works such as Bishop J. A. T. Robinson's *Honest to God* (1963) in Great Britain, and Harvey Cox's *The Secular City* (1965) in the United States. Critical self-examination abounded in Protestantism, Roman Catholicism, and Judaism; important works included Martin Marty's *The Second Chance for American Protestants* (1963), Edward Wakin and Joseph F. Scheuer's *The De-Romanization of the American Catholic Church* (1966), and Richard Rubenstein's *After Auschwitz* (1966). This discourse had very real ramifications for the culture. Testing the boundaries of freedom in the 1960s, a "new morality" was present in demands by university students for greater freedom. It was marked by increasingly open hostility toward traditional authority, including the state and church. Notably, the "civic religion" detailed by Herberg in the mid-1950s was more and more a target for the young as they sought less formal and legalistic expressions of their spirituality (Ahlstrom 447–48).

Contrary to Herberg's predictions, polls over the period indicate the widespread perception that religion was becoming less central to the nation's culture. By the late 1960s, 57 per cent held this opinion, and by 1970 the percentage had increased to 75 per cent (Hudson 415). Many religious conservatives perceived the march of science as a direct threat. In the century before, the notion of providential design had increasingly given way to a naturalism based in Darwin's evolutionary theory, and historians, anthropologists, psychologists, and sociologists more and more explained behavior in scientific terms. If the full force of these arguments had been somewhat blunted by a special sense of destiny in the United States in the immediate aftermath of World War II, as manifested in the rise of an anticommunist civil religion and the presence of Billy Graham and Norman Vincent Peale in the halls of power, the 1960s were a period in which America's *specialness* would be questioned. A more educated population, as well as an omnipresent mass media (notably, television), brought traditional religious views and structures under greater scrutiny. Additionally, immigration and the urban explosion of the twentieth century had chipped away at the Protestant consensus.

Unprecedented economic expansion and rapid social change experienced in the United States in the aftermath of World War II set the stage for the moral and religious transformation of the 1960s. Rapid urbanization created problems with which American political and fiscal systems could not cope, contributing to poverty, crime, pollution, and other societal maladies. Technological developments in agriculture and industry fostered migrations of people that led to an electorate in opposition to the Protestant establishment and WASP dominance, typified in the growing political power of Roman Catholics and African Americans. And humanity's technological capabilities, exemplified in the Apollo space program, seemed to have no limits. This belief was magnified in an increasingly educated population. Yet, the war in Vietnam exposed the inequities inherent in the nation's conscription policy. To many, America's traditional church culture appeared to be an obstacle to solving the country's problems, particularly those related to civil rights and the Vietnam conflict (Ahlstrom 450–54).

America's traditional religious culture was under assault. As Wuthnow (1995) notes of the religious climate of the 1960s, college-educated individuals were less likely to attend services on a regular basis or to believe in a literal interpretation of the Bible. They were also more interested in "new religions," like Transcendental Meditation, Zen Buddhism, and Hare Krishna, than those who had not attended college, who remained committed to traditional views of the Bible and religion (Wuthnow 379). Mainline Protestant churches and the Roman Catholic church, in a state of growing disarray sparked by dissension over the proper role of faith in the modern world, experienced an ever-accelerating decline in membership as the middle and latter part of the decade were reached (Hudson 415–17).

Within this context, the response to Lennon's statement can be seen for what it was: one of the opening salvos in a culture war marked by an increasing generational divide and fought over the role of institutionalized Christianity and other established institutions of control. Lennon's comments were publicized in the United States just months after *Time* ran its "Is God Dead?" cover story, which described the current state of the debate among theologians over the meaning of God, and sparked public discussion of faith and doctrine. Lennon, an avid reader of history and religion, was undoubtedly aware of the controversy.[18] Lennon's statement provided an opportunity for traditionalists to vent their anger, and fundamentalist wrath was unleashed throughout the South and Bible Belt. Hoping to salvage the American tour, Lennon flew into Chicago for its start, and to respond to rising hostility. The *New York Times* quoted Lennon as saying, "I suppose if I had said television is more popular than Jesus, I would have got away with it. I am sorry I opened my mouth." He continued, "I'm not anti-God, anti-Christ or anti-religion. I was not knocking it. I was not saying we are greater or better" ("Lennon of Beatles" 38).[19] Lennon's apology was apparently accepted by a majority of Beatles fans, for the next day the *New York Times* reported that the Chicago concert, the first of the American tour, was a sold-out success ("Just the Usual" 10). The Vatican City newspaper, *L'Osservatore Romano*, also accepted Lennon's apology, even noting that "there was some foundation to the latest observations of John Lennon about atheism or the distraction of many people" ("Vatican" 13). A *New York Times* editorial wondered how "such an articulate young man could have expressed himself imprecisely in the first place" ("What He Meant" 38).

The Beatles weathered the storm—perhaps because they had already been defined as four individuals, starting with the *National Record News* Capitol had distributed for its first promotion of the band. There, in fact, Lennon had been called the "angry young man" of the group, a reference associating Lennon with the literary and theatrical movement that had emerged in the late 1950s as a critique of the British class system and the domination of British culture by London and the south. Lennon had further distinguished himself with release of his first book, *In His Own Write*, a work noted for its wordplay and absurd humor, in spring, 1964. Add to this the fact that the Beatles were expected to be irreverent and to say shocking things. The Beatles' reputation, and Lennon's acknowledged intellect, created a space for his comments. Except in the South, noted *Time*, the scandal proved "less than consequential": "During the Beatles' only personal appearance below the Mason-Dixon line, in Memphis, a Christian Youth Rally was scheduled simultaneously. The free-admission protest exhibition drew more than 8,000 people; the Beatles (in two performances) pulled 20,128 at $5.50 a head" ("Is Beatlemania Dead?" 38).

While the scandal appeared "less than consequential," it clearly illustrates the vast differences between the youth cultures of the 1950s and the 1960s. Though following a well-trod course in their rise to stardom, that is, a successful career as singers creating an opportunity to enter motion pictures, Elvis Presley and the Beatles— more correctly, their images—were on different trajectories, particularly in their post-touring incarnations. Presley's image was modified to be less controversial, especially once he began his career in film, an enterprise that took up far more of his effort in the 1960s than did touring. The Beatles' image, however, consistent with the youth culture to which it appealed, became increasingly subversive.

Rock and roll's emergence was viewed by many to be another stone in the path to damnation for the nation's teenagers, alongside comic books and Hollywood's exploitation of that young audience. Films of the period included *Blackboard Jungle* (MGM, 1955), in which a young high school teacher, played by Glenn Ford, battles urban toughs; the fact-based *The Wild One* (Columbia Pictures, 1953), wherein a motorcycle gang, led by Johnny (Marlon Brando), takes over a California town; and *Rebel Without a Cause* (Warner Brothers, 1955), starring James Dean as Jim Stark, the troubled teen at the center of the film's depiction of alienated youths. Into this mix came Elvis Presley, whose image embodied perhaps the most distressing aspect of delinquent culture: Alongside the appeal of brooding Brando and angst-ridden Dean was the raw sexuality of Elvis Presley, perceived by many as a sign of "blackness" and an unwelcome development in a country still segregated along racial lines. In the most controversial year of Presley's rise to stardom, 1956, his performances on national television, notably on *The Milton Berle Show*, *The Steve Allen Show*, and *The Ed Sullivan Show*, raised the ire of some of the nation's most influential critics. In September, the *New York Times*'s media critic, Jack Gould, assailed an entertainment industry that he called "mercenary" in promoting Presley:

> Mr. Presley initially disturbed adult viewers—and instantly became a martyr in the eyes of his teen-age following—for his striptease behavior on last spring's Milton Berle program. Then with Steve Allen he was much more sedate. On the Sullivan program he injected movements of the tongue and indulged in wordless singing that were singularly distasteful.
>
> . . . With congested schools, early dating, the appeals of the car, military service, acceptance by the right crowd, sex and the normal parental pressures, the teen-ager has all the problems he needs.
>
> . . . To resort to the world's oldest theatrical come-on just to make a fast buck from such a sensitive individual is cheap and tawdry stuff. . . . If the profiteering hypocrite is above reproach and Presley isn't, today's youngsters might well ask what God do adults worship. (Gould, "Elvis Presley")

The *Times* reported that Cardinal Spellman of New York, quoting from Gould's article, warned, "A new creed has been patterned by a segment of the young people of America—a creed of dishonesty, violence, lust and degeneration," and condemned "today's teen-age craze for suggestive TV performers and performances" ("Spellman in Plea to Save U.S. Youth" 32). Emblematic of increasing attempts to impose civic control over Presley's performances, *Life* reported that a Jacksonville, Florida juvenile court judge—alarmed by the behavior of young fans who "nearly ripped all his clothes off"— prepared warrants for Presley's arrest for "impairing the morals of minors" should Presley repeat the "torso-tossing spectacle of his earlier visits." Presley dutifully modified his performance ("Elvis—A Different Kind of Idol" 108).

The fact of Presley's threat, however, was never universally conceded, and it was short-lived. While Presley may have been the bane of principals and parents all over the country, even at the height of critical scorn and condemnation he had his defenders. The consternation sparked by Presley's performance on *The Ed Sullivan Show* was countered by John Sharnik, writing in *House and Garden* magazine, who opined that rock and roll was "probably no more than background music in the war between the generations." He continued:

> Somehow we accept with amused tolerance the whistles and mutterings of the boys [ogling Marilyn Monroe], including a good many boys of advanced age. But the squeals of the girls embarrass us, and, in the context of the controversy over Rock 'n' Roll, we are frightened of what we imagine to be the consequences.
>
> ... What is really bothering us *adults*, I suspect, is not that television has chosen to satisfy this teen-age audience but that such a distinctive audience exists at all, that within our own society there is a large, well defined group whose standards of taste and conduct we find baffling, and even terrifying. (Sharnik 40–41)

For some, Presley was even a positive image for youths. The *New York Times* reported in October 1956 that the singer, in New York City for a television appearance, had received his polio inoculation: "He is setting a fine example for the youth of the country," said one doctor, who further explained "only 10 percent of the city's teenagers had received inoculations." The physician hoped Presley's example would inspire his fans to get shots ("Presley Receives A City Polio Shot" 33).

Apparently unfazed by the scorn initially poured upon its most famous son, in September 1956 Presley's hometown of Tupelo, Mississippi, honored the singer; Governor J. P. Coleman said that the state was "proud" of him and presented him with a scroll ("Hometown Honors Presley"). The following April the *Times* reported that a Canadian convent had decided to reinstate eight pupils expelled for attending a Presley performance. The Notre Dame Convent, located in Ottawa, ended the expulsions due to the "extenuating circumstances" that some of the pupils' parents had approved their attendance at the Presley show ("Convent Yields on Presley"). It is, in fact, informative to note how short-lived Presley's affront to society had been. His "taming" was accelerated when he turned his attention to the movies.

Once delivered to the Hollywood star-making machine, Presley's image was carefully tuned to maximize his market appeal as a movie star. As Peter Guralnick notes in *Last Train to Memphis: The Rise of Elvis Presley* (1994), upon release of Presley's first film, *Love Me Tender*, *Time* described the singer's new packaging, asking, "Is it a sausage?" of Presley's new image (Guralnick 362). The magazine wrote in late 1957, "As befits a solid citizen (possible 1957 gross: $1 million), he has lately eschewed fist-fights and steady starlets, projected a 15-acre Elvis Presley Youth Foundation in Tupelo, Miss., his birthplace" ("The Rock is Solid" 50). Particularly after starting to make films, Presley's image was crafted along lines suitable to the movie star, a business that Hollywood had been in for half a century. As such, much of the press was content to discuss his rise to fame and describe the riches following that success. The final act of "assimilation" for Presley was, of course, his induction into the U.S. Army in 1958, an event covered by the mainstream press and media. When Presley returned to civilian life, it was with an image suited to the needs of the Hollywood movie industry. The threat had effectively been removed from Presley's image. In effect, publicity had outpaced Presley's early promotion, defining him before the music and film industries took back control of the message.

By contrast, in the Beatles' case the carefully constructed image promoted by Epstein and Capitol in 1963 and 1964, increasingly had to contend with and accommodate publicity generated by the press and a greater assertiveness on the part of the Beatles. Unlike Presley, the Beatles' image started from a "safe" and standardized position, that of the teen idol, and followed patterns that had been worked out in Hollywood decades earlier. Their early success, marked by their rise from obscurity to unprecedented commercial achievement, closely tracked the American myth of success. In addition to their hit records, the Beatles were admired for their quick wit and irreverence, and while they and their fans may have baffled some onlookers, they failed to raise concern in any but the most reactionary quarters. The Beatles were also refreshingly candid, and while largely muzzled by Brian Epstein from speaking at length on controversial issues, during the touring years the Beatles were hounded into discussing issues of concern to many of their young fans, including the hostilities in Vietnam, civil rights in the United States, and so on.

The "more popular than Jesus" palaver was another manifestation of the battle being joined across generational lines, and the Beatles, representatives of a burgeoning youth culture, increasingly found themselves at the center of public dialogue on that culture. Lennon's remarks and the vitriol they had ignited had clearly drawn a cultural line in the sand, and Lennon and the Beatles located themselves squarely against tradition and cultural conservatism, and further developed the rebellious aspect of their image.

The failure of the scandal to become more than a localized event (across the South and the Bible Belt) can, perhaps, be viewed as evidence of the degree to which Americans' confidence in the traditional religions had already been shaken. It provided an avenue to test the limits of that generation's insertion of itself into the discussion on topics as varied as fashion and politics: for the first time in the country's history, youth would assume a separate and distinct identity from that of the adult/establishment world with which it increasingly found itself at odds. The "more popular than Jesus" controversy came in like a lion and left like a lamb largely because American society accepted the premise of Lennon's offending statement and/or was willing to admit representatives of the youth culture into the current debate on the role of religion in society. (It is worth noting that, in the midst of the controversy, no promoter accepted Epstein's offer to cancel any show.[20]) The incident ushered in an era in which youth and their representatives (including musicians; often the Beatles) actively spoke out on pertinent issues of the day, from civil rights to Vietnam. In the following years, the Beatles would become a focus of discussion by, for, and about the youth culture—indeed, for some the Beatles would become not only models to be emulated but leaders of the youth culture. The full force of this shift of youth allegiance from tradition and leaders of the establishment to the values and personalities of their own generation was yet to be felt, but the forces were aligning.

The tour ground on. In Memphis the Beatles were pelted with fruit, firecrackers, and other debris as they performed ("Debris" 11). Adding to the group's misery, a performance in Cleveland occasioned another mishap in which nearly 3,000 fans stormed the stage, forcing a temporary stop to the show and causing extensive damage to Cleveland Municipal Stadium ("Beatles Beat a Retreat" 35).

The Beatles made a successful return to Shea Stadium, although at 45,000 the crowd was about 10,000 below capacity (Montgomery, "Beatles Bring Shea" 40). The tumult on this last American tour, and the generally less fanatical response of the nation's teenagers to the Beatles, led *Time* to speculate on the end of Beatlemania. Reasons included the fact that three of the four (Lennon, Harrison, and Starr) were now married; also, as manager Brian Epstein himself noted, the Beatles simply were not the "novelty" they had once been. Noting that "only" 500 fans had gathered at the Beatles' New York hotel, compared to 10,000 the year before, *Time* concluded, "Clearly, Beatlemania has seen greater heights" ("Is Beatlemania Dead?" 38–39). After three years of pandemonium, Beatlemania had lost its luster. The last tour ended on August 30 at San Francisco's Candlestick Park. From then on, the Beatles were primarily a studio group.

Of the Beatles' achievements in Britain, Inglis (1995) notes that, "in successfully adhering to the demands of a popular music industry largely organized around transient phenomena and immediate expectations, the Beatles quickly constructed a position for themselves of considerable power and influence, their status deriving essentially from their perceived competence" (67). Though describing the Beatles within the context of the British popular music industry, these comments could equally be applied to their status in the U.S., in terms of chart success and their perceived artistic supremacy. The Beatles' chart domination was unequalled in the 1960s, and for the period 1964–66 this command was even more pronounced in relation to other youth-oriented acts. In spite of the fact that the Beatles did not launch a tour of the U.S. until six months after their first *Ed Sullivan Show* appearance, their singles and albums remained atop the charts. During the Beatlemania phase of their careers, twelve singles topped the *Billboard* chart; nine albums reached number one on the *Billboard* album chart (Whitburn, *Top Pop Singles* 38–39; Whitburn, *Top 40 Albums* 28–29). These statistics are even more impressive when one considers that over the same period, the Beatles' archrivals, the Beach Boys and Rolling Stones, had only three number one singles and one number one album apiece (Whitburn, *Top Pop Singles* 36–37, 521; Whitburn, *Top 40 Albums* 27, 263); Bob Dylan did not have a number one single or album. The Beatles were the top-selling artists of the decade in terms of both singles and albums. With regard to singles, they were followed by Elvis Presley, Ray Charles, Brenda Lee, the Supremes, and the Beach Boys, in that order, and in sales of albums by Presley, Frank Sinatra, Herb Alpert and the Tijuana Brass, the Kingston Trio, and Andy Williams (Whitburn, *Top Pop Singles* 847; *Top 40 Albums* 377).

Also impressive was the quantity of music produced in this period. In the twenty-four months following the summer 1964 tour and release of the film *A Hard Day's Night*, Capitol released nine singles (seven reaching number one in the *Billboard* charts) and six albums of new Beatles recordings. (In total, eight albums were released, including *The Beatles' Story*, a collection of interviews and other items of interest primarily to fans, and *The Early Beatles*,[21] Capitol's rerelease of the Vee-Jay recordings.) The Beatles stayed atop the charts with Lennon and McCartney's songwriting, and demonstrated mastery of a wide variety of music in their song selection.

Their "tough" sound continued to dominate on *Beatles '65*. The Beatles' rock and roll roots were evident in "Rock and Roll Music," a barnstormer made even more so than Chuck Berry's original by Lennon's frantic plea, "Just let me hear some o' that rock and roll music. . . ." "Everybody's Trying to Be My Baby" features Harrison on lead vocal and guitar, paying tribute to Carl Perkins on this cover version. "I Feel Fine" and "She's a Woman" (previously released together as a single) featured more guitar-driven rock and roll, with one of rock and roll's most memorable guitar riffs opening the former, and McCartney continuing to expand and demonstrate his range with the latter, a rhythm and blues–inspired rocker. Lennon's songwriting, too, continued to evolve, to a more inward-looking form of expression: "I'm a Loser," "Baby's in Black," "No Reply," and "I'll Be Back" all focus on the dark side of relationships.

Lennon, influenced by Dylan, was forging a new kind of rock poetry based less on conventions of boy-girl relationships and glorious
youth and more on his own experience.

Far from the direct address of the female audience that was a
mark of Lennon and McCartney's early compositions, the protagonist of "I'm a Loser" cannot even communicate with the object
of his affection, and is left crying on the shoulder of a confidant.
Here, rather than being the hopeful focus of the protagonist's love,
the "girl" is something that has already been lost and, rather distant from an innocent ideal, had been a competitor in the game of
love; Lennon "should have known she would win in the end." She
has left him broken, someone who has lost everything. "Baby's in
Black" is a darkly comic waltz in which the protagonist's true love
mourns for the love of another: "Oh dear, what can I do? Baby's in
black, and I'm feeling blue. Tell me, oh, what can I do?" Even "No
Reply," which more closely follows the formula of direct address of
the female audience, is about a relationship that is over, and recounts
the frantic efforts of the boy to reclaim the love that is irrevocably lost
to another, for "you walked hand in hand with another man in my
place." As Lennon acknowledged, he went through a "Dylan phase"
in which his music began to become more self-revelatory. Dylan is
often credited with forcing this change in Lennon's songwriting,
challenging Lennon to "say something." Undoubtedly this is true,
but it is also the case that Lennon's work quickly became even more
recognizably autobiographical than Dylan's, for Dylan had little interest in revealing himself to his audience, while Lennon came to
believe such revelation essential to his status as an artist.

The next Capitol release, *Beatles VI*, was heavily laden with rock
and roll, the tough sound present on "Kansas City"/"Hey-Hey-
Hey-Hey!," "Bad Boy," and "Dizzy Miss Lizzy." While retaining
this hard edge, the Beatles continued to demonstrate their facility
with the ballad. Lennon's "Yes It Is" is a showcase for the group's
close harmonies. *Beatles VI* finds the Beatles, or rather Capitol, in a

holding pattern, awaiting the release of *Help!* As such, the song selection was a safe retreat to a proven mixture of heavy rock and roll, ballads, and singles.

While the inclusion of the electric guitar–driven hit single "Ticket to Ride" gives the album an edge that connects the Beatles to their "tough" roots, *Help!* indicates a shift in focus that would be fully realized on their next album. Lennon hints in that direction on his acoustic guitar–based title tune, which was far more personal than anyone realized at the time;[22] and "You've Got to Hide Your Love Away" presents an introspective Lennon at his most Dylanesque. Lennon, arguably the most hardcore rock and roller in the band, was leading the band into its next phase. Where the Beatles previously utilized the acoustic for background rhythm to their rock and roll–based songs, the next album stepped away from their rock and roll roots toward a sound more fully entrenched in the country and folk traditions from which new American bands such as the Byrds, the Lovin' Spoonful, and Buffalo Springfield derived inspiration. The band, and Capitol, fashioned an album that would successfully take on the American bands on their own turf and, in so doing, would present a new aspect of their image. The Beatles' perceived supremacy would no longer be simply a function of their domination of the sales charts;[23] perceptions of the band's artistry would become an increasingly important component of the image.

By the time of the recording sessions for *Rubber Soul*, in October and November of 1965, studio two at Abbey Road Studios was used almost exclusively for Beatle business. The source of EMI's £3 million profit, the Beatles were free to create as it suited them. They were no longer "on the clock," so to speak (Norman, *Shout* 258–59). With this newly won freedom, the Beatles set about expanding the boundaries of popular music. Commented *Newsweek* of the latest album: "In 'Rubber Soul,' the Beatles blend gospel, country music, baroque counterpoint and even French popular ballads into a style that is wholly their own. Says McCartney: 'Our best influences now are ourselves. We are so well established that we can bring fans along with us and stretch the limits of pop'" ("Bards of Pop" 102).

The Beatles already had proven themselves amazingly adept not only at pacing the competition, but also at surpassing it. For instance, in early 1965, as noted by MacDonald, challenged by the tougher sound of British groups like the Yardbirds, the Kinks, the Rolling Stones, and the Who and by the appearance of guitar virtuosos like Jeff Beck and Eric Clapton, Lennon answered with "Ticket to Ride" (113). Faced with a growing number of rivals in the United States, individuals and bands drawing on the American experience for inspiration, the Beatles would go them one step further on *Rubber Soul*, incorporating American influences and an artistic vision colored by their use of marijuana. In this environment, the Beatles were "always looking for new sounds," as George Martin put it (The Beatles 196).

Experimentation would mark this period of the Beatles' careers, one dominated by the studio, not the road. The Beatles had shown their penchant for experimentation early on. "I Feel Fine" (released November 1964), for instance, opened with guitar feedback, perhaps its first intentional use in a rock and roll recording. On *Rubber Soul*, their first U.S. album without a single, Lennon's "Norwegian Wood" featured George Harrison on sitar, an instrument that quickly became commonplace. Each successive single (and, increasingly, album) was viewed both by its audience and by critics/commentators to be a progression. Consistent with its practice to this point, Capitol limited the album to twelve tracks to limit its fees to the Beatles' publisher. The label dropped a number of the heavier electric songs on the British release, including "If I Needed Someone," "Drive My Car," and "Nowhere Man." What is left is one of the Beatles' most distinctive albums, one awash in acoustic guitars and a perfect riposte to the burgeoning folk-rock scene then beginning to enter the American charts.

Also important to the album's success and historical significance was the photo by Robert Freeman, who had shot the cover for *Meet the Beatles!* Freeman was showing the band some photographs that might be used when a shot of the band was accidentally distorted as it was projected onto a cardboard placard (standing in as an album cover) that had slipped out of position. The Beatles insisted that this "mistake" be utilized for the album cover. As Harrison put it years later, "I liked the way we got our faces to be longer on the album cover. We lost the 'little innocents' tag, the naivety, and *Rubber Soul* was the first one where we were fully-fledged potheads" (The Beatles 197). In short, the album was more than a collection of songs: it was a hint of things to come, a nod in the direction of a countercultural lifestyle that would become an explicit feature of the image.

Capitol had released one album of new Beatle music every December, June, and August in 1964 and 1965. The next year was no different, and *Rubber Soul*'s release in December 1965 was followed by the release of *"Yesterday"* . . . *and Today* in June. The album compiled the three latest American singles, "Yesterday"/ "Act Naturally," "We Can Work It Out"/ "Day Tripper," and "Nowhere Man"/ "What Goes On;" from the British *Rubber Soul* came "Drive My Car" and "If I Needed Someone." However, the album represented more than a mere holding pattern in anticipation of the Beatles' summer release: With a June debut, American fans heard a number of songs before their British counterparts, who had to wait until the release of *Revolver* in August to hear "I'm Only Sleeping," "And Your Bird Can Sing," and "Doctor Robert." Given the time span represented on the album, with recording for "Yesterday" and "Act Naturally" completed on June 17, 1965, and "I'm Only Sleeping" completed on May 6, 1966, it is not surprising that the album displays the work of a number of phases in the Beatles' development. The country-inflected "What Goes On," along with a version of Buck Owens' "Act Naturally," both sung by Ringo, were from the vein of American country and folk that the Beatles mined on *Help!* and *Rubber Soul*, as is "We Can Work It Out." "Nowhere Man," "Day Tripper," and "And Your Bird Can Sing" are musically reminiscent of the tough early sound of the band but lyrically point toward the drug-inflected euphoria of *Sgt. Pepper's Lonely Hearts Club Band*. "Nowhere Man" was Lennon's autobiographical criticism of himself for whiling away the hours in drug-induced inactivity, "sitting in his nowhere land" and making his "nowhere plans for nobody." "And Your Bird Can Sing" is an early example of the kind of wordplay that characterized much of British psychedelia, and takes a rather more positive view of Lennon's solitude and consciousness, now worn as a badge of enlightenment: You may have seen "seven wonders," but "you can't see me," sings Lennon. You may have heard all there is to hear, but "you can't hear me." At this point, few fans had "tuned in" to the fact that the Beatles were active in the drug culture, but many were beginning to deduce it from the sonic experiments and increasingly surreal lyrics.

The remaining tracks taken from the British *Revolver* most straightforwardly present the then-current preoccupation of Lennon. His recreational drug-induced lethargy is reflected both in the plea "Please don't wake me. No, don't shake me, Leave me where I am" of "I'm Only Sleeping" and in "Doctor Robert": "If you're down he'll pick you up—Doctor Robert. . . . Well, well, well, you're feeling fine . . . he'll make you—Doctor Robert." The subject matter and musical content of these songs have more in common with the recordings that would follow, on *Sgt. Pepper's Lonely Hearts Club Band*, than with those that came before. "I'm Only Sleeping" exemplifies the Beatles' new, experimental approach. Harrison, a master of guitar tone throughout his career, devised an ingenious backwards guitar part that augmented the basic track's dreamy quality (Lewisohn, *Complete* 218). "Doctor Robert," a drug song referring to a New York doctor known for his extracurricular prescriptions, would have fit nicely with "character songs" such as "Lovely Rita" and "Lucy in the Sky with Diamonds."

In June 1966 Capitol released advance copies of *"Yesterday"* . . . *and Today* to disk jockeys, distributors, and reviewers. The cover of the album contained the infamous "Butcher" photo, taken by Bob Whitaker, of the band wearing white butcher smocks and covered in raw meat and dismembered dolls. The Beatles, particularly Lennon, delighted in the surreal photograph and submitted it for use on the cover of the new album. Though anxious about the shocking nature of the photograph, Capitol, with the release date of the album quickly approaching, had little choice but to issue the album with the cover. Negative reaction from disk jockeys, distributors, and newspaper and magazine reviewers led the company to pull the album and rerelease it with a new, less controversial cover (Spizer, *Beatles Story, Part Two* 111–22). Butcher cover aside, the collection of recordings was a comfortable segue from the moptops of Beatlemania to the new Beatles. Popular with the fans, it dethroned Frank Sinatra's *Strangers in the Night* at number one in the album charts, remaining there for five weeks before being displaced by their next album.

With the release of *Revolver* on August 5, 1966, the Beatles broke decisively with their moptop past. Gone were the paeans to boy-girl relationships and the standard setup of two guitars, bass, and drums. An eclectic assortment of instruments and effects were brought to bear on songs with lyrics that were at once more introspective, poetic, and surreal than anything that Lennon, McCartney, and Harrison had ever attempted. The results were dazzling. Recording sessions began in early April 1966, with the recording of Lennon's "Tomorrow Never Knows." The lyrics were based on a flyer distributed by Timothy Leary,[24] the LSD guru: Lennon invites the listener to "Turn off your mind, relax, and float downstream," and to "surrender to the void." In contemplating his new song, Lennon had imagined "thousands of monks chanting," and the Beatles and producer George Martin set about finding the means of capturing the ethereal quality sought by Lennon (The Beatles 270). The Beatles, Martin, and engineer Geoff Emerick achieved Lennon's eerie vocal by running his microphone line through a revolving Leslie speaker usually used with a Hammond organ, an innovation exemplifying their collective creativity. A type of song new to Western ears, and obviously influenced by the Indian music that filled much of the Beatles' free time, the song dispenses with the standard rock and roll song structure in favor of a tamboura drone which runs throughout, propelled forward by Starr's hypnotic drumming, the basic C opening each verse giving way to the B-flat that closes them. In addition, influenced by the music of the German avant-garde composer Karlheinz Stockhausen, McCartney led his bandmates into the world of electronic music. The resulting tape loops[25] were combined with varispeed recording and backwards tapes. The song also makes the first use of Artificial Double Tracking, or ADT, which was created by Abbey Road engineers at the Beatles' request and is now standard equipment in recording studios (Lewisohn, *Complete* 216–17). Experimentation ruled the day as the group attempted to realize fully the potential of their acid-inspired creations.

The Beatles' music reflected their current altered state(s) of mind, a point not lost on many within the growing drug culture. Although they had yet to come out publicly on the subject of their drug use, the Beatles had been "under the influence" for years. They had powered their lengthy sets in Hamburg with amphetamines washed down with beer. While Bob Dylan is widely believed to have "turned on" the Beatles to marijuana during the Beatles first full-blown tour of America, they had experimented with it by the time they first visited the States (The Beatles 158; Bramwell 102). Nevertheless, the experience with Dylan, in August 1964 was formative for the band members and may well have been their first shared experience of being "stoned." They were certainly devout potheads by the time of their second film, *Help! Revolver* followed up the marijuana euphoria of *Help!* and *Rubber Soul* with the psychopharmacological mysteries of lysergic acid diethylamide. While *Sgt. Pepper's Lonely Hearts Club Band* is often referred to as the Beatles' LSD album, *Revolver* was the earliest result of the band's, and especially Lennon's, heavy use of the hallucinogen. The Beatles did not publicly admit to using the drug at the time; they would do so just weeks after the release of *Sgt. Pepper*, in June 1967.

Elsewhere on the album, McCartney sheds his bandmates, as he had on "Yesterday," for the hauntingly effective string octet on "Eleanor Rigby." The song featured some of his darkest and most surreal lyrics to date, telling the story of the title character who, waiting at the window, wears "a face that she keeps in a jar by the door."²⁶ "All the lonely people," sings McCartney, "Where do they all come from? . . . Where do they all belong?" McCartney's talent as a balladeer is highlighted on the beautiful "For No One" and "Here, There, and Everywhere." He also contributes "Good Day Sunshine," with its barroom piano, and the Motown-inspired "Got to Get You Into My Life." Harrison offers a bit of early social commentary with "Taxman," a song prompted by his realization that the British treasury was claiming most of his income. Harrison also wrote "Love You To," his first attempt to write a song specifically for Indian instrumentation, and the riff-based "I Want to Tell You." "She Said She Said,"²⁷ inspired by an acid trip that Lennon had had while in California, featured varispeeded recording and alternate guitar tuning to achieve the distinctive guitar sound. Starr is spotlighted on Lennon and McCartney's whimsical children's song "Yellow Submarine," which tells the story of a "man who sailed to sea," to return to tell of the "land of submarines," prompting the singer to journey himself to the "sea of green" and to "live beneath the waves" in the yellow submarine. "We all live in a yellow submarine," sings the chorus. A simple children's song? Perhaps, but, as with the other tracks on *Revolver*, its dependence on studio processing made it all but impossible to bring it to the stage. The technical limitations of live performance weighed heavily in the group's disenchantment with live shows. After the rigors of touring came to an end on August, 29, 1966, at San Francisco's Candlestick Park, the Beatles entered into their most creative period, pushing the experimentation displayed on *Rubber Soul* and *Revolver* to new heights and, in so doing, elevating rock and roll music to the status of art. Their image evolved as a clear statement of that fact.

In the mid-1960s there was a growing willingness to speak of popular music as an art form. Lennon and McCartney, in particular, were recognized for their songwriting talents. In March 1966 *Newsweek*, in addition to presenting the standard litany of success, captured the band's burgeoning status as artists: the "Beatle bards" had composed eighty-eight songs that had spawned nearly three thousand cover versions, sold close to 200 million copies, and garnered total sales nearing half a billion dollars. "The songs sell because they carry the Beatles' golden name," noted the article; importantly, it continued, "They also sell because they are as brilliantly original as any written today." As proof, the piece described the music's growing respectability among acknowledged artists, including "discriminating jazz groups like the Ramsey Lewis Trio" and "peerless vocalists like Ella Fitzgerald" ("Bards of Pop" 102). The Beatles had a foothold in the world of art; in the months that followed, their efforts would lead to the full acceptance and legitimization of rock and roll as an art form.

The Beatles' success also translated into influence within the youth culture. On the 1966 American tour the Beatles, who at Epstein's urging had shied away from public pronouncements on issues such as racism, religion, and the Vietnam conflict, were more vocal than they previously had been. They had grown weary of dodging the questions that were inevitably asked. For example, at a press conference at New York's Warwick Hotel, held earlier in the day of that year's Shea Stadium concert, they commented upon the Vietnam conflict in unison, "We don't like war, war is wrong." When asked why his comments on Christ had caused such a commotion in America, Lennon replied, "There are more people in America so there are more bigots also. You hear more from American bigots." He quickly added, "Not everyone in America is bigoted" (Dallos 30). Lennon's comment about Jesus Christ, and the ensuing furor, were far more important for what they exposed about the growing influence of the youth culture than for their content: For the first time, a pop star had spoken out on an issue normally held outside the scope of acceptable comment for entertainers or young people, and had gotten away with it, even garnering some empathy from establishment pundits. From this point on, pop stars and other representatives of the youth culture would be asked to comment on issues and would be viewed by many within and outside that culture as speaking for it.

If the youth market was being exploited by marketers and advertisers, the same strategies that targeted teens as a specific consumer group also contributed to their awareness of themselves as belonging to a cohesive group with its own interests, interests often at odds with the adult world and establishment. One young commentator said of the Beatles' second appearance at Shea Stadium: "All of us took dates; some of them were the very same girls we were with when all the trouble started. And even in 1966, when the Beatles sang, the looks in the girls' eyes were faraway. It was different, though. This time, we boys were almost as entranced, and the experience was more unifying than dividing" (Westcott 14). Perhaps an innocent observation, but it hinted at the role that the Beatles were playing in the lives of American youths. Increasingly, rock and roll was becoming an organizing principle for the youth culture. This feature of the Beatles' image, as a rallying point for that culture, is echoed by Todd Gitlin (1987), a media critic and Columbia professor of journalism and sociology, in his description of early attempts to bring the counterculture and New Left together to pursue common concerns: "In December 1966, the Berkeley campus administration sent police to evict an antiwar recruiting table from the student union. At a mass meeting about a campus strike, someone started singing the old union standby, 'Solidarity Forever.' Then someone started 'Yellow Submarine,' and the entire roomful rollicked into it, chorus after chorus. With a bit of effort, the Beatles' song could be taken as the communion of hippies and activists, students and nonstudents, all who at long last felt they could express their beloved single-hearted community" (*The Sixties* 208–9). Gitlin, once the president of the Students for a Democratic Society, also noted the prompt response of Free Speech Movement veteran, Michael Rossman, who ran off a leaflet that showed a little submarine with the words "NO CONFIDENCE" (in Berkeley's administration): "The Yellow Submarine was first proposed by the Beatles, who taught us a new style of song. . . . Last night we celebrated the growing fusion of head, heart and hands; of hippies and activists; and our joy and confidence in our ability to care for and take care of ourselves and what is ours. And so we made a resolution which broke into song; and we adopt for today this unexpected symbol of our trust in our future, and of our longing for a place fit for us all to live in. Please post, especially where prohibited. We love you" (*The Sixties* 210). Thus, by the time the Beatles stopped touring there were numerous hints of the direction their image was moving, from moptops eliciting an exuberantly youthful mania to that of a unifying presence among American (and Western) youth, one displaying their mores and values.

The Beatles' image was in its most purely and intentionally commercial form with its introduction to American audiences in late 1963 and early 1964. That is to say, in the period before the press and other media were mobilized to follow the band's progress, promotional material provided to them presented an image consistent with the commercially proven model of the teen idol. Over the ensuing months and years, however, the image moved beyond its "boy next door" limitations to accommodate an increasingly inquisitive press and the temporal and intellectual maturation of the Beatles. Whatever the wishes of Capitol and Epstein, the press was interested in the Beatles' views on a wide range of topics important to the American public, particularly the nation's youth. Never comfortable with the vacuity of their teen idol façades, the Beatles asserted themselves as individuals with opinions and beliefs quite beyond the limits of their manufactured selves. In the process, they assumed a defining role in the youth culture.

For many the Beatles would be pied pipers, leading their young fans on the search for meaning, first through hallucinogenic drugs, and then through the investigation of Eastern belief systems. As described in the next chapters, the Beatles' musical artistry and supremacy would be the basis for legitimizing popular music as an art form, and for legitimizing the lifestyle of the counterculture. These, of course, were paramount concerns of Jann Wenner, as reflected in his magazine, *Rolling Stone*, the topic of chapter 5. However, the mainstream press had already begun to describe the Beatles and their influence in these terms, and the Beatles' image evolved to reflect their unequaled position of artistry, celebrity, and influence, a process that accelerated with the release of "Penny Lane"/ "Strawberry Fields Forever" in February 1967.

FOUR

"The Mood of the Sixties"
The Beatles as Artists, 1966–68

IN THE POST-BEATLEMANIA PERIOD following the end of touring, the Beatles attempted to leave behind their show-business image and to make their public image more authentic and consistent with their perceptions of themselves. The Beatles' new image broke with the "Fab Four" of the Beatlemania years and instead presented them as artists and committed counterculturalists. This chapter examines various aspects of the image that emerged in the mainstream media in the years 1966–68.

To be sure, the image created and fostered during the days of Beatlemania continued to exert an influence over perceptions of the band and its importance. In the years following the end of touring, however, notions of the Beatles' artistic supremacy (compared to other popular music artists) and of their role in the legitimization of pop music as an art form were increasingly important facets of the evolving image, as were perceptions of their leadership of the youth culture.

In late 1966 and early 1967, the Beatles set out to destroy their images as lovable moptops. McCartney went so far as to tell the *Sunday Times* that the Beatles might be breaking up: "Now we Beatles are ready to go our own ways. . . . I'm no longer one of the four mop-tops." He called his recently debuted mustache "part of breaking up the Beatles. I no longer believe in the image" ("Paul McCartney Predicts" 29). In reality, while the band was willing to leave the press guessing, by the time of the interview in January 1967, the Beatles were together in the studio in the midst of sessions for their next album, *Sgt. Pepper's Lonely Hearts Club Band*. Now, they actively sought to distance themselves from the image that had been part of their phenomenal success. The necessity for change was felt strongly within the band. Thirty years later, McCartney candidly recalled to Barry Miles: "We were fed up with being the Beatles. We really hated that fucking four little mop-top boys approach. We were not boys, we were men. It was all gone, all that boy shit, all that screaming, we didn't want anymore, plus, we'd now got turned on to pot and thought of ourselves as artists rather than just performers" (Miles 303).

That is not to say that the "Fab Four" disappeared immediately or completely. While the Beatles had begun to react to contemporary issues, the teen magazines held fast to the teen idol image of the Beatles. With article titles like "Beatles Personal Letters," "The Girls Who Invade the Beatles Privacy!," and "Beatles: What They Really Say About U.S. Teens!,"[1] much of the copy of fan magazines remained dedicated to presenting the Beatles as the stuff of female adolescents' dreams. Emblematic of the approach is the April 1966 issue of *Tiger Beat*, featuring a letter from a fan to Ringo. Included in the magazine's "Love Letters to the Stars!" section, the letter declared the writer's undying love for the drummer:

> I am writing this letter to you because I know you would love me if you found me so here I am. Just last week I was voted the most popular girl in the school system. All my life I have dreamed of you, and now is my chance to get you (finally)! I am desperate and feel that you should divorce Maureen. I feel that this would be the right move since I am more capable of fulfilling your needs. Please don't think I am stuck-up; it's just my love for you shining through.
>
> Every Saturday I watch your "Beatles" cartoon show. I don't

think they are making fun of you like some people. I feel if we were married I could be a valuable addition to the show. I went to your performance in Seattle and when you glanced roughly in my direction I knew you were staring at me with longing eyes. Don't you remember?

All my deepest love and greatest affection, Willa

("Love Letters" 40–41)

In the same issue the magazine's publisher, Charles Laufer, responded to a reader's letter from the previous issue that had stated that if any Beatle were expendable, it would have to be Ringo or George, because John and Paul were irreplaceable. The publisher unequivocally refuted the claim, in capital letters for emphasis: "THE EDITORS OF TIGER BEAT MAGAZINE BELIEVE THE BEATLES ARE EQUAL. WITHOUT RINGO, JOHN, PAUL, AND GEORGE WORKING TOGETHER AS A TEAM, THERE COULD BE NO BEATLES. NOT ONE OF THEM COULD EVER BE REPLACED." Then, to demonstrate just how equal the band members were, a chart was provided comparing the Beatles in terms of hair and eye color, height, weight, collar, chest, waist, and shoe size. Very similar, indeed! "In every way, these boys are fantastic! And it's a gift to us all," wrote Laufer, "that such greatness can come in four equal packages!" (Laufer 8). *Tiger Beat*, *16*, and numerous other publications, while gradually coming to terms with the maturation of the Beatles, continued to promote the Beatlemania-era image even as the band was replaced at the top of the teen idol pile by the new heartthrobs, the Monkees.

Television continued to offer various versions of the Beatlemania-era Beatles. ABC presented *The Beatles* cartoon on Saturday mornings, while NBC broadcast perhaps the single most viewed version of the "Fab Four," as they appeared in *A Hard Day's Night* and *Help!*, on the half-hour comedy *The Monkees*. Airing at 7:30 p.m. on Monday nights from September 1966 to August 1968, the show was broadcast early enough in the evening to capture both the adult and youth audiences, and created the sort of chaotic energy that had sparked the two Beatle films. Mickey Dolenz, Mike Nesmith, Peter Tork, and Davy Jones starred in the series and sang on the recordings (which otherwise featured studio session players). The brainchild of Don Kirshner, whose Aldon Publishing and Brill Building pop had been a powerful force in the early 1960s, the Monkees were soon the darlings of the teen magazines and at the top of the charts. They quickly eclipsed the Beatles with the number one single for 1966, "I'm a Believer"; they also spent more time at number one in the album charts in 1966 and 1967 (Whitburn, *Top Singles* 882; Whitburn, *Top 40 Albums* 391). The Beatles may have been pursuing individual projects, no longer willing to continue in their roles as lovable moptops, but the market nevertheless met the demands of those members of the audience for whom that image remained attractive. As if to signal the transfer of the pop throne, the June 1967 issue of *16* magazine giddily proclaimed, "THE MONKEES & BEATLES MEET."

After years of touring, the Beatles had indeed gone their own ways. Harrison immersed himself in study of the sitar and Hindu philosophy. McCartney and producer George Martin wrote the score for the film *The Family Way* (Jambox Films, 1966). Starr enjoyed family life and the London club scene. Lennon acted in Richard Lester's antiwar black comedy *How I Won the War* (Petersham Films, 1967). Lennon indicated his discomfort with the Beatles' image to *Look* magazine while on location for the film in Madeira, Spain:

I don't want people taking things from me that aren't really me. They make you something that they want to make you, that isn't really you. They come and talk and find answers, but they're their answers, not us. We're not Beatles to each other, you know. It's a joke to us. If we're going out the door of the hotel, we say,

"Right! Beatle John! Beatle George now! Come on, let's go!" We don't put on a false front or anything. But we just know that leaving the door, we turn into Beatles because everybody looking at us sees the Beatles. We're not the Beatles at all. We're just us. (Gross 62)

Lennon bemoaned the concessions that the band had made to meet the expectations of the music industry. "We weren't as open and as truthful when we didn't have the power to be. We had to take it easy. We had to shorten our hair to leave Liverpool and get jobs in London. We had to wear suits to get on TV. We had to compromise." As with the other three Beatles, for the first time in his adult life he was pursuing individual interests and contemplating life away from "Beatling": "I feel I want to be them all—painter, writer, actor, singer, player, musician. I want to try them all, and I'm lucky enough to be able to. I want to see which one turns me on" (Gross 59).

Lennon's comments are interesting for a couple of reasons. First, Lennon was beginning to press his status as an artist, a feature that would become more pronounced in the Beatles' image as time passed. In fact, artistic achievement and supremacy would be a central theme in the band's evolving image to the end of their career. Second, Lennon clearly hints at a more authentic Beatles in which the image of the band is less tied to the necessities of the music industry and more a revelation of the band members as they really are. Their next single, and the promotion accompanying it, presented the band with an opportunity to introduce the new, authentic Beatles.

The previous three years had seen the Beatles rise to the top of the entertainment industry. Their unrivaled success had been fueled by endless touring, movies, and a remarkable number of recordings over a relatively short span: fifteen singles and nine albums of new Beatles material. Capitol had rarely gone more than three months between Beatles singles, and never more than three months without releasing a single or album. But since the delivery of "Eleanor Rigby"/"Yellow Submarine" and *Revolver* in August 1966, the Beatles had not released any new music. The band's hiatus had predictably led to press speculation that the Beatles were breaking up.

In February 1967 the Beatles released their most ambitious single yet, the double-A-side "Penny Lane"/"Strawberry Fields Forever." Regarded by many to be the greatest rock single of all time, it displays all the ingredients of British acid rock, including bells, violins, sound collage, and surreal lyrics. "Strawberry Fields Forever," one of the Beatles' most impressive recordings, is the more experimental of the two. Lennon had worked on the song while on location in Madiera. The lyrics, at times resembling a stream of consciousness, reflected the alienation Lennon felt following the "more popular than Jesus" controversy, as well as a certain sense of resignation to that isolation. Nevertheless, as Lennon pointed out in an interview in 1980 (Sheff 135–36), the song was positive, for, in spite of the apparent disaffection, in Strawberry Fields there is "nothing to get hung about." The song was introduced by Lennon to the band and George Martin in late November 1966, and sessions for the recording were the first of those intended for the next album, destined to be called *Sgt. Pepper's Lonely Hearts Club Band*. No longer limited by what could be played before a live audience, the band and Martin extended their earlier experiments on *Revolver*. Numerous and varied versions of "Strawberry Fields Forever" were attempted; it was the first song the Beatles had ever redone. The song was finally edited from two separate takes that were brilliantly pulled together by the Beatles' production team. Lennon liked the first minute of the band's original take, but otherwise preferred the more somber orchestration of another, and told Martin that he wanted the two sections joined. Unfortunately, the versions of the song were in different keys and tempos. Lennon told Martin to "fix it." To Martin's surprise, the speeds of the two segments could be varied to bring the tempos and keys into *near* alignment, giving the recording its dreamy quality (Lewisohn, *Complete* 235).

Like "Strawberry Fields Forever," "Penny Lane" was a product of experimentation, both with the possibilities of the studio and with the mind-altering substances that had consumed more and more of the Beatles' time over the last two years. The recording, McCartney later recalled for *Anthology* series cameras, was intended as art: "(T)he nice thing is, a lot of our stuff then started to get a little bit more surreal. And then 'Penny Lane' was a little bit more surreal, too, you know, the 'fireman with his hourglass,' and all that sort of stuff was us trying to get into a bit of art, a bit of surrealism" (*The Beatles Anthology*, episode 6). For Ian MacDonald, in his superb analysis of the Beatles' recordings, *Revolution in the Head* (1994), the song captured the heady atmosphere of the period: "With its vision of 'blue suburban skies' and boundlessly confident vigour, 'Penny Lane' distils the spirit of that time more perfectly than any other creative product of the mid-Sixties" (177). Deceptively simple, the recording is an intricate amalgam of varispeeded and multilayered sound and effects benefiting from an expanded pallet of instruments.[2] McCartney's growing fascination with experimental music was also evident in its detailed arrangement (Ian MacDonald 177–79; Lewisohn, *Complete* 240–41).

Weary of the tedium of promoting their latest singles with television appearances, the Beatles had been producing promotional clips since November 1965. Having been at the forefront in creating promotional films, primarily lip-synched performance clips, the Beatles now turned to nonperformance/nonrepresentational filmmaking. Produced for NEMS Enterprises,[3] the clips for the single were important for a number of reasons. First, in presenting the Beatles in these "mini movie(s)," visual renderings of the story of the songs, they were among the first promotional clips to dispense with the usual lip-synched "performance" in favor of conceptual pieces; as such, they were precursors to today's storyboard music videos (Bramwell 181; Neaverson 120–21). Second, the clips also presented the Beatles' new look. Instead of the clean-shaven, cheery lads in designer suits, the Beatles were now sporting mustaches and donning fashions that placed them squarely in "hippiedom." This new look, a break with the established (and successful) image, was the focus of much comment. And third, the clips helped strengthen the connection between the Beatles and the experimental and avant-garde art community, a preoccupation of McCartney's especially, and an important element of the Beatles' image in this period.

Tony Bramwell, a boyhood friend of the Beatles who was involved in many of the Beatles' entertainment activities, including film production, brought in Swedish television and pop film director Peter Goldman to direct the promotional films (Bramwell 181–82). Goldman later recalled his excitement and trepidation in approaching the shoots for the clips: "Everything went so fast. It wasn't until I sat on the plane for London [that] I realized what I was up to. . . . How in the world should I be able to make something [funny enough], bizarre, clever, crazy, sophisticated to satisfy the Beatles" (Goldman). Despite his anxiety, Goldman effectively presented the new Beatles. For "Strawberry Fields Forever," the more experimental of the two new films, the newly mustachioed Beatles are shown in a field standing around a piano under a tree, the piano attached to the tree with strings. The Beatles are shown both in daytime and at night, with the latter offering a particularly potent environment for Goldman's experiments. McCartney is shown running toward the tree and jumping up onto a limb. In fact, the segment had been shot in reverse as McCartney dropped from the branch and ran *backwards* away from the tree—which is also shown in the clip. Goldman brings a full complement of avant-garde camera techniques and editing effects to bear, including the use of varispeed techniques, reverse motion, and so on. The Beatles, having been at the forefront of sound experimentation, quickly grasped the possibilities of the camera and would apply what they had learned to their own experimental film, *Magical Mystery Tour*, later that year.

"Penny Lane," with establishing shots filmed in Liverpool, focuses on Lennon (wearing his new "granny glasses," the National Health Service specs he had first started to wear while filming *How I Won The War*), and presents what would become an iconic image: Lennon walks the streets of London's East End (standing in for Liverpool), aloof, taking in the city streets but unaffected by them or the pedestrians who spin around, their attention captured by the passing Beatle. Michael Lindsay-Hogg had explored this aura of regal detachment in his direction of the promo clip for "Rain," released in May 1966. In the nonperformance sections of that film the Beatles are there to be taken in by the viewer, meant to be observed along with the other art and artifacts on the grounds of Chiswick House: their interaction with those around them, including the fans kept at bay beyond the gate, is minimal. Visually, both films capture a quality then being established in the image of the band: The Beatles, in an unrivaled position of commercial and artistic supremacy, were a new kind of royalty, emulated, venerated, and infallible.

In America, the broadcast rights for the "Strawberry Fields Forever" and "Penny Lane" films went to ABC, which debuted the clips on *The Hollywood Palace* on Saturday, February 25, 1967, and aired them again in mid-March on Dick Clark's *American Bandstand*, where audience opinion was split as to the Beatles' new look and sound. The variety show debut is interesting, capturing a moment in television that has long vanished. Though passing out of favor in the 1970s, in the 1960s the variety show retained its long held popularity. Here, in primetime, a whole host of entertainers were brought together in a way that seems inconceivable in today's niche-driven world of entertainment. On this night the host, actor Van Johnson, welcomed anti-establishment comic George Carlin, Judy Garland's young daughter Liza Minelli, a Vietnam pin-up girl, and Hollywood stalwart Mickey Rooney, who joined the host for a baseball skit. The mixing of such disparate genres, arts, and generations, though largely unheard-of today, was the standard fare of the variety show. In the midst of this very "showbiz" presentation came the Beatles, with their new look and new sound. "They made a special film for *The Hollywood Palace* about a Liverpool street called 'Penny Lane,'" began Johnson's introduction of the clip before a studio audience full of screaming girls, "I think it's the most imaginative treatment of a song I have ever seen...." As this first clip ended, Johnson tempted the audience: "If you think that one was far out, wait until you hear their next one, 'Strawberry Fields Forever'" (*Hollywood Palace*, February 25, 1967). At the end of the show, Johnson introduced the second clip, another one filmed "especially" for *The Hollywood Palace*: "And believe me, these strawberries are really wild."[4] The crowd shrieked as the clip began.

Wild strawberries, indeed. The single was welcomed as a new direction in the Beatles' music, as well as a unique contribution to pop music. *Time* applauded the "astonishing inventiveness" displayed on the new single. The magazine also noted McCartney's "passion" for the work of electronic music composer Karlheinz Stockhausen, an early example of the promotion of perceptions about the Beatles' growing connections to "art" that became essential to their new image. The article concluded of the single, "*Strawberry* is full of dissonances and eerie space-age sounds, achieved in part by playing tapes backward and at various speeds. This is nothing new to electronic composers, but employing such methods in a pop song is electrifying" ("Other Noises" 63).

Richard Corliss, later a senior writer at *Time* magazine but then writing for the Catholic publication *Commonweal*, located the single within the evolution of the Beatles' recordings: "But the Beatles aren't simply getting gamier; their songs have improved tremendously. Each succeeding album has had fewer mediocre cuts. *A Hard Day's Night, For Sale,* and *Help!* (featuring the astounding

'Yesterday') deepened the group's exploration of pop horizons; *Rubber Soul* broadened it. *Revolver*, their latest LP, made startling new gains, and their latest single, 'Penny Lane' and 'Strawberry Fields Forever,' has consolidated those gains" (235). Indicative of the increasingly widely held perception of the Beatles' centrality to contemporary art and culture, such plaudits were emblematic of the reception the Beatles were receiving across a wide spectrum of American media. Acclaimed for its achievement, the single was a harbinger of things to come.

The Beatles, especially Paul McCartney, frequently visited the art galleries of 1960s Swinging London. The galleries were a staple meeting place in which Britain's new elite, the pop musicians, could mingle with each other and with other artists. This was a time in which the arts were invigorated by the youth culture, and in which the art of the youth culture began to both follow and direct creative currents within the art world. Musicians began to regard the artist with fascination and, perhaps, envy; many consciously attempted to create art. Few, if any, were as successful as the Beatles in this endeavor. By integrating a wide swathe of current artistic values and concepts into rock and roll, the Beatles changed the parameters of what was possible, and acceptable, on a pop recording. The artistry exhibited by the Beatles on their next album, *Sgt. Pepper's Lonely Hearts Club Band* (released in June, 1967), and its reception, were central elements within the Beatles' evolving image. With *Sgt. Pepper*, the Beatles' credentials as the period's preeminent artistic and social force were fully established.

Given not only their related artistic programs and shared experience, but also the egalitarian mores they held in common, it was only natural that British pop artists and pop musicians would gravitate towards each other. Many of the young musicians had attended British art schools, one of the few avenues of upward social mobility open to working-class youths.[5] In addition, many British pop artists shared common backgrounds with the musicians. The 1960s were a period when the working class appropriated and dominated British culture as they had in no other period. British film star Michael Caine, who rose from a working-class background to become a star during the 1960s, commented on this change: "The sixties have been misunderstood: they should not be judged by standards of talent, skill, artistry or intelligence, or by the great works or artists that those years produced. The reason for their notoriety is far more simple than that. For the first time in British history, the young working-class stood up for themselves and said, 'We are here, this is our society and we are not going away. Join us, stay away, like us, hate us—do as you like. We don't care about your opinion any more'" (159). This view was (and is) held by many of the British pop artists and musicians who came to prominence during the period.

Many of the top pop artists and musicians pursued an art of combination, so to speak, in which disparate elements from various sources were joined together to form strikingly new forms. The result could simply be an "anthropology of popular taste," as Frith and Horne (1987) describe artist Peter Blake's (and the Beatles' and the Kinks') definition of "Britishness." It could also be a comment on mass media and consumption, as often pursued by Richard Hamilton, or Peter Townshend of the Who (Frith and Horne 107). Thus, given their common interests (and geographic proximity), it was quite reasonable that Blake and Hamilton, among Britain's top pop artists, and the Beatles, the most celebrated pop group of the period, would eventually cross paths, as they did on *Sgt. Pepper's Lonely Hearts Club Band* and the "White Album."

Every technique perfected in the last three years was brought to bear on what many consider to be the greatest rock album ever recorded. As music historian Paul Griffiths (1988) notes, the music of the Beatles, particularly their later work, "occupies a rare and privileged position, in that it was exceedingly popular and yet free to be as imaginative as its creators knew how" ("Music" 79). Very few artists in the era of mass art have been able to pursue an artistic vision unencumbered by restrictions imposed by those funding the effort. In the 1920s and 1930s, Charlie Chaplin, due to his unprecedented commercial success, was able to spend unheard of amounts of money and, especially, time, making films for his own production company. Such creative control was rare in the mass arts, however. Unique among their contemporaries, the Beatles were left to create as they saw fit; the bean counters were held at bay by the expectation that, whatever the costs, the benefits would outpace them. With this freedom, the Beatles and producer George Martin brought their full creative and technical prowess to bear in creating an album on which the influence and concerns of British pop art are everywhere, and which is widely held to be the first rock (as distinct from rock and roll) album—the point at which pop music was established as a legitimate mode of artistic vision.

Sgt. Pepper's Lonely Hearts Club Band encapsulates the pop art concerns first listed by Hamilton and his colleagues in the Independent Group (see discussion in chapter 3): The album was popular, in that it was designed for a mass audience; it was mass-produced; it was aimed at the young; it was witty, sexy, gimmicky, and glamorous; and it was the product of big business. Though undoubtedly the product of a culture industry dependent upon the "transient," and the endless fueling of consumption through style obsolescence, the album confounded contemporary expectations about the longevity of rock and roll. The Beatles avoided becoming obsolete by continually pushing the parameters of what was possible in the studio and within the pop idiom, thus demonstrating that, in fact, rock and roll was an evolving form that could accommodate a wide range of influences, both old and new.

Ian MacDonald (1994), Alan Moore (1997), and Mark Lewisohn (1992), among others, provide excellent discussions of the music on the album and the means employed in its creation. It is not necessary here to delve deeply into this well-mapped terrain except as it relates to the Beatles' image and contemporary artistic culture. The album is often referred to as the first "concept album," though the ubiquitous caveat that follows is that what started as a conceptual work reverted to simple recording of tracks. Certainly, McCartney's original intention that the album present a musical revue headlined by the Lonely Hearts Club Band was quickly jettisoned. Yet, at its core the album remains a conceptual work: It is self-consciously and unapologetically Art, fearless and self-assured in its purpose. The Beatles' confidence in the enterprise is demonstrated in their decision not to release a single from the sessions. "Strawberry Fields Forever" and "Penny Lane" were recorded first, and the Beatles acquiesced to Capitol's request for product (it had been six months since the release of the previous single and three months since the release of *Revolver*), but by design the remainder of the sessions produced no singles. The five months between the release of "Strawberry Field Forever"/"Penny Lane" and its follow-up, "All You Need Is Love"/"Baby, You're a Rich Man," was an unprecedented gap in the release of Beatles singles, which, with rare exception over the previous three years, had come at a rate of at least one single every two to three months. Additionally, the four-month gap between release of the single and the album was something new, with the music industry and fans for the first time in three years having to go more than two or three months without the release of new Beatles recordings. At any point between the release of the single in February, and the album in June, the Beatles could have released recordings and quashed discussion of their demise. Yet they chose not to, and went so far as to demand that Capitol release the album in America as programmed by the Beatles and George Martin, with no alterations to the track listing. This all speaks to the Beatles' determination that this new album remain an artistic whole, in effect shielding the album from commerce with an eye toward acclamation of their work as art.

The album opens with the sound of an orchestra tuning up before the start of a performance. This reminder of a classical past is suddenly disrupted as the first notes of "Sgt. Pepper's Lonely Hearts Club Band" blast in, the electric guitars and amplified beat a clear statement of the present. The orchestra (and parts thereof) is not finished. Musical references to bygone eras pepper the album. In fact, old and new, high art and low, nostalgia and expectation, are intertwined throughout: a brass quartet graces the hard-edged electric sound in the opening track; strings elevate McCartney's "She's Leaving Home," and combine with sitar in Harrison's "Within You Without You"; a music hall ensemble propels McCartney's "When I'm Sixty-Four; Lennon's "Being for the Benefit of Mister Kite" benefits from Martin's production and a sound collage of organ music composed from recordings of numerous instruments, sectioned into small pieces, scattered, and then assembled willy-nilly; and, of course, an orchestra carries the album to its chaotic and overwhelming finale on "A Day in the Life."

As always, each Beatle has at least one song on the album; the opening track segues into "With a Little Help from My Friends," the Lennon and McCartney song selected as Starr's vocal contribution. The next track, "Lucy in the Sky with Diamonds," though inspired by a drawing by Lennon's young son Julian, demonstrates the influence of *Through the Looking Glass*, by Lewis Carroll, one of his favorite authors (Ian MacDonald 190). Lennon's fascination with Lewis Carroll was shared by many within the counterculture who, as Ian MacDonald notes, "canonized" the Alice books for their "surreal wit and drug-dream undertones" (190).[6] Many pointed to the acronym of the song's title, LSD, as a clear statement of the Beatles' involvement in the drug culture. And, of course, by this time the Beatles were well aware of the hallucinogen's effects, Lennon and Harrison having been "dosed" by a dentist friend at a dinner party in 1965. Eventually all of the Beatles experimented with the drug; Lennon, in particular, spent much of his spare time in a state of drug-induced euphoria or torpor. In any event, this song was banned from the BBC for its drug references, (as was "A Day in the Life"—

"I'd love to turn you on"). The song, awash in droning instrumentation, reverb, echo, varispeed, and other studio effects, brilliantly appealed to the counterculture's nostalgia for the childlike innocence embodied in Carroll's books, while at the same time invoking hallucinogen-induced ecstasy and expanded consciousness.

Another song demonstrating the Beatles' attachment to the counterculture is Harrison's "Within You Without You," which opens side two of the album. As a protest against the establishment and tradition, counterculturalists often adopted the customs and values of historically oppressed groups. While much of the American counterculture adopted the dress and, often, beliefs of Native Americans, British hippies looked to the former colonies (particularly India) for inspiration (Moore 21).[7] Great Britain's popular culture abounds with examples of the British fascination with empire: consider the popularity of Rudyard Kipling's works ("Gunga Din," 1892; *The Jungle Book*, 1864), H. Rider Haggard's Allan Quatermaine and Ayesha novels of the 1880s–1920s, Edgar Wallace's *Sanders of the River* series (1910s–1920s), or the "empire films" of the Korda brothers in the 1930s (*Sanders of the River*, *The Drum*, and *The Four Feathers*, released in 1935, 1938, and 1939, respectively). In fact, the imperial period of British history fascinated British and American audiences. In the 1960s, however, far from celebrating empire, many looked to the fashions, faiths, and philosophies of the East as part of the countercultural critique of Western society. Harrison's love of Indian culture and his devotion to Hinduism must be understood within this cultural context.

The following track, "When I'm Sixty-Four," exemplifies one of McCartney's, and the Beatles', great strengths—a facility with pastiche, a respectful, though perhaps humorous, act of imitation. Here, McCartney pays homage to the pre–World War II music-hall style of George Formby. This penchant for imitation can be seen on earlier recordings such as "Eleanor Rigby," with a string arrangement inspired by Bernard Herrmann's score for Francois Truffaut's film

Fahrenheit 451, and "Yellow Submarine," with its Goons-inspired effects and brass band (Everett 51–57), and is also displayed on numerous later recordings, including McCartney's tribute to flapper-era jazz, "Honey Pie," and Lennon's "Yer Blues," a send-up of the contemporary British blues scene (both from *The Beatles*). This ability not only to imitate but to surpass was a talent shared by few of the Beatles' contemporaries.

Encoding its context into its content, some of the album's tracks display the pop art preoccupation with mass media. Lennon's "Good Morning Good Morning," for instance, emerged from the mass-mediated experience of his everyday life. A product of Lennon's habit of working with the television on, it took its inspiration from a Kellogg's Corn Flakes commercial, and contains a reference to a British television show of the time, *Meet the Wife*. Ending with a sound collage of animal noises, "Good Morning Good Morning" segues into "Sgt. Pepper's Lonely Hearts Club Band (Reprise)," the bleating of a fox hunt horn magically transforming into a distorted guitar to begin the number. In essence the Beatles' alter ego, the "Lonely Hearts Club Band" bookends the album, with a cheering crowd closing the "Reprise" and ushering in "A Day in the Life."

This last song's lyrics are a kind of record of human communication as experienced by Lennon: "I read the news today, oh boy . . ." / "I saw the photograph . . ." / ". . . having read the book" / "I saw a film today, oh boy. . . ." Primarily a Lennon song, with McCartney contributing the section between the first orchestral buildup and Lennon's final verse, "A Day in the Life" contains the Beatles' most explicit lyrical statement of their involvement in the drug culture, with Lennon singing, "I'd love to turn you on," and McCartney adding, "Found my way upstairs and had a smoke / somebody spoke, and I went into a dream." Along with obvious countercultural overtones, the song also displays pop art's collapsing of the barrier between high and low art. In particular, the Beatles' awareness of the musical avant-garde is put on display, as McCartney recalled years

later: "Because of all this Cage and Stockhausen stuff . . . I thought
'OK. I'd try this idea on John' and I said let's take 15 bars, count 15
bars and we'll do one of these avant-garde ideas. We'll say to all the
musicians, 'You've got to start at the lowest note on your instrument,
which is like a physical limitation, and go to your highest note'" (*The
Paul McCartney World Tour Book* 52). The orchestra was recorded
four times playing the segue and climactic buildup, and the tracks
were combined, thus creating the monumental finale of the song.

The product of months of experimentation and development,
the aurally stunning *Sgt. Pepper's Lonely Hearts Club Band* needed
something equally dramatic for its packaging. Peter Blake was recommended to the Beatles by West End gallery owner Robert Fraser. Blake and the Beatles proved to be a perfect fit, with Blake's artistic interests coinciding to a large extent with those of the Beatles.
In her biography of the artist, Marina Vaizey (1986) notes that Blake
"makes of the ephemeral something that is simultaneously classic
and nostalgic. He has said that 'pop art is often rooted in nostalgia;
the nostalgia of old, popular things.'" Blake was "'always looking
back at the source of the idiom'" while simultaneously "'trying to
establish a new pop art, one which stems directly from our time'"
(Vaizey 38). The Beatles, too, mined their British past for inspiration, and what Vaizey wrote of Blake and his art of combination
could surely be said of the Beatles: They often assumed the role of
"editor of the real and the imaginary, of past and present" (16). In
fact, much of what the Beatles recorded was reminiscent of Blake's
art. For instance, "Lovely Rita," who in uniform looked "a little like
a military man," suggests Blake's penchant for costumes and badges,
as is apparent in his *Self Portrait (In RAF Jacket)* (1952–53), *On the
Balcony* (1955–57), and *Self Portrait with Badges* (1961); "Being for
the Benefit of Mister Kite" reminds one of Blake's circus series of
the late 1950s and his wrestlers collages of the early 1960s.

Once committed to designing the album's package, Blake and
his partner (and wife), Jann Haworth, were allowed to listen to the

songs that had been completed, and conceived of the cover as a collage. Collage—that is, the addition of various ephemera such as newspapers and other printed work to painting—was a crucial element of the art of many British pop artists, including Richard Hamilton and Peter Blake. Hamilton's *Just what is it that makes today's homes so different, so appealing?* (1956) is emblematic of the collage of the movement: images from mass media, such as a magazine advertisement for canned ham, a picture of a bodybuilder (perhaps from a bodybuilding magazine), a comic book cover, and a movie marquee advertisement for *The Jazz Singer* are all brought together by means of commercial graphic design techniques in a comment on American mass media and progress. Whereas Hamilton had tended to stand firmly in the present with his art, Blake often used art as a means of defining "Britishness"; his collages and paintings often depicted souvenirs of a bygone era in tandem with contemporary images. *Toy Shop* (1962) combines some of the toys Blake had collected with images of Elvis Presley, the Union Jack, and the instruments of the artist's craft. Likewise, *Couples* (1959) combines both old and new postcards for its statement.

Blake immediately picked up on the band's notion of creating an alter ego, that is, Sgt. Pepper's Lonely Hearts Club Band, and arranged to borrow the waxwork figures of the Beatles standing in Madame Tussaud's Wax Museum. Thus, on the cover the Beatles could look upon the Lonely Hearts Club Band, along with everyone else. Creating the album cover collage and center gatefold—itself an innovation—was a collaborative affair. The Beatles had had their colorful Northern brass band uniforms made even before Blake came aboard. For the "audience" joining Sgt. Pepper's Lonely Hearts Club Band on the cover, Lennon, McCartney, and Harrison provided Blake with lists of people they wanted in attendance. Blake, Haworth, and Robert Fraser also contributed lists. Blake, consistent with British pop art's immersion in American popular culture, included Leo Gorcey and Huntz Hall of the Bowery Boys,

Dion DiMucci of Dion and the Belmonts, and a waxwork of former heavyweight boxing champion Sonny Liston. Fraser selected several artists (which may explain the inclusion of Larry Bell, Wallace Berman, and Richard Lindner, among others), some of whom had appeared at his gallery. Lennon's choices included the proponent of the black arts, Aleister Crowley, Liverpool footballer Albert Stubbins, Jesus, Adolf Hitler, and Lewis Carroll (or was this Blake's choice?). Harrison was responsible for the inclusion of a dozen gurus, and one suspects that Stockhausen was among those included on McCartney's list, along with Hollywood musical star and dancer Fred Astaire and beat author William Burroughs. Starr was quite content to let the others design the sleeve (Martin and Pearson 114–16; Trynka 259).

Blake and Haworth enlarged photographs collected from magazines and other materials, of the various individuals that had been selected for inclusion on the cover, and pasted them onto hardboard. Then they set about creating the collage that would adorn the album cover. Haworth built the background, then affixed the photographs to poles, spacing them on tiers one foot apart to create the illusion of depth. Haworth also did all of the hand-tinting on the photographs. Consistent with McCartney's original cover idea, that the band could be shown being given a formal presentation by the Lord Mayor, Haworth added the flowerbed that stands in the foreground of the album cover, thus maintaining the "band in the park" idea. Blake asked fairground artist Joe Ephgrave to paint the drum skin, which was suitably carnivalesque (Martin and Pearson 116). The album had a gatefold sleeve, with the lyrics printed on the back (a first for a pop album), and came with a page of cutouts designed by Blake, including a Sgt. Pepper badge. The inclusion of the lyrics indicates the degree to which the Beatles intended the album to be received as something of permanence, that is, as "art." With this album we have, in a sense, a musical as well as graphic rendering of many of the concerns shared by the Beatles and Peter Blake, and present in much British pop art: the juxtaposition of old and new, the fascination with the fantastic, and a focus on mass media.

U.S. record dealers, it was reported in *Time*, placed orders for more than one million copies of the album prior to its release on June 2, 1967 ("Mix-Master" 67). Notices were unanimously positive, or nearly so, a notable exception being Richard Goldstein's review in the *New York Times*. He found the album "precious but devoid of gems," an album of "special effects, dazzling but ultimately fraudulent," characterized by an "an obsession with production coupled with a surprising shoddiness in composition" ("We Still Need the Beatles" 24). Goldstein's sentiments evoked an immediate and critical response. In fact, another writer for the *New York Times* was so incensed by Goldstein's review of the album that he refuted it in a review appearing in the *Village Voice*. Applauding the Beatles for turning the record album into an art form, Tom Phillips countered Goldstein's claim that the album was an "undistinguished collection of work," calling the album the "most ambitious and most successful album ever issued, and the most significant artistic event of 1967" (15).

Reaction to Goldstein's review was so vast and negative that Robert Christgau, in an article appearing in *Esquire* magazine, devoted a section of his analysis of contemporary music to a discussion of the Goldstein piece and the reaction it elicited ("the largest response to a music review in its [the *New York Times*'] history"). Contrary to Goldstein's view, Christgau found the Beatles to be "inordinately fond (in a rather recondite way) of what I call the real world. They want to turn us on, all right—to everything in that world, and in ourselves." He applauded the Beatles' "genius," and praised their refusal to "prostitute themselves for their fans" in constructing an album that was "for the people" (284–85).

As is apparent from the commentary of the time, Goldstein's views had little or no constituency. Critical praise was heaped upon the Beatles' new work. *Time* noted of the Beatles that they had "moved onto a higher artistic plateau" and that, in so doing, they were "leading an evolution in which the best of current post-rock sounds are becoming something that pop music has never been before: an art form." "'Serious musicians'" were listening to the Beatles and "marking their work as a historic departure in the progress of music—any music." Among those "serious musicians" were Leonard Bernstein and Ned Rorem, the "composer of some of the best of today's art songs," who said: "'They are colleagues of mine, speaking the same language with different accents.'" On the album's "cunning collages," "the Beatles . . . piece together scraps of tension between the generations, the loneliness of the dislocated '60s, and the bitter sweets of young love in any age. At the same time, their sensitivity to the absurd is sharper than ever." The album, which sold a "staggering" 2,500,000 copies in the first three months of its release, was found by *Time* to demonstrate "note for note, word for word, the brilliance of the new Beatles" (Porterfield and Birnbaum 60–61).

Newsweek's Jack Kroll, who compared the Beatles to Lord Tennyson, Charlie Chaplin, and poet Edith Sitwell, and likened "A Day in the Life" to T. S. Eliot's *The Waste Land*, asserted the album's status as art. He wrote that the Beatles "have lost their innocence, certainly, but loss of innocence is, increasingly, their theme and the theme of more 'serious' new art from the stories of Donald Barthelme to the plays of Harold Pinter" ("It's Getting Better" 70). The *New Yorker* elicited the response of a number of members of the audience for its piece on the album. A disc jockey summarized his listeners' reaction: "Not much . . . They're unprepared. Just as people were unprepared for Picasso. That's because this album is not a teen-age album. It's a terribly intellectual album." One record buyer maintained that the music of the Beatles went "beyond making you feel good, although it does do that. It has aesthetic appeal. It conforms more to my conception of art." Calling the record a "musical *event*, comparable to a notable new opera or symphonic work," another opined, "there is more going on musically in this one record than has gone on lately almost anywhere else." Like Duke Ellington, the Beatles were "working in that special territory where entertainment slips over into art" ("Sgt. Pepper" 22–23). From a critical standpoint, then, the Beatles' status as artists was at a high point, and their appeared to be no limit to the band's creativity.

On June 25, just weeks after the release of the album, the Beatles' status as hippies was on display in the global satellite broadcast of the band recording their new single, "All You Need Is Love." For the event, they were decked out in the finest hippie fashions and surrounded by friends (among them Mick Jagger and other pop luminaries) and balloons and colorful signs declaring the song's eponymous message in numerous languages, all to the strains of the orchestra assembled for the recording. The Beatles' new album and single epitomized the ethos of the Summer of Love, and firmly established within the Beatles' image their countercultural leanings. But the Beatles' impact on culture expanded beyond the influence they exerted on the youth culture to which they first appealed. It was discussed seriously among the intelligentsia. Noted composer and critic Ned Rorem, in a January 1968 essay appearing in the *New York Review of Books*, opined: "The Beatles have, so to speak, brought *fiction* back to music, supplanting criticism. No, they aren't new, but as tuneful as the Thirties with the same exuberance of futility that Bessie Smith employed. They have removed sterile martyrdom from art, revived the sensual" (Rorem 27). In his essay, "Learning from the Beatles," which appeared in the *Partisan Review* in the fall of 1967, influential modernist critic Richard Poirier lamented the inadequacy of criticism of rock produced by the "youth establishment," academic conservatives, and the old-left literati, in dealing with popular music as art. He called *Sgt. Pepper's Lonely Hearts Club Band* "an eruption, an accomplishment for which no one could have been wholly prepared" (109). He noted that the Beatles shared with T. S. Eliot and James Joyce an "allusiveness both in their direct references and in their styles." He recognized a "range of musical familiarity" lacking in the work of their chief rivals, the Rolling Stones (112–13).

Ralph Brauer, in "Iconic Modes: The Beatles" (1978), maintains that it was the "love of the intellectuals which helped to kill the Beatles," for the apparent acceptance of the band by the establishment called into question their legitimacy among students, their greatest "devotees" (153). This is a questionable conclusion. As discussed in the next chapter, the band's fall from grace with the more radicalized elements of the youth culture was more a function of their characteristically countercultural apathy toward politics and their continued adherence to a countercultural ideal based on notions of brotherhood and love. The Beatles enjoyed the support of students and intellectuals well into 1968, at which point, in the midst of presidential primaries, mounting casualties in Vietnam, and an increasing number of draft calls, the apolitical brand of counterculturalism came to be viewed by many students as an ineffectual response to the excesses of the establishment. Prior to that, assumptions about the Beatles' artistry, supremacy, and standing as a vehicle of progress—concepts integral to their image— were essential components of the youth culture's self-definition and -legitimization (more fully discussed in the next chapter). With *Sgt. Pepper's Lonely Hearts Club Band* the Beatles established once and for all their artistic preeminence in the world of youth-oriented musicians and bands. They also seized positions within the world of "serious" music and art.

While amassing an unprecedented record of commercial achievement, they had shown a consistent pattern of improvement with every album, a process that accelerated with the issue of *Rubber Soul*, continued with *Revolver*, and culminated in *Sgt. Pepper's Lonely Hearts Club Band*. Moving beyond that which had proven so commercially successful, the Beatles explored new and commercially unproven terrain, thereby expanding the parameters of pop.

With the release of that album, acceptance of their artistic primacy and influence within pop music was all but universal, a point highlighted in *Time*: "As the Beatles moved on, absorbing and extending Bob Dylan's folk-rock hybrid and sowing innovations of their own, they were like musical Johnny Appleseeds; wherever they went, they left flourishing fields for other groups to cultivate." One producer commented, "[N]o matter how hard anybody tries, no matter how good they are, almost everything they do is a cop on the Beatles." *Time* found their example to be "liberating." Musicians were in agreement. Art Garfunkel, of Simon and Garfunkel, commented, "They were saying 'If you want to get better, here's the route.'" "Mama" Cass Elliot, of the Mamas and the Papas, said of the Beatles, "They're untouchable" (Porterfield and Birnbaum 62). The *Time* article discussed the group's unmatched ability to successfully introduce current artistic concepts and techniques into pop music, a capacity of which they were well aware. Producer George Martin likened the Beatles' accomplishments to the shift from representational art to abstraction, noting, "Until recently . . . the aim has been to reproduce sounds as realistically as possible. Now we are working with pure sound. We are building sound pictures" (Porterfield and Birnbaum 68). Freed of the financial constraints burdening most popular entertainers, the Beatles were pushing the boundaries of recorded music and, in so doing, were perceived by a wide swathe of contemporary American society to have profound influence on contemporary art culture.

An essential aspect of the new image was the notion that, more than any other artists, the Beatles were transforming pop music into an art form, and they were increasingly discussed in terms of "serious" artists. As reported in *Time*, one educator in UCLA's school of music found that "the Beatles have taken over many of the electronic concepts in music that have been worked on by the German composers of the Cologne group.[8] They've made an enormous contribution to electronic music" (Porterfield and Birnbaum 68). There was also a notion that the Beatles were knocking down the barrier between high and low art. *Newsweek*'s Jack Kroll noted the Beatles' unique mixture of commercial success and critical acclaim: "Earlier this year the Beatles' 'Sgt. Pepper' album exploded the notion that pop music was just . . . well, pop music. The sounds the Beatles made, the words they sang, reached such levels of irony, allusiveness, wit, poetry and put-on that the mighty Liverpudlians could be said to have come through with the first modern work that blended all heights of brow and levels of culture. The album sold by the millions and was analyzed ecstatically by critics who had previously concentrated on the subtleties of Henry James and John Donne" (Kroll, "Beatles vs. Stones" 62). The perception that the Beatles' music represented a progression in popular music positioned them as prime movers in the process of legitimizing rock music as an art form.

Bernard Gendron, professor of philosophy at the University of Wisconsin–Milwaukee, and author of numerous articles and books on the cultural meaning of music, speaks of "cultural accreditation" in his discussion of the Beatles in *Between Montmartre and the Mudd Club* (2002). By "cultural accreditation," he means "the acquisition of aesthetic distinction as conferred or recognized by leading cultural authorities, which, in the case of performers, means the acquisition of the status of 'artist' as opposed to 'entertainer'" (Gendron 161). In particular, Gendron demonstrates how the "cultural accreditation" of rock music began with the arrival of the Beatles in the United States in 1964 and reached its apex with the release of *Sgt. Pepper's Lonely Hearts Club Band* in 1967. In 1964, Gendron maintains, the music of the Beatles was treated with utter disdain by the American cultural establishment; treatment of the band focused on their status as a social phenomenon. By 1967, however, the Beatles were recognized for their artistry (Gendron 162–63). "Cultural accreditation" is a useful term for describing the process by which popular music won acceptance from established cultural critics, thereby transforming "entertainment" into "art." Rather than speaking solely to the accreditation of the form "rock and roll," I use the term "legitimization" here to mean the process by which the art of the Beatles and the cultural ethos they exemplified came to be accepted by members of the youth culture and, at least in part, by establishment critics and intellectuals.

Even with their first visit to America, the Beatles had won at least some level of acceptance from the cultural guard. Recall Stokowski's assessment of the Beatles and his charge to the young Carnegie Hall audience, just days after an appearance there by the Beatles: The Beatles "give the teen-agers something that thrills them, a vision.... I like anything that makes for self-expression.... We are all looking for the vision of ecstasy of life. I am too.... Whatever you enjoy doing, do it" (Shepard 13). Stokowski may have spoken more to the effect than the music, but this cultural acquiescence was an important beginning for the process of legitimization. The disturbance among the young may have been of interest to the American public, but for the most part it was not a matter of great concern, as had been the reaction to Elvis Presley's earliest appearances. The amused, and oftentimes bemused, reaction of the cultural authorities to the phenomenon of Beatlemania was followed by recognition of the Beatles' music for its musicality.

First and foremost among the Beatles' early champions was Leonard Bernstein, the brash young director of the New York Philharmonic who was well known to American audiences. He composed the music for the Broadway production *West Side Story*, which was later turned into an Oscar-winning film with a soundtrack recording that is still among the top-selling albums of all time. Further, Bernstein may well have been the most visible and popular proponent of high art to grace television screens across the country. During a period in which the networks brought stage productions and classical performances to the public, Bernstein frequently directed concerts on CBS's *Omnibus* series. Additionally, he entertained and educated his audience on the Emmy-winning *Young People's Concerts* (CBS) of the 1950s and 1960s. Thus, by the time that Bernstein started peppering his *Young People's Concerts* with references to the Beatles and other youth-oriented acts, he was well established among the general public as a cultural authority. Gendron discusses Bernstein's use of the Beatles' music to demonstrate features of classical music, thus attracting "young people" to classical music; he also notes that the conductor's positive take on the band was circulated largely through rumor and in the society pages, rather than the music section (Gendron 172).

Bernstein, however, championed the musical merits of the Beatles' compositions and recordings in a very direct way with the airing of the CBS news special *Inside Pop—The Rock Revolution*, in April 1967. Here, between the release dates of the number one single, "Penny Lane"/"Strawberry Fields Forever," and *Sgt. Pepper's Lonely Hearts Club Band*, Bernstein set about answering two questions: "Why do adults hate it (pop music) so?" and "Why do I like it?" Maintaining that only "five percent" of this youth-oriented music was "good," Bernstein described that five percent with examples including the music of Bob Dylan, the Association, the Left Banke, and the Rolling Stones. Clearly, however, given the breadth and depth of his description of the band's music, his real passion was for the Beatles. Bernstein, sitting at his grand piano, begins with a discussion of "Good Day Sunshine," a "cheery bit" that does something "new" when it drops a beat, arbitrarily changes key, and goes into "a sort of round" as the song concludes. All this is emblematic of the Beatles' music, which is "always unpredictable and a bit more inventive than most." He continues with a discussion of "She Said She Said," from *Revolver*: "You know a remarkable song of theirs . . . that goes nicely along in four. There's again a sneaky switch to three-quarter time. . . ." He then sings and plays the verse, followed with an airing of the Beatles' recording: "Such oddities as this are not tricks or show-off devices. In terms of pop music's basic English, so to speak, they are real inventions." Later, he compares "Got to Get You into My Life" to the work of archetypal Romantic composer Robert Schumann. He sings and plays the song, commenting: "It's so expansive and romantic . . . and notice how the range of the melody has been expanded. Most pop tunes have in the past been restricted to an octave or so owing to the limitations of pop singers' vocal ranges. But not so anymore. Our pop generation reaches and spreads itself, grasping at the unattainable, and this is one of the things I like most about it." Finally, he praised pop music's eclecticism, as exemplified in the trumpet on "Penny Lane," the string quartet of "Eleanor Rigby," and the raga of "Love You To" (not to mention the "arab café" of the Rolling Stones' "Paint it Black") (*CBS News Special: Inside Pop*). Bernstein's insight was borne out in the aftermath of *Sgt. Pepper's Lonely Hearts Club Band*, when the Beatles' commercial and artistic success would prompt numerous other bands to explore new instrumentation and non-Western music styles. Among the bands shifting their focus were the Moody Blues, the Jefferson Airplane, the Rolling Stones, Procol Harum, and Strawberry Alarm Clock. Ultimately, the introduction of so many new elements would open the way for the art- and glam-rock movements, from which emerged artists such as Yes, Emerson, Lake and Palmer, Elton John, and David Bowie in the late 1960s and early 1970s.

The environment was thus prepared for a wider acceptance of the Beatles' music among cultural authorities and for the dissemination of these views among the general public. Legitimization of the Beatles' music—and thereby pop music—as art often took the form of comparisons to recognized works of art and artists, whether to Schumann, Donne, or James. Calling *Rubber Soul*, *Revolver*, and *Sgt. Pepper* "volumes of aural poetry in the McLuhan age," Jack Kroll's review of *Sgt. Pepper* for *Newsweek* captures the artistic weight given the album by observers:

The new Beatles are justified by the marvelous last number alone, "A Day in the Life," which was foolishly banned by the BBC because of its refrain "I'd love to turn you on." But this line means many things. . . . John's wish to "turn you on" is a desire to start the bogged-down juices of life itself. This point is underscored by an overwhelming musical effect, using a 41-piece orchestra—a growling, bone-grinding crescendo that drones up like a giant crippled turbine struggling to spin new power into a foundered civilization. This number is the Beatles' "Waste Land," a superb achievement of their brilliant and startlingly effective popular art. ("It's Getting Better" 70)

Evidence of the seriousness with which the album was received is found in Kroll's reference (noted above) to T. S. Eliot's allusion-filled classic of modernist poetry, *The Waste Land* (1922), one of the most commented-upon poems of the twentieth century.

Acceptance by recognized artists was also an essential part of the legitimization of the Beatles' music as art, and mass-market magazines brought the opinions of intellectuals to the general audience. *Time* reported, "Ned Rorem, composer of some of the best of today's art songs, says. . . . 'She's Leaving Home'—one of twelve songs in the *Sgt. Pepper* album—'is equal to any song that Schubert ever wrote.' Conductor Leonard Bernstein's appreciation is just as high; he cites Schumann. As Musicologist Henry Pleasants says: 'The Beatles are where music is right now'" (Porterfield and Birnbaum 60).

Look's Patricia Coffin found similar enthusiasm for the Beatles' accomplishments among classical and avant-garde composers:

Serious musicians dig them too. Italian composer Luciano Berio, currently teaching at New York's Juilliard School of Music, admires the Beatles for their depth and range. "On a poetically limited scale," says Berio, "they are recapitulating an important phase in the history of our music." Aaron Copland says more simply: "When people ask to recreate the mood of the sixties, they will play Beatle music." John Cage, whose break with tradition in 1952 is now musical history, applauds the revolutionary influence the Beatles have on our culture. Serious musicians, he feels, would do well to follow their example. The revolutionary mix that marks the Beatle product is as complex as a computer—with soul. Music of the past mingles with dissonant space-age sounds achieved by the manipulation of electronic tapes. (Coffin, "The Beatles" 32)

Copland, of course, with compositions including *Billy the Kid* (1938), *Rodeo* (1942), *A Lincoln Portrait* (1942), *Fanfare for the Common Man* (1942), and *Appalachian Spring* (1944), was the great proponent of a distinctly American classical music; Bernstein had brought him to the mass audience as never before in his televised *Young People's Concerts*. Cage, perhaps best known for *4'33"* (1952), in which the composer sat at a piano passively for four and a half minutes, was an influential experimental composer and pioneer of "chance" and electronic music. Berio, an innovator of electronic music and avant-garde composition techniques, was a contemporary of Karlheinz Stockhausen and Pierre Boulez. Their acceptance of the Beatles as a musical and cultural force helped open up new terrain for popular music's acceptance and development.

The following two passages from *Time* and *Look*, respectively, indicate a widespread notion that the Beatles' music both reflected and encapsulated its time:

Like all good popular artists, the Beatles have a talent for distilling the moods of their time. Gilbert and Sullivan's frolics limned the pomposities of the Victorian British Empah [sic; "Empire"]; Cole Porter's urbanities were wonderful tonics for the hung-over '30s; Rodgers and Hammerstein's ballads reflected the sentiment

and seriousness of the World War II era. Today the Beatles' cunning collages piece together scraps of tension between the generations, the loneliness of the dislocated '60s, and the bitter sweets
of young love in any age. At the same time, their sensitivity to
the absurd is sharper than ever. (Porterfield and Birnbaum 60)

To the fractured sixties, the Beatles are what the painter Toulouse-
Lautrec was to Paris in the nineties, what freewheeling novelist
Scott Fitzgerald was to America in the twenties. They are inter-
preters and innovators—Lennon, McCartney and Harrison, especially. They reflect and influence many of the movements stir-
ring in all the arts today. (Coffin, "The Beatles" 32)

The Beatles had been viewed as models, both good and bad, for
their generation even before winning the approval of establishment
intellectuals. With acceptance by the intellectuals secured, this status came to take on more purpose. No longer were the Beatles mere
models of acceptable fashion and behavior for the young; increasingly, those within the youth culture posing political and lifestyle
programs looked to the Beatles, the most visible and influential
members of that culture, to lead. This leadership was an important
part of the image presented in the nation's mass media.

Notions of the Beatles' leadership of the youth culture were
widely publicized in the wake of *Sgt. Pepper*. Presentation of the
Beatles as leaders, even lifestyle revolutionaries, is most explicit in
Rolling Stone (detailed in the following chapter), but their status as
such was widely attested to in the mainstream press. In September
1967 *Time* noted, "Even the Beatles' nonmusical utterances tend
to take on the tone and weight of social prophecy." Concert promoter Sid Bernstein, who had booked the Beatles for their Carnegie Hall performances in 1964 and the two Shea Stadium concerts
in 1965 and 1966, commented, "Only Hitler ever duplicated their
power over crowds. . . . I'm convinced they could sway a presidential

election if they wanted to." If that was "far-fetched," concluded *Time*, "the fact remains that when the Beatles talk—about drugs, the war in Viet Nam, religion—millions listen, and this is a new situation in the pop music world" (Porterfield and Birnbaum 62).

In July of that year, the *New York Times'* John Leo reported that one educator, addressing a conference of music teachers and administrators on the topic of how to make music studies more relevant for the day's youth, said, "If you want to know what youths are thinking and feeling, . . . you cannot find anyone who speaks for them or to them more clearly than the Beatles" (Leo 29). "Kids," wrote *Time's* Porterfield and Birnbaum, "sense a quality of defiant honesty in the Beatles and admire their freedom and open-mindedness; they see them as peers who are in a position to try anything, and who can be relied on to tell it to them straight—and to tell them what they want to hear." Even some parents joined their children in welcoming the Beatles' opinions on contemporary issues. Said one father of three, "The Beatles are explorers, trusty advance scouts. I like them to report to my kids" (Porterfield and Birnbaum 62).

Not all aspects of the Beatles' leadership were embraced, however. The *Time* article drew a connection between the Beatles' singular artistic achievement and their influence with the nation's youths, particularly with regard to the recreational use of drugs. Other bands, including the Doors, the Grateful Dead, the Jefferson Airplane, the Paul Butterfield Blues Band, the Byrds, and Cream, had so far failed to match the "distinctiveness and power of the Beatles' mixture—which, after all, is responsible for having boosted them into their supramusical status." Thus, their "flirtation with drugs and the dropout attitude," embodied in songs like "A Day in the Life," "disturb[ed] many fans, not to mention worried parents" (Porterfield and Birnbaum 62).

By the time that the mainstream press began to take account of the Beatles' involvement in the drug culture, however, the Beatles were already moving beyond it (at least publicly). The Beatles' pub-

lic disavowal of drugs in late 1967 and early 1968 followed quickly
on the heels of McCartney's acknowledgment, in June 1967, that he
had taken LSD. Harrison, in discussing a recent visit to San Francisco's hippie center, Haight-Ashbury, with *Look*'s Patricia Coffin,
in the January 9, 1968, issue, lamented that "so many of the young
ones . . . think they have to go on [LSD] trips all the time." Harrison
had a better path: "Yoga and discipline, that's the way to get high."
He continued, "There was a yogi who was born before Christ. He
is still living today, in the same body, up in the Himalayas. He casts
no shadow, and he leaves no footprint. He and Christ are watching over the world." All would be revealed through the "happy pop
scene." Harrison's comments prompted Coffin to observe, "In this
connection, perhaps the Beatles' most significant recent announcement is that LSD and mysticism don't mix. They were made Members of the Order of the British Empire for being 'a national asset'
(all those records sold abroad) in 1965. For damning drugs they
should be knighted" (Coffin 41).

Thus, in late 1967 the Beatles, flush with the acclaim for *Sgt. Pepper's Lonely Hearts Club Band* and widely acknowledged to be leaders of the youth culture, felt at the top of their powers and capable of
anything. Their status as artists was discussed by fans and intellectuals alike. The Beatles, however, had a sense of themselves as artists that went beyond their demonstrated mastery of music and recording. The Beatles considered a great deal of their activities to be
avant-garde. The concert program for McCartney's late 1980s tour of
the United States makes it clear that establishing his and the Beatles'
avant-garde credentials remained important to him: "The funny
thing is John's ended up as the one . . . that's the avant-garde guy
because he did all that with Yoko. . . . I helped start *International
Times* . . . helped start the Indica Bookshop and Gallery. . . . So I
had a very rich avant-garde period which was such a buzz, making movies and stuff" (*The Paul McCartney World Tour Book* 50–
51). In discussing the breakup of the Beatles with *Rolling Stone*'s

Jann Wenner, in 1970, Lennon, though assaulting the myth in virtually every other sense, nevertheless took pride in their musical experimentation: "I know it was very strange and avant-garde music
is a very tough thing to assimilate and all that, but I've heard the
Beatles playing avant-garde music when nobody was looking for
years. But they're artists" (Wenner, *Lennon Remembers* 69). The
Beatles clearly considered much of their work avant-garde, and a
notion of the avant-garde permeates their image.

The Beatles reinvented themselves following the end of touring in 1966, and their image evolved to accommodate their status
as counterculturalists, or "beautiful people," and artists. Two values that emerge as core elements in the image of this period are opposition and artistry. In 1967 and 1968, the Beatles undertook numerous projects challenging the establishment and its institutions,
many of which are discussed in the next chapter. Here, two examples should suffice: the making of the *Magical Mystery Tour* film,
and the creation of Apple Corps, Ltd., in 1968. The first, obviously
influenced by the Beatles' immersion in the counterculture and en-
joyment of mind-altering substances, employs experimental film
techniques to target the establishment and its institutions. The second, while intended as a tax shelter, was nevertheless an attempt to
bring art to its audience in a new way, or, as McCartney described
it, a "kind of western communism." This section examines the status of the Beatles as artists and its effect on the evolution of the image. Can they be construed as *avant-gardistes*? In particular, can the
film *Magical Mystery Tour* (1967) be considered an avant-garde statement? And may the creation of Apple Corps in 1968 be understood
in avant-garde terms?

For all their success, 1967 was a year of great turmoil for the
Beatles. Perhaps most important to the band's ultimate dissolution,
Brian Epstein, the Beatles' manager since the beginning of their rise
to stardom, died of an accidental overdose in August. Moving into
the vacuum that was created by Epstein's death, Paul McCartney at-

tempted to rally the band, but the Beatles never recovered from the
loss of their manager. What followed were a series of missteps, cor-
rections, and scores of ideas that never went much further than the
discussion stage. One project instigated by McCartney was the television special *Magical Mystery Tour*.[9] While the soundtrack album it
spawned, comprising numerous tracks from the *Sgt. Pepper* sessions
and material recorded since that album's release, was another chart-
topper for the band, the film was less favorably received.

If *Sgt. Pepper's Lonely Hearts Club Band* was the pinnacle of
the Beatles' achievements in 1967, *Magical Mystery Tour* was the
low point of the Beatles' professional career. Inspired by the adventures of Ken Kesey's bus-riding Merry Pranksters, chronicled
in Tom Wolfe's *The Electric Kool-Aid Acid Test*, McCartney decided that the Beatles should make a film. With the other Beatles in
agreement, production began in the fall, with the Beatles loading up
a bus full of extras and setting out across the English countryside
in search of a story. Conceived as a series of vignettes, *Magical Mystery Tour* reveals the organizational ineptitude of the Beatles in the
absence of the steady hand of Brian Epstein. They had depended
upon Epstein to handle all logistical and organizational aspects of
their careers, just as they depended on George Martin's expertise in
the studio. With little planning, the *Magical Mystery Tour* caravan
caused traffic jams and work stoppages wherever it went. There was
no shooting script. Editing, which was to have taken only a couple
of weeks, ballooned into eleven weeks when the Beatles failed to
book time at Shepperton Studios and had to settle for time as it became available. And it was maddeningly disorganized: McCartney
would come in in the morning to find his editing from the previous day reedited by Lennon, and vice versa. In spite of the mistakes,
however, the Beatles' had high hopes for the film.

Although shot in color, the film was broadcast in black and
white over the Christmas holiday, and was lambasted by the critics.
It was the Beatles' first popular and critical failure. The BBC had

expected at least 20,000,000 people to view its first telecast on December 26, 1967; only 13,000,000 tuned in to its primetime showing.
Further, as reported in *Variety*, far from the expected holiday high
point, the show failed to make it into the top ten shows for the week
of its broadcast ("Beatles' TV Spec" 1). *Time*, the American magazine, termed the show "chaos," and provided a litany of comments
from across the British press: " 'Tasteless nonsense,' 'blatant rubbish,'
'a great big bore,' howled the London critics" ("Fab? Chaos" 60–
61). British criticism scared away American companies from broadcast rights negotiations; it was not broadcast in the United States and
had only limited theatrical screenings in Los Angeles and San Francisco in May 1968 (Harry 66).

The film's hostile reception in Great Britain didn't preclude the
film from furthering the Beatles' counterculture credentials, however. Obviously influenced by their experimentation with LSD and
other mind-altering substances, the film put on display the Beatles'
own countercultural values.[10] It stood as an example of counterculture art in the ongoing effort to legitimize that art and the youth
culture from which it sprang (an effort discussed in depth in the
next chapter). *Rolling Stone*'s Jonathan Cott, writing in February
1968, was critical of the Beatles' editing of the film, which they had
not "developed . . . in the ways that Stan Brakhage and Bruce Con-
nor have," but nevertheless insisted on comparing the Beatles' work
to that of notable contemporary avant-garde filmmakers. That is,
while the Beatles may have "missed the mark," Cott (and *Rolling Stone*) still argued that their work was correctly viewed as serious art (Cott 22). Further, in expectation of the film's broadcast in
the United States (still a possibility in April 1968), the magazine
reported that the second broadcast of the film in Great Britain, in
color, was "widely-praised, even by some of those who had put it
down the first time around" ("Flashes: Mystery Tour Making Local Stops" 4). Rather than the comeuppance of an artistic blunder,
argued Jonathan Cott, the film's critical reception was a product of

the establishment British press, whose analysis was "bitter, ignorant, and demented" (Cott 22). Cott's review was emblematic of the "us versus them" editorial stance adopted by underground publications when describing the establishment media. As discussed in the next chapter, for *Rolling Stone*'s young founder and editor, Jann Wenner, the Beatles were the supreme example of the countercultural lifestyle he was attempting to popularize and legitimize. An important part of his efforts entailed establishing rock music as a legitimate art form, and Cott's pieces were among the most consciously concerned with the aesthetics of rock music and culture.

The Beatles intended that the film be received as art. A NEMS Enterprises press release countered criticism of the film, stating, "*Magical Mystery Tour* is being accepted all over the world as an important and successful experimental film" ("Beatles reply" 2c). Whatever its reception, *Magical Mystery Tour* displays a preoccupation with formalism and specificity—defining characteristics of the experimental film and art of the 1960s. While there is little evidence that the Beatles conceived of their art in terms of the theoretical discourse described below, there can be no doubt that they were influenced by the artistic currents of the time, through their own backgrounds (Lennon, for instance, attended art school) and their mingling with contemporaries in the art world, many of whom were deeply involved in the theoretical debates of the time. *Magical Mystery Tour* displays the Beatles' familiarity with the formal values of avant-garde cinema, values defined by filmmaker Maya Deren in her influential essay, "Cinematography: The Creative Use of Reality" (1960).

In an era when medium specificity carried with it shadings of ideology and politics, Deren compared film to other art forms, and noted the medium's unique capacity to make "its statement as an image in movement" (Deren 54). Film, according to Deren, is in exclusive possession of a number of elements. For instance, it can microscope time through slow-motion which, when used properly, can be "a statement of either ideal ease or nagging frustration" (Deren 39). Reverse motion may create a sense of the "undoing of time" when applied to a photographic image; it was employed in the promo clip for "Strawberry Fields Forever," and the Beatles used the technique in the "I Am the Walrus" and "Fool on the Hill" sequences of *Magical Mystery Tour*. "I Am the Walrus" also benefited from the use of filters and polarization of the moving image, another process exclusive to the motion-picture medium that the Beatles employed to heighten the sense of otherness.

For Deren, manipulation of time and space is a major part of the filmmaker's task, and she writes specifically of that type of orchestration that "becomes itself part of the organic structure of a film" (Deren 59–60). Deren notes that editing can be used to manipulate time and space through the creation of relationships between separate times, places, and persons. Examples of this can be seen in Deren's *Meshes of the Afternoon*, notably in the sequence in which Deren progresses with each step from sand to grass, onto pavement, and finally onto a rug. Similarly, Kenneth Anger's influential, experimental trance film[11] *Fireworks* (1947) presents us with a sequence in which the protagonist exits his bedroom through a door marked "GENTS" to enter into a netherworld of night, excess, and violence. This type of fragmentation of space is evident in *Magical Mystery Tour*: As an army sergeant (played by Victor Spinetti) barks orders to the tour group milling about his office, the camera zooms in to his open mouth, fading to black; when the camera zooms back out, the sergeant and tour party are in a field.

While the Beatles do not seem to have theorized the medium in any great detail, they do exhibit an awareness of avant-garde themes and techniques throughout the film. For instance, "Aunt Jessie's Dream," a segment devised by Lennon, puts on display his fascination with surrealism, and perhaps his familiarity with the trance film. The sequence is a mixture of psychic violence and humor. Aunt Jessie, starving on the bus, dreams of her next meal: She and other Magical Mystery Tourists are in a rather surreal restaurant in which passengers and crew, in various stages of dress, bunny hop through the dining tables; a stuffed cow stands atop the back wall of the room; and Lennon, as Pirandello, serves mounds of spaghetti onto Aunt Jessie's plate. No longer hungry, she is being tormented by the gleefully sadistic waiter. As the sequence ends, Pirandello escorts Aunt Jessie upstairs, at which point the location suddenly becomes unclear; apparently it is above the room, for the tour bus courier, "Jolly Jimmy" Johnson, stands with the stuffed cow. Shirtless, but still wearing his courier's cap, he enjoys a glass of milk while a London bobby and another keeper of the peace lean on the cow as if standing at a bar. Jolly Jimmy is starkly lit against a black, featureless void. The shot is reminiscent of Kenneth Anger's "other world" in *Fireworks*, in which muscle-bound sailors violate the protagonist (Anger) and a starkly lit sailor pulls down his zipper and retrieves a lit roman candle. With its sadistic elements and severe lighting, it is difficult to imagine that Lennon had not seen the Anger film or similar trance films. Harrison's "Blue Jay Way" sequence also employs a number of experimental film techniques: A slide of a cat's face is projected onto Harrison's face; footage of Harrison, playing a "keyboard" that has been drawn on the floor, is superimposed over a man's naked torso upon which is scribbled "Magical Mystery Boy"; and, in the close of the scene, a multilayered projection onto Magical Mystery Boy's chest is viewed by Lennon, who rocks vigorously in the saddle of a rocking horse (a nod to surrealism).

The Beatles, at least initially, fully expected to be lauded for their brilliance on film, considering themselves artists capable of moving freely and successfully within several mediums. The film's public debacle put an end to any aspirations the group held of joining the cinematic avant-garde.[12] However, Neaverson (1997) convincingly argues that the film, as a countercultural statement, is a prolonged assault on the establishment and its institutions and conventions, including the state, the military, censorship, filmmaking practice, and commercialism (61–65). Further, *Magical Mystery Tour* was influential in the development of the cinematic language of pop music: The film's rejection of narrative causality influenced the development of the pop video, and pointed the way for other rock and roll films, including the Monkees' *Head* (1968), Led Zeppelin's *The Song Remains the Same* (1976), Frank Zappa's *200 Motels* (1971), and the Who's *Tommy* (1975). In sacrificing narrative, the Beatles sacrificed audiences but also rendered obsolete the cheery naïveté of the traditional pop musical and pointed the direction for future rock musicals and video. Finally, the film's fragmented structure and rejection of the "real" was also an important influence on *Monty Python's Flying Circus* (1969–74) and the *Python* films of the 1970s and 1980s (Neaverson 121).

While *Magical Mystery Tour* displays an assault on the mores of straight society, the creation of Apple Corps represents the Beatles' greatest effort to apply their countercultural principles to the economics of art production and distribution. The formation of the company in February 1968 was intended to provide an outlet for artistic expression normally at odds with the profit-driven interests of corporations. McCartney explained the purpose of Apple on NBC's *The Tonight Show*, when he and Lennon appeared on May 12, 1968: "It's a controlled weirdness, a kind of western communism. We want to help people but without doing it like a charity. We always had to go to the big men on our knees and touch our forelocks and say, 'Please, can we do so and so . . . ?' We're in the happy position of not needing any more money, so for the first time the bosses aren't in it for a profit. If you come to me and say, 'I've had such and such a dream,' I'll say to you 'Go away and do it'" (Brown and Gaines 303). Lennon also saw benefits coming to both the Beatles and their fans: "The aim isn't just a stack of gold teeth in the bank. We've done that bit. It's more of a trick to see if we can get artistic freedom within a business structure—to see if we can create things and sell them without charging five times our cost" (Brown and Gaines 303–4). According to Lennon, Apple would accommodate "people who just want to make a film about anything without going on their knees" ("Beatles' film and music company" 7h). Among the divisions envisioned were Apple Music, Apple Electronics, Apple Boutique, Apple Films, and Zapple.[13]

Initially, the company aggressively recruited new talent, enlisting James Taylor, Jackie Lomax, and Badfinger, among others. Ultimately, however, the Beatles lacked the cohesiveness to pursue their vision. While Apple was for the most part a failed dream, it nevertheless evinced the Beatles' leanings toward the avant-garde and away from the establishment. This experiment was unsuccessful, nearly bankrupting the Beatles, though the corporation found its health in the 1970s and continues to this day as a traditionally-conceived entity.

The film and the corporation manifest the band's artistic and ideological claim to be *avant-gardiste*, clearly important to Lennon and McCartney. Certainly, the *Magical Mystery Tour* film was intended as an avant-garde statement, as the term was understood by the Beatles; yet what does "avant-garde" mean? One influential effort at definition comes from Peter Bürger, in his *Theory of the Avant-Garde* (1984). He notes that "historical avant-garde movements" [i.e., early-twentieth century movements such as Futurism, Dadaism, Surrealism, etc.] rejected the notion of autonomous art[14] and attempted to wrest it from the marketplace and return it to everyday life, or the "praxis" of life (Bürger 53–54). For the historical avant-garde, art was to be used as a critique of society; as such, the *avant-gardiste* attempted to remain separate from the market system and employed techniques and concepts geared toward attaining and maintaining this independence. Bürger argues that the avant-garde's time has passed, for attempts to continue the tradition of the avant-garde movements can no longer have the same shocking effect they once had. Rather, a "neo-avant-garde" has emerged that, contrary to the historical aims of the avant-garde, attempts to establish avant-garde art as art, something distinct from the "praxis" of life (Bürger 57–58).[15]

Writing specifically of the artistic environment of the 1960s, however, Andreas Huyssen, in his edited volume *After the Great Divide* (1986), notes that, despite its "cooption through commodification," the pop avant-garde "retained a certain cutting edge in its proximity to the 1960s culture of confrontation." He continues, "No matter how deluded about its potential effectiveness, the attack on the institution art was always an attack on hegemonic social institutions, and the raging battles of the 1960s over whether or not pop was legitimate art prove the point" (Huyssen 193). That is, while the pop avant-garde was firmly rooted in the marketplace, it nevertheless opposed the "hegemonic social institutions" of the establishment. Thus, while Bürger's definition revolves around art's independence from the marketplace and its integration into everyday life as an end in itself ("praxis"), Huyssen stresses the confrontational aspect of the avant-garde.

Magical Mystery Tour was intended as an avant-garde statement; Apple Corps was intended as a revolutionary new model for bringing art to the marketplace and challenging its status as mere commodity. Regardless of their intentions, however, the Beatles' efforts do not fit into the narrow definition of the avant-garde proposed by Bürger. Beyond the fact that they emerged four decades after Bürger's historical avant-garde, the Beatles self-consciously sought the status of art for their work. By Bürger's definition the Beatles, far from integrating art back into life, sought to "institutionalize avant-garde art as art" (Bürger 58). While trying to fashion a new art— even a new society—based on countercultural values, the Beatles nevertheless sought success within the marketplace. For the Beatles and many of their contemporaries in the counterculture, I suggest, "avant-garde" was a nebulous, often heroic term comprising artistry and opposition to the establishment, clearly two qualities at the core of the Beatles' image and perceptions of their leadership of the youth movement and counterculture. The Beatles retained (as Huyssen said of the pop avant-garde) "a certain cutting edge" in their "attack on the institution art." They retained an oppositional status that was understood to be reflected in their art and lifestyle choices. As such, they were, in Huyssen's terminology, part of a pop avant-garde.

While *Sgt. Pepper* presented the Beatles at the height of their cohesiveness as a band and in the full flowering of their artistic powers, the fifteen months after its release saw them drifting apart as a group. The process quickened with the death of Brian Epstein in 1967. McCartney stepped forward to attempt to give the band direction, but the others bridled under his leadership. Concurrently, the entrance of Yoko Ono, Lennon's girlfriend, into the inner sanctum of the Beatles caused further deterioration of relations within the band.

It was in this atmosphere that *The Beatles* was produced. Despite the malaise that had set in over the preceding months, the Beatles demonstrated that they were still capable of commanding the top of the charts. The first single released by Apple, in August 1968, was "Hey Jude"/"Revolution," with the first track becoming the Beatles' biggest-selling American hit. Despite the single's success, and the cohesiveness this was assumed by many observers to demonstrate, the album that followed was the most disparate collection that the group ever recorded. A product of a band in disarray, *The Beatles* exhibits more than any other album the individual interests of the band members. On this so-called "White Album," the Beatles' efforts canvass much of the scope of popular music: Lennon lampoons the white British blues of John Mayall and Eric Clapton on "Yer Blues"; McCartney's "Honey Pie" pays tribute to songs of the 1920s and 1930s; the Beatles try their hand at heavy rock with "Helter Skelter"; McCartney adds a country flavor with "Blackbird," "Mother Nature's Son," and, especially, "Rocky Raccoon"; and the

Beatles turn to Hollywood kitsch with "Goodnight." Lennon, with the help of Ono and Harrison, presents "'Revolution 9,' the world's most widely distributed avant-garde artifact" (Ian MacDonald 230). While demonstrating the band's incredible creative capacity, the album also displays the unwillingness of band members to cut their own songs from the album, to put the whole before its parts, so to speak. Though producer George Martin advised them to prune their production down to fourteen of the best tracks, in the end everything was delivered to the public in a two-disk set that, despite Martin's concerns, became one of the top-selling albums of all time (Whitburn, *Top 40 Albums* 381–83).

When it came time to create the packaging for the album, the Beatles turned again to Robert Fraser, the West End gallery owner who had recommended Peter Blake to them for the design of the *Sgt. Pepper's Lonely Hearts Club Band* sleeve. Fraser had advised numerous of his artists, including Richard Hamilton, to take commissions to design record sleeves. Hamilton had focused on the pop elite with his *Swingeing London 67* and related works immortalizing the February 1967 narcotics arrest of Rolling Stones Keith Richard and Mick Jagger, along with their friend Robert Fraser. One such work was a poster copied from a collage of numerous press clippings and photographs, as well as material concerning Fraser's gallery. The Beatles were familiar with the poster, and asked Hamilton to design the packaging for *The Beatles*. Consistent with his notion that pop art should be "popular," Hamilton was drawn to the project by the possibility that distribution of the edition could reach 5,000,000 units. He promptly accepted the Beatles' offer (Hamilton, *Richard Hamilton* 78–83; *Collected Words* 104).

For Hamilton, designing the package was an intellectual exercise, an effort to imbue the package with a structural unity. Richard Morphet has observed that, for Hamilton, the "interaction between motif and structure is an integral part of the 'subject.'" He continues, "It is as though he feels that the more the content of a work can be focused by a clear containing device, the more fully that the content can be animated and opened up to examination" (Morphet 20). As earlier noted, Hamilton's collage *Just what is it that makes today's homes so different, so appealing?* (1956) was emblematic of what was to become known as British pop art. Hamilton's design for *The Beatles* included the sleeve, one loose photograph of each Beatle, and a collage to be composed of photographs supplied separately by each band member. In some ways reminiscent of his Marilyn Monroe portrait, *My Marilyn* (1965), the collage for *The Beatles* made use not only of photographs, but also of different types of photographic marks. Hamilton retained the Beatles' own marks of acceptance and rejection, as he had Monroe's in realizing the earlier piece (Field 1983, 27–28). While McCartney worked closely with the artist in producing the final product, Hamilton's concern with the structure of the collage is evident from his description of his artistic goals for the project:

> Inside the album was a give-away "print". Most of the design effort and expense went into this. Each of the Beatles provided me with a large dossier of personal photographs and I selected from this material to make a collage. Because the sheet was folded three times to bring it to the square shape for insertion into the album, the composition was interestingly complicated by the need to consider it as a series of subsidiary compositions. The top right and left hand square are front and back of the folder and had to stand independently as well as be a double spread together. The bottom four squares can be read independently and as a group of four. They all mate together when opened up and used as wall decoration. (Hamilton, *Collected Words* 105)

Obviously, the piece was the product of a clear intellectual program systematically described—as noted by Morphet, a distinguishing characteristic of Hamilton's work.

Hamilton suggested a plain white sleeve in order to "avoid the issue of competing with the lavish design treatments of most jackets" (Hamilton, *Collected Words* 104). The title *The Beatles* was embossed on the stark white sleeve, and the serial number of each unit, appearing directly beneath the title, was rendered in such a way that it appeared to have been done by a hand numbering machine. Hamilton later recalled: "I suggested a plain white cover so pure and reticent that it would seem to place it in the context of the most esoteric art publications. To further this ambiguity I took it more into the little press field by individually numbering each cover" (Hamilton, *Collected Words* 104–5).

While the artistic concerns and goals of Blake and the Beatles were similar, in some instances verging on identical, it is readily apparent that Hamilton's package stands more as an exemplar of his own artistic values than those of the Beatles. The choice of a white sleeve was primarily the product of practical concerns: following the example of *Sgt. Pepper's Lonely Hearts Club Band*, the rock and roll market was saturated with psychedelic imagery and album covers. Hamilton wanted to differentiate the cover from this mass. With regard to Beatle involvement in design of the packaging, McCartney took an active part in designing the collage, yet one has the impression that he was more or less "along for the ride," acting principally as an advisor. Certainly the finished collage retains the characteristics of a Hamilton work.

Less the product of a group effort than any of their previous releases, *The Beatles* received mixed notices. Jann Wenner, *Rolling Stone*'s founder and editor, wrote, "Whatever else it is or isn't, it is the best album they have ever released, and only the Beatles are capable of making a better one" (Wenner, "The Beatles" 10). Richard Goldstein, the music reviewer of the *New York Times* who had evoked so much resentment among critics for his review of *Sgt. Pepper's Lonely Hearts Club Band*, applauded the Beatles' turn away from technology to songwriting: "In terms of melodic and lyrical diversity, it is far more imaginative than either 'Sergeant Pepper' or 'Magical Mystery Tour.'" Both of those albums had relied on the "surrogate magic of studio technique," while song composition was neglected. "This time," wrote Goldstein, "the Beatles have dared to be restrained" ("The Beatles" 33, 37). Other critics were less impressed, however. *Newsweek*'s Hubert Saal was critical of its unwieldy nature: "With 30 arrows of song, it's hard to see how the brilliant quartet could have missed their marks so often. Unlike previous albums, the bull's-eye of variety in lyrics, wit, ease of style that made changing keys or tempi natural, lovely love songs, and adventures in electronics is rarely bit in 'The Beatles'" (Saal, "Double Beatle" 109). *Time* was equally dismissive of the uneven quality of the album, which they termed an example of the band's "mannerist phase": "Skill and sophistication abound, but so does a faltering sense of taste and purpose. The album's 30 tracks are a sprawling, motley assemblage of the Beatles' best abilities and worst tendencies" ("Mannerist Phase" 53). Still, many rock critics and fans, disgusted by a seemingly endless stream of feeble attempts to recreate the studio artistry of *Sgt. Pepper*, welcomed the Beatles' turn toward simplicity, a trend apparent in much of rock and roll in the late 1960s. Criticisms aside, the album was a huge success, selling more than a million copies in the first five days of release, and the Beatles enjoyed a popular rebound from the disappointment of *Magical Mystery Tour*.

Reaching its high point, so to speak, with 1967's "Summer of Love," the heyday of the counterculture was overwhelmingly positive, exciting, life-altering—and short-lived. Intensification of the hostilities in Vietnam, and repercussions at home, led to a growing radicalism within the youth movement. By the summer of 1968, the counterculture was increasingly perceived as incapable of bringing political change, and many students and young people were joining the more activist New Left in direct confrontation of the system.

While the countercultural program lost much of its appeal, the countercultural ideal that the Beatles' image embodied remained popular with the general audience. It was during this period that the purest, most arresting, and most popular statement of that ideal came in the form of a Beatles film that, interestingly, drew little support from the Beatles.

The animated feature *Yellow Submarine* debuted in London in July 1968 and in the United States in November. The film is a Beatles product more by way of inspiration than participation. An Apple Films and King Features production with distribution by United Artists, the film could draw no more than apathetic support from the Beatles, who never fully approved of their animated television series representation (also produced by King Features). Nevertheless, the film is an inspired amalgam of animation styles that, using Beatles music and mythology as its starting point, provides the audience with a rich audio and visual experience while promoting the Beatles' connections to a family-friendly countercultural ideal (lots of love; no drugs).

Yellow Submarine tells the story of the Beatles' journey to Pepperland aboard the Yellow Submarine. The Beatles have been called upon to rescue Pepperland from the Blue Meanies, who have invaded and destroyed all beauty and positive energy, in the process imprisoning Sgt. Pepper's Lonely Hearts Club Band. After numerous adventures aboard the Yellow Submarine, the Beatles arrive in Pepperland, where they battle the Blue Meanies. They are able to free the Lonely Heart's Club Band and, together, they beat back the forces of negativity. While *Magical Mystery Tour* displayed many of the values of the counterculture, *Yellow Submarine* presents a more explicit statement of the countercultural ideal at the core of the Beatles' post-touring image, and is a kind of hippie parable about the power of love. As such, it promoted a distinctly Beatlesque, yet sanitized version of the counterculture—one based explicitly around an ideal of love and community. The film debuted as the counterculture was losing some of its potency, many adherents forsaking hippie disengagement from society in favor of a more radical challenge to the political system(s) of the West. However, as detailed in the next chapter, the Beatles never embraced this new activism and, in fact, continued to espouse countercultural views on a range of topics. *Yellow Submarine*, the premise of which is based on an ideal that was increasingly out of favor within the youth movement, nevertheless provides the period's most cogent, widely accessible, and popular argument for that ideal, an ideal firmly entrenched in the Beatles' image.

Top animators were employed in making the film, including director George Dunning and animator Heinz Edelmann. At his TVC TV Cartoons studio in London, Canadian George Dunning helped establish Great Britain in the 1960s as a center for internationally recognized animation. The director started his career in 1943 as one of the first group of animators to be hired by John Grierson to work under Norman McLaren at Canada's National Film Board. Dunning pursued major animation research throughout the 1960s, beginning with *The Flying Man* (1962) and culminating with *Yellow Submarine*. Heinz Edelmann, the project's designer, created the animated Beatles, the Flying Glove, the fighting "YES" and "NO," and other memorable characters. While Edelmann was responsible for the film's overall design, numerous segments, including "Eleanor Rigby" and "It's Only a Northern Song," departed from his master plan as other animators contributed to the film's final form.

The film drew on various sources, among them op art, the antiwar movement, and the counterculture. Memorable quotes from contemporary culture abound, from the pop art of the Claes Oldenburg–style burger and coke that decorate the lair of the Lennon/Frankenstein's monster, to the Beardsley-like Apple Bonkers. In realizing this pop vision, the animators made use of various techniques, including polarized filtering, multi-plane, stills animation, traveling mattes, live-action superimpositions, and silk screening, to name a few. Perhaps the most visually stunning segment, "Lucy in the Sky with Diamonds" was the product of rotoscoping, a process first developed by Disney Studios in the 1930s, in which a live-action film is projected onto celluloid sheets one frame at a time, each frame is traced and painted, and then is rephotographed as with ordinary animation. In Disney's *Snow White and the Seven Dwarfs* (1937), Prince Charming and Snow White were rendered via rotoscoping. *Yellow Submarine* utilized Busby Berkeley clips from the 1930s in creating the "Lucy in the Sky" segment (Bowman 175).

Yellow Submarine has been credited by many commentators with having saved the feature-length animation form, or at least creating an alternative to the Disney approach.[16] A *New York Times* reviewer noted: "'Yellow Submarine' presents the strongest case for animated feature-length films since "Fantasia" . . . The fact that the Beatles have chosen to make one . . . and that Heinz Edelmann has drawn it, for the most part, so beautifully ought to help animation along" (Adler 14). The *New Yorker*'s influential film critic Pauline Kael commented that the film, "with its bright Pop flourish and inventiveness, restores the pleasure of constant surprise, which has always been the fun of good animation" (134–35). She correctly, if somewhat sarcastically, bemoaned the transformation of "yesterday's outlaw idols of the teenagers" into "a quartet of Pollyannas for the wholesome family trade" (135). That trade extended beyond the movie theater. Besides spawning a vast number of tie-ins, from lunchboxes to alarm clocks, from coloring books to posters, the popularity of "Yellow Submarine art" with graphics-design houses clearly displayed the orientation of the market. As the president of one large advertising firm told the *New York Times*, the art "has a great influence on young people. . . . And companies want to be 'with it' today because young people influence everyone else" (Sloane 15).

As with so many of their endeavors, the involvement of the Beatles often acted as a catalyst for change and redirection within society. Though able to provide little more than a patchy selection of recordings for the soundtrack and a snippet of screen time at the very end of the film (and though increasingly fraught with discontent, apathy, and hostility), with *Yellow Submarine* the band preserved its association with new and innovative currents in the world(s) of art and commerce. The film presented an ideal, if sanitized, vision of the counterculture, with the Beatles at its center. That ideal was far from a children's fantasy, however. For one counterculture periodical, in particular, the Beatles were the archetypal hippies, providing those within and outside the youth movement with a model of the counterculture lifestyle. Jann Wenner tied the fortunes of *Rolling Stone* to the Beatle ideal. As we shall see, he had a receptive audience for his program.

FIVE

"Beatlepeople"
Rolling Stone, 1967–70

WRITING IN LATE 1968, JANN WENNER, the young founder and editor of *Rolling Stone*, made no bones about the importance of the Beatles to the youth culture of the 1960s: "In considering the Beatles, . . . we are actually considering several much bigger things: we are, of course, considering the Beatles as individuals; we are considering their impact on the world; we are considering the whole question of 'rock and roll'; we are considering the world we live in and we are considering ourselves." Wenner's concept of the Beatles was, in fact, so inextricably bound to his vision for the counterculture that it is impossible to conceive of one without the other. The Beatles were, in essence, a fount from which the counterculture flowed: "'The Beatles' have been an influential part of everyone's lives. It has been incredible. Think of all the changes in the world that have occurred in the last five years, and so many of them, especially for the young of my age, are attributable directly to the Beatles" (Wenner, Rev. of *The Beatles: Authorized Biography* 17).

The Beatles, central to Wenner's assault on "straight" society and the mainstream press, emerge in the pages of *Rolling Stone* as the standard-bearers for countercultural values. Striking back at a mainstream "'press' [that had] distorted the picture of being . . . Beatlepeople,"[1] Wenner argued, "What they are doing is putting their responsibilities on us. . . . That is how corrupt the press, magazines, newspapers, television and media in general has become. And every-

178

one suspects it. The Beatles know it, and thus are contemptuous of the press and not piously grateful." And Wenner's competitors did not escape his critical eye: "This contempt spills over to the pop critics and reviewers. And this has been deserved. So much ineptness, it's incredible" (Rev. of *The Beatles: Authorized Biography* 17–18). Wenner time and again called on the Beatles, literally and otherwise, to fortify his countercultural claims and position his magazine as the dominant underground publication of the period. His exploitation of the Beatles ultimately contributed to the success of *Rolling Stone* beyond its initial audience and facilitated its transformation from the most successful publication catering to the counterculture into a successful commercial publication espousing counterculture values, in essence demonstrating the acceptance of aspects of the counterculture into mainstream culture. By 1969, when the magazine's circulation reached 100,000, readership surveys indicated that for many of readers it was the sole source of information on matters of interest to the youth culture (Draper 94). Of particular interest to us is how the Beatles' image was developed within the pages of the magazine:[2] How was the image defined for Wenner's counterculture audience? How was the image utilized to bolster Wenner's countercultural program?

Wenner relied heavily on the Beatles' image in promoting his magazine and the counterculture lifestyle. As this chapter will demonstrate, the Beatles' image clearly provided the counterculture model implicit, and often explicit, in the editorial pieces written by Wenner and Ralph Gleason, Wenner's mentor. Further, the Beatles were often invoked in explaining the editorial positions of the two. Wenner viewed the Beatles as leaders of the counterculture, and promoted this view within his staff and to his readers. Importantly, as discussed in the previous chapter, this belief also had great currency in the mainstream media. The Beatles were the vehicle by which the counterculture ideal was conveyed not only to committed counterculturalists, but also to the general public.

A useful tool for analyzing media messages is the concept of media frames. Todd Gitlin, in his 1980 study of the mainstream media's coverage of the New Left during the 1960s, *The Whole World is Watching*, defines frames as "persistent patterns of cognition, interpretation, and presentation, of selection, emphasis, and exclusion, by which symbol-handlers routinely organize discourse, whether verbal or visual" (Gitlin, *Whole World* 6). Robert Entman describes the process of framing: "To frame is to *select some aspects of a perceived reality and make them more salient in a communicating text, in such a way as to promote a particular problem definition, causal interpretation, moral evaluation, and/or treatment recommendation* [Entman's emphasis] for the item described" (Entman 52). Frames adopted by an underground publication in the period under consideration would be openly biased in advocating the views of the community to which, and for which, it spoke.

Rolling Stone adopted an "us versus them" approach in its reportage, setting itself against both the mainstream media and establishment (Atkin 188–90). Within this oppositional frame, certain aspects of the Beatles' image were stressed, including the band's artistic superiority to other bands and the exceptional artistry of their albums. Also important was the notion that the Beatles were an engine for artistic and societal progress. For *Rolling Stone*, the Beatles performed the essential function of legitimizing rock and roll as an art form, and at the same time acting as archetypal counterculturalists. A product of all these assigned attributes, the image promoted in *Rolling Stone* positions the Beatles as leaders of the counterculture—and the Beatles image attains its most consistently antiestablishment bearing in the pages of *Rolling Stone*.

The word "counterculture," for our purposes, is defined as "a culture created by or for the alienated young in opposition to traditional values,"[3] and refers specifically to the youth-centered oppositional culture of the 1960s and early 1970s. Kenneth Cmiel, in his article "The Politics of Civility" (1994), describes those who, in the

name of communalism and authenticity, "[argued] for the liberation
of the self," and advocated an "alternative politeness, one not based
on the emotional self-restraint of traditional civility but on the ex-
pressive individualism of liberated human beings"(Cmiel 270–71).
Also informative is the depiction of the counterculture provided by
Jack Whalen and Richard Flacks in their 1989 study, *Beyond the
Barricades: The Sixties Generation Grows Up*:

> Parallel to the emerging New Left there was, of course, the
> emerging counterculture, a much larger number of youth who,
> while not necessarily interested in defining a political position,
> were self-consciously rebelling against a wide variety of norms
> and practices commonly called middle class. Hippie outfits ex-
> pressed identification with all cultures that stood outside of
> or were being destroyed by western industrial society—from
> American to East Asian Indians, from cowboys to European
> peasants, from farm grandmothers to black slaves. Long hair,
> beads, painted faces, androgyny—all expressed not only a gener-
> alized desire to shock, but to shock in a particular way. For hip-
> pie styles all denied the superiority of conventional measures of
> status—the middle class, the adult, the male, the urban. (Whalen
> and Flacks 11)

They further describe the centrality of drug use:

> The use of illegal drugs, combined with explicit identification
> with the drug culture announced by one's appearance, inevita-
> bly got many white middle-class youths in trouble with the law.
> Such trouble reinforced fantasies of identification with the out-
> law, which in turn further polarized "hippie" and "straight"
> sensibilities. To be seen as a hippie in the mid-sixties was, ac-
> cordingly, not simply to be part of a new fashion trend; it was
> instead interpreted by many as a commitment to an alternative

life course, a sign that one had made a break with the values and ways of life defined by one's parents, school, and community. (Whalen and Flacks 11)

In practice, then, the counterculture's rejection of society was displayed in shoulder-length hair on men, alternative clothing styles, open sexuality, a rise in the use of scatological language, and the widespread use of drugs (Caute 64–65; Whalen and Flacks 270).

Herbert Marcuse, the Frankfurt School social theorist and philosopher and a seminal influence on the politics of the New Left, commented, "I have tried to show that any change would require a total rejection . . . of this society. And that it is not merely a question of changing the institutions but rather . . . of totally changing human beings in their attitudes, their instincts, their goals, and their values" (Marcuse 29). While many of those influenced by Marcuse chose to confront the political system, the counterculture instead chose to challenge the attitudes and values of the establishment and straight society. This "hippie" sensibility was at the core of the countercultural program espoused by *Rolling Stone* during the peak of its underground period, from 1967 to 1970 (Atkin 188). The counterculture, however, was not monolithic, nor was it static. Cmiel argues convincingly that the counterculture, at its most utopian, and run through as it was with the theme "love," was simply too *nice* to secure systemic change (Cmiel 271–72). There is general agreement that the counterculture peaked during the years 1967–70 and afterwards declined rapidly (Cmiel 269; Caute 64). The escalation of the war in Vietnam brought about an increase in the influence of the New Left, particularly among students, and the revolution in consciousness championed by the hippies gave way in the late 1960s to confrontational, often violent, tactics (Whalen and Flacks 10–15). The Students for a Democratic Society (SDS) fragmented badly as the decade came to a close, and zealots within the dissident faction Weatherman, among others, pursued a campaign of bombings and disruptions. Between September 1969 and May 1970, for instance, there were at least 250 bombings of ROTC buildings, draft boards, and other federal offices (Patterson 716–17). Numerous underground publications intended for a counter-culture audience arose in the 1960s. The underground papers, with their uninhibited style and content and their philosophical ties to the counterculture, recorded and participated in the rebellion against the establishment and against the mass media. In their history of the American press, Emery and Emery (1978) note that the "best" underground papers "did a capable job of criticizing both . . . The immediate stimuli were the four letter word movement, the sex revolution, the generation and credibility gaps that created the anti-establishment ear, and above all, the bitter antiwar protest typified by the March on the Pentagon" (Emery and Emery 379; quoted in At-kin 186). The underground press was instrumental in defining not only the establishment and opposition to it but also, as a corollary, the values and aspirations of the counterculture. Very soon after its debut, notes Atkin of *Rolling Stone*, "the publication emerged as a leader among the alternative, or underground, press, fusing the mu-sic and politics of America's New Left" (Atkin 185). As with other cultural underground papers, *Rolling Stone* questioned the utility of violence for bringing about change (Atkin 191). As the efficacy of the counterculture's largely apolitical stance increasingly fell into disrepute, the magazine's founder and editor, Jann Wenner, main-tained his, and hence the magazine's, antipathy toward violence. Proposing rock and roll as the organizing principle for the youth culture, Wenner persevered in his insistence that the magazine re-tain its counterculture/lifestyle orientation, even as many of his writ-ers and editors became more politically motivated in their views of music and American culture.

Under Wenner's editorial control, the magazine was the most widely read publication promoting the ideals of the counterculture, and opinions by and about rock stars were important expressions of the magazine's stands on social and political matters. Wenner utilized the Beatles' image not only to increase the magazine's circulation but also to promote his counterculture ideal (Anson 172). It should be noted that the foundation and establishment of *Rolling Stone* as *the* countercultural magazine coincided with the peak of the lifestyle strand of the counterculture (most visible in the hippies) and, importantly, with the height of the Beatles' influence, in 1966–68. The Beatles actively promoted the values of the counterculture, and *Rolling Stone* often exploited their image in the service of countercultural claims. The Beatles themselves, and their image, became the focus of strong, if infrequent, criticism as the youth movement was radicalized and the counterculture began to disintegrate. While Wenner and his mentor, Ralph Gleason, continued to present the Beatles as counterculture ideals, other *Rolling Stone* writers and editors considered the Beatles to be, as Cmiel said of the counterculture, too *nice*, and championed instead other music personalities (notably, the Rolling Stones) as leaders and/or spokespersons for the youth culture. Wenner's views remained dominant, however. The timbre of both the celebration and criticism of the counterculture was a function of the diverse views of the magazine's editors and staff, and of the singular position held by the magazine within the counterculture.

While its origins were underground, most historians differentiate between *Rolling Stone* and other underground tabloids in that it "went beyond politics, extending into the realm of popular culture" (Anson 186). Glessing discriminates between two categories of underground press. The political papers "emphasize radical politics and believe the underground press should be used as tools for a political revolution. The cultural papers, on the other hand, are interested in the total complex of relations between all people in the movement and work toward a general awareness in American society" (98). Based on Glessing's characterization, then, Atkin classifies *Rolling Stone* as a cultural underground newspaper at its inauguration in November 1967 (Atkin 186). *Rolling Stone*, Atkin notes, "never espoused the revolutionary solutions commonly preached in radical underground papers. In this regard, it served more of a cultural than a political function. We see, instead, a consistent focus on politics as a function of music" (Atkin 190–91). Jann Wenner, the magazine's founder and editor, disliked politics and doubted its utility for bringing about societal change. His views and those present in the content of *Rolling Stone* mirrored the program of the counterculture described by Cmiel: recreational use of drugs was advocated, scatological words and phrases were rampant, and rock and roll music was the centerpiece of the magazine in much the same way that it formed an organizing principle for the counterculture (Cmiel 269–71).

Wenner's antipathy toward politics and activism is apparent in the magazine's tenth issue. Wenner denounced the efforts of the Yippies (Youth International Party) to draw students and musicians to the 1968 Democratic convention in Chicago. "The Yip protest— in methods and means—is as corrupt as the political machine it hopes to disrupt," he wrote. "Rock and roll is the *only* way in which the vast but formless power of youth is structured, the only way in which it can be defined or inspected" (Wenner, "Musicians Reject" 22).[4] Draper observes that "Wenner stuck to his belief that kids spoke through music, not with ballots or bricks. The new lifestyle would subvert the old order. Revolution began at the dinner table. Manifestos were bullshit, like gathering moss" (Draper 121). As a result, New Left radicals mistrusted Wenner and *Rolling Stone*.

Wenner's fascination with celebrity and status as a "super-fan"[5] were evident in the content of the magazine; rock stars (most notably the Beatles) implicitly, and often explicitly, were positioned as leaders of the counterculture. The Beatles and *Rolling Stone* shared a symbiotic relationship that went beyond the advertisement that financed the magazine and promoted the band. Hoping to draw on the group's success, Wenner had put Lennon on the cover of the first issue. Perhaps more important to the success and survival of the magazine, the November 23, 1968, issue's cover bore a photograph of the naked backsides of Lennon and then-girlfriend Yoko Ono, while the inside contained a full frontal nude picture of the couple; the two pictures also adorned the back and front, respectively, of their album of experimental music, *Unfinished Music No. 1—Two Virgins* (Tetragammaton/Apple, November 1968). Urged to do so by his mentor, Ralph Gleason, Wenner had contacted Apple Corps and requested the nude photos. Derek Taylor, press secretary to the company, was happy to oblige, and the pictures appeared in the magazine's first anniversary issue, as did an interview with Lennon. Lennon welcomed the opportunity to shock the sensibilities of the establishment. The cover was enough to place the struggling magazine within American consciousness.

By 1969, the magazine was flourishing as its competitors fell by the wayside. *Crawdaddy!* debuted on the East Coast in February 1966, and was an important early voice on the music and culture of the time. Perhaps more closely tied to the underground than Wenner's later publication, *Crawdaddy!* brought artistic criticism and the drug culture fully into play: issue #11 (September/October 1967) included an essay by Richard Meltzer, "My Sergeant Pepper Trip," that seemed little more than acid-induced stream of consciousness; Don McNeil's article, "Report on the State of the Beatles," provided a serious look by a counterculturalist at the artistic culture into which the album was released (*Crawdaddy!* #11). The magazine was the first to specialize in rock criticism and was the starting point for numerous rock critics, notably Jon Landau, who later went to *Rolling Stone*. In at least one reader's opinion, however, *Crawdaddy!* was simply too intellectual—or so thought Jann Wenner (Draper 58). In contrast, *Rolling Stone* was intended from the start to be entertaining. By the end of the decade, while other rock and roll magazines such as *Cheetah*, *Eye*, *Scene*, and *Crawdaddy!* were struggling to continue publication (and for the most part failing), *Rolling Stone* found success (Draper 121). Thus, while the radical left viewed Wenner and his magazine with suspicion,[6] the periodical was nevertheless an important and increasingly unique source of information and entertainment for members of the youth culture in general, and the counterculture, specifically.

But what of the Beatles' image? The magazine attached numerous qualities to the "Beatles," among them notions of the group's superiority to other bands, their exceptional artistry and status as an engine of progress, their function in the legitimizing of rock as an art form, and their status as leaders of the counterculture. Essential to Wenner's notion of progress within the counterculture, and underpinning his use of the Beatles in defining the counterculture ideal, was his belief, shared by many, in the Beatles' supremacy in the realm of music and art. Central to this assumption of superiority was the influence of the album *Sgt. Pepper's Lonely Hearts Club Band*. In December 1967 Wenner wrote: "How they do it is anybody's guess, but I recall a conversation in the back of the Avalon Ballroom about what the Beatles might do after *Sgt. Peppers* [sic]. Someone suggested that they would set the bible to music. 'Ah no,' was the reply, 'They'll write their own.' And the reply to that was that if we had just come up with the idea, the Beatles would be doing something well beyond that" (Wenner, "Rock and Roll Music" 16).

Interestingly, the Beatles' chief rivals, the Rolling Stones, were among the first to feel the sting of post-*Pepper* criticism. In December 1967, the Rolling Stones released the album *Their Satanic Majesties Request*. The album, widely held to be the Stones' attempt to create their own *Sgt. Pepper*, was a disappointment to many. Jon Landau, reviewing the album for *Rolling Stone*, maintained that the album put the Stones' status in jeopardy: "They have been far too influenced by their musical inferiors and the result is an insecure album in which they try too hard to prove that they too are innovators, and that they too can say something new" (Landau, "Stones" 18). Landau, in implicitly criticizing the Beatles, was one of the few critics to do so. Despite the sentiment, shared by Landau and a number of others writing for *Rolling Stone*, that the Rolling Stones were more "authentic" in their music and image than the Beatles, under Wenner's direction publication of criticisms of the Beatles remained infrequent.

Wenner celebrated what he viewed to be artistic and cultural progression in *Sgt. Pepper* and other Beatles work. By comparison, in previewing the Stones' next album, *Beggar's Banquet*, Wenner called *Satanic Majesties* the "prototype of junk masquerading as meaningful," and continued, "the Stones fell hook, line and sinker into the post–Sgt. Pepper trap of trying to put out a 'progressive,' 'significant' and 'different' album, as revolutionary as the Beatles. But it couldn't be done, because only the Beatles can put out an album by the Beatles" ("Rolling Stones Comeback" 1).

The Rolling Stones were not the only band to draw criticism for emulating the Beatles. Wenner, while celebrating the accomplishments of the Beatles, also took the opportunity to lambaste other groups, particularly the Beach Boys, for getting "hung up in trying to catch the Beatles":

> The Beatles have introduced to rock and roll all the new ideas, devices and new instruments currently in use. The sitar is one prominent example; electronic music is another. But whenever the Beatles have used a new instrument, a new technique or a sound or style that is outside the normal rock and roll complement (and rock and roll can take such additions perfectly) they have always used it in such a way that it is musically integral to what they are saying and fits the purpose of the song. All the freaky noises that the Beatles have made are not for the sake of being freaky, far out, advanced or avant-garde, but because they have made sense in the context of what they are trying to do. ("Rock and Roll Music" 16)

A product of the San Francisco music scene's mistrust of the music establishment centered in Los Angeles,[7] the marked hostility to the Beach Boys was also present in Ralph J. Gleason's "Perspectives" column of January 20, 1968. Lamenting the Beach Boys' inability to go beyond being a mere reflection of "Southern California hot rod, surfing and beer-bust fraternity culture" (and disregarding their pioneering use of the theremin on 1966's "Good Vibrations"), Gleason set the Beatles in contrast as a band that, blessed with "major talent four deep," was successful in the move into electronic music; that is, the Beatles were viewed as progressive ("Perspectives: The British Group Syndrome" 10). The breadth and depth of these views would become even more apparent as Gleason and Wenner argued against the radicalization of the counterculture, a matter taken up later in this chapter.

Wenner and Gleason took the superiority of the Beatles for granted, and the band served as a benchmark of progress. Commenting on the debt owed black music by "important groups" such as the Beatles and Jefferson Airplane, Gleason noted that the Beatles had moved beyond imitation. By contrast, the Rolling Stones "have not made it as far as The Beatles (after all, the lads are incredibly talented individually as performers, comics, writers, players and all that) and they may not make it." The greatest criticism was reserved for the Beach Boys who, viewed as a product of the Los Angeles–based music industry so reviled within the Bay-area music scene, were "a logical extension of Pat Boone and Ricky Nelson (as well as Paul Anka). They look like and perform like summer resort boozers, Fort Lauderdale weekend collegians. They sound like that, too" (Gleason, "Perspectives: Changing With Moneychangers" 9).

In dismissing the Beach Boys and the Rolling Stones, Gleason and Wenner effectively placed the Beatles in a unique position of superiority over their only true competition, and a competition it was, for the bands of the 1960s were acutely aware of the work of other bands. The Beach Boys' *Pet Sounds* displayed bandleader Brian Wilson's all-consuming desire to best the Beatles' album *Rubber Soul* (Miller, "Beach Boys" 195). McCartney viewed *Sgt. Pepper's Lonely Hearts Club Band* as a riposte to *Pet Sounds*. And the Rolling Stones, often listening to *Sgt. Pepper* for inspiration, intended *Their Satanic Majesties Request* to critically and commercially outdo their rivals' masterpiece (Norman, *The Stones* 192, 224). The Beach Boys never attained the kind of recognition in the United States that the Beatles did; the Rolling Stones did fully regain their credibility with *Rolling Stone*'s critics with the release of *Beggar's Banquet*. For Wenner and Gleason, the Beatles stood alone in their artistic achievement.

Wenner was ecstatic over the release of *The Beatles*, in November 1968. Referring to the band as the "perfect product and result of everything that rock and roll means and encompasses," Wenner judged the "White Album" "the best album they ever released, and only the Beatles are capable of making a better one." He went so far as to term the album "more perfect" than *Sgt. Pepper*, the "history and synthesis of Western music" (Wenner, Review of the sound recording, *The Beatles* 10). The notion that the Beatles were superior to other bands and that they were ushering in a new era in the development of music and culture is implicit, and often explicit, in the vast majority of articles and news items found in *Rolling Stone*, particularly from the magazine's inception in November 1967 well into 1969, when the Beatles' *de facto* breakup took place. During that period, drawing upon *Sgt. Pepper*'s acceptance by establishment art critics, *Rolling Stone*'s writers attempted to bolster rock's status as an art form.

Commentary on the Beatles within *Rolling Stone* was often geared toward legitimization of the counterculture's music and production as art; it was intended to continue the process started with the near-unanimous acclaim of the mainstream press for *Sgt. Pepper's Lonely Hearts Club Band*. This effort is most pronounced in articles written by *Rolling Stone*'s London correspondent, Jonathan

Cott. Cott's commentary consistently dealt with rock music and musicians in terms of Art with a capital A. That is, Cott viewed his subject as one legitimately considered alongside high art rather than simply as the product of a popular art. In his review of John Lennon's and Yoko Ono's album *Two Virgins*, released in early 1969, Cott wrote: "Obviously, John and Yoko's music circulates in that musical air inhaled by composers such as Luciano Berio, Robert Ashley, Gordon Mumma, La Monte Young, Morton Feldman, Cornelius Cardew, and John Cage—composers who generally emphasize sounds over pitches, a mixed-media interacting environment over a performer-listener concert hall ritual, the unfolding of musical events—the way a waterfall falls—over the structuring and permuting of rows and series (as in the music, for example, of Milton Babbitt, Harvey Sollberger, or David Del Tredici)" ("Two Virgins" 20). Although one suspects a certain amount of vanity in Cott's cataloguing of experimental artists, it is also apparent that he has a program, and that is to knock down the barrier between high art and low. At one point, he compares the feelings engendered by the sounds on the album to those stimulated by Bartok's *Out of Doors Suite* and Ravel's *L'Enfant et les Sortileges*. The opening of side two reminds him of the duck's lament inside the belly of the wolf in Tchaikovsky's *Peter and the Wolf*. He concludes:

> The East/West tension [i.e., that engendered by the occidental Lennon and the oriental Ono] dissolves in the music. And if you hear the lightest of echoes of Satie, Virgil Thomson, Swedish herding tunes, *Visage*—(aside from the obvious quotations and your own music), why not? As in Stockhausen's *Telemusik and Hymen*, all music is heard as one. The confrontation becomes an anastomosis—a running together, as of two streams. The music creates a story, there is a contest, but the music wins—especially those ubiquitous returning rhythms, like those of a person breathing in dreams. ("Two Virgins" 20)

Cott was not alone in accepting Lennon and Ono's status as experimental artists. In reviewing the premiere of their films *Two Virgins* and *Number Five* at the Chicago International Film Festival in late1968, Roger Ebert stated that *Two Virgins* would undoubtedly "find its way into the repertory of 'basic' underground films with Nelson's 'Oh, Dem Watermelons,' Palazzolo's 'O,' Emshwiller's 'Relativity' and Brakhage, Markopoulis, Anger and the rest" (Ebert 15). He further applauds Lennon and Ono for moving beyond Godard and Warhol:

> But now Yoko Ono has advanced it [i.e., breaking down the distance between the film and the audience by exposing the filmmaking process] one step farther, and in doing so has demonstrated that Warhol [in his film *Empire*] was moving in the wrong direction. The thing about Godard has always been his artistry, his craftsman's regard for his materials. His films are constructed like good handmade shoes. . . . What Yoko Ono and John Lennon have accomplished is two things at once: They have created a film record (real time equals film time) with its own peculiar atmosphere of reality, and they have done it lovingly, with artistry. Instead of pointing their camera and stepping aside (the Warhol approach), they have pointed their camera and then tried to make the picture it sees and the sounds it hears as beautiful as possible. And beauty is as real as the Empire State Building, and more durable. (Ebert 30)

The idea that the Beatles were superior vehicles of progress, within not only rock music but art and society in general, was an essential element in Wenner's arguments for the validity and promise of the counterculture lifestyle. Wenner's promotion of the Beatles as counterculture ideals and leaders was fostered by the widely held belief among youth that the band possessed a seemingly infinite ability to create. The mantle of leadership was one the Beatles explicitly rejected but that was nevertheless foisted upon them. Their celebrity, coupled with their artistic supremacy, all but guaranteed that their earnest pronouncements on any number of issues important to the counterculture would be widely circulated.

Until Lennon's peace campaign in 1969, however, the Beatles were reluctant to assume the role of leaders. In late 1968, for instance, McCartney was asked by a Black Power leader to speak at a rally to, as Apple press officer Derek Taylor commented, "state the case for white people." McCartney declined, replying, according to Taylor, that he was "not responsible for, and did not represent, all whites" ("Beatles May Do Free Concert" 1). McCartney was not alone in resisting attempts to make the Beatles into leaders or models. Hunter Davies quoted Lennon in the authorized biography, *The Beatles*: "I never felt any responsibility, being a so-called idol. It's wrong for people to expect it. What they are doing is putting their responsibilities on us, as Paul said to the newspapers when he admitted taking LSD. If they were worried about him being responsible, they should have been responsible enough and not printed it, if they were genuinely worried about people copying" (Davies 292). Wenner, as noted above, derided the establishment press for expecting the Beatles to assume responsibility for the behavior of their fans, and thus distorting "the picture of being Beatlepeople" (Wenner, Review of *Authorized Biography* 17). Nevertheless, the Beatles, largely through Wenner's efforts, emerge within the pages of *Rolling Stone* as leaders promoting the values of the counterculture and representing the youth culture in opposition to the establishment and its institutions.

Their image comprised, in part, two seemingly inconsistent qualities: They were exceptional and they were identifiable as "us," meaning youth and the counterculture. Thus, while their uniqueness was assumed, they nonetheless were viewed "whether they like it or not," as "mirrors of ourselves." Wenner actively promoted this view of the Beatles: "In considering the Beatles . . . we are considering the world we live in and we are considering ourselves" (Review of *Authorized Biography* 15, 18). Of course, notions of the Beatles' uniqueness and their being "one of us" are not necessarily contradictory; for leaders often arise out of their cohort, and such a development is consistent with Gramsci's notion of the intellectual and its leadership function. To summarize, Gramsci, the "theorist of consent as legitimization,"[8] maintained in his theory of hegemony that only weak states rely upon domination or the threat of force for legitimization. In a strong state, the hegemonic class rules through a series of alliances in which its interests are universalized and "become the interests of the other subordinate groups" (Gramsci, *Selections from the Prison Notebooks* [hereafter *SPN*] 181). Hegemony is ever-changing in its composition as different groups drift in and out of the hegemonic class. The struggle for domination between cultural elites, that is, between "organic" and "traditional" intellectuals (counterculture and the establishment intellectuals, respectively), culminates in either restoration of the old hegemony or the establishment of a new hegemony. Wenner, through *Rolling Stone*, I would argue, nominated the Beatles to the role of "organic" intellectuals: It was in the pages of that magazine where the Beatles most explicitly emerged as leaders speaking to and for the counterculture.

In July 1967 the Beatles joined sixty-five luminaries of British society (among them Members of Parliament, Graham Greene, Dr. R. D. Laing, and critic Kenneth Tynan) on a petition appearing in the *Times* (London) calling for the legalization of marijuana. It was widely believed, and rightly so, that the Beatles had paid for the one-page advertisement (Miles 387, 393). Even before the band's use of the hallucinogen was verified in June 1967, it was widely believed within the counterculture that the Beatles used LSD. By the time that the Summer of Love was in full swing, the Beatles removed all doubt. The June 16, 1967, issue of *Life* magazine noted that McCartney was "deeply committed to the possibilities of LSD as a universal cure-all": "After I took it, it opened my eyes. . . . We only use one tenth of our brain. Just think what all we could accomplish if we could only tap that hidden part! It would mean a whole new world. If the politicians would take LSD, there wouldn't be any more war, or poverty or famine" ("New Far-Out Beatles" 105). With the inception of *Rolling Stone* in November of that year, the Beatles had a direct outlet to the counterculture through which to further clarify their view(s) on the use of drugs and a host of other issues of interest to the youth culture and the counterculture. The Beatles provided the magazine with a highly visible and powerful vehicle for promoting the values of the counterculture.

Initially, it was Starr and Harrison who were the most vocal in their support for the recreational use of drugs. In February 1968 Starr, in an interview reprinted in *Rolling Stone*, was asked by Jack Hutton, editor of England's *Melody Maker*, how he could condone the use of illegal drugs. Starr responded, "It used to be legal until a couple of fellas got round a table and said we'll make it illegal. . . . I don't see why the law suddenly says you can't have it." He further chided the authorities for, in essence, promoting drugs: "They think it's great you know if the police raid a place. But fifty million people have read about it again and a couple of thousand will say 'I'll take drugs.' . . . So they're building the case for it, more than against it, because of their silly attitude." Harrison attributed his religious conversion to his use of "acid": "It's really only after acid that it pushes home to you that you're only little—really" (Hutton and Jones 12–13).

Even when the Beatles themselves were not advocating the use of drugs, their image was closely linked to the drug culture. The February 1, 1969, issue of *Rolling Stone*, with its "It Happened in 1968" article, contained a small photograph of Lennon's smiling face with the inscription "Would you buy a lid[9] from this man?"; the photograph, with its caption, appeared twice in that issue ("It Happened in 1968" 15, 19). A 1970 article opens with a picture of Lennon holding what appears to be a joint, though no mention is made of drugs in the accompanying piece (Yorke, "A Private Talk" 22). Finally, there was the famous *Rolling Stone* interview with John Lennon, by Wenner, appearing in two installments in January and February 1971, in which Lennon was quite candid about his and the other Beatles' drug use.[10] Clearly, the Beatles' image encompassed their recreational use of drugs, and this aspect of their image was promoted and described time and again as part of Wenner's advancement of the counterculture lifestyle.

The 1960s were a period in which traditional forms of Western religion were forsaken for other models of faith and worship, among them those of the East. The exploration of Eastern philosophies was a widespread practice of the counterculture, and the Beatles were among its most visible proponents. It was largely through their patronage of the Maharishi and Transcendental Meditation [TM] that the belief system was able to take hold in the West among the youth culture. The Beatles' religious journey, so to speak, was widely covered in the mainstream press[11] and broadcast media. In March 1968, for instance, the Beatles' "Lady Madonna" clip debuted on *The Hollywood Palace* in support of the new single. Jimmy Durante, one of the most beloved entertainers of the twentieth century, introduced the film, complete with his trademark malapropisms: "It takes place in a recording studio they made right after they 'medicated' with the Mah——rishi in India [audience laughter]. The newspaper says that Ringo Starr [screams from the audience] walked out on the rest of 'em. You know, it wasn't that he disliked the Maharishi; he had to get home to get things ready in the recording studio" (*Hollywood Palace*, March 30, 1968).

As with drug use, Harrison was the most vocal of the Beatles in his support of TM, and in promoting a Beatles metaphysic, one based largely upon counterculture values. In early 1968 he told *Rolling Stone*'s Nick Jones that it was deficits among the Christian faithful that prompted him to look to the East:

When you're young you get taken to church by your parents and you get pushed into religion in school. They're trying to put something into your mind. But it's wrong you know. Obviously, because nobody goes to church and nobody believes in God. Why? Because religious teachers don't know what they're teaching. They haven't interpreted the Bible as it was intended. . . . For Christianity, it's the people who profess to be the religious teachers who screw the whole thing up. They're the people who create the sectarianism, the prejudices and the hate that goes on. You know, those people who are supposed to be propagating the Lord's word—they're screwing it all up. (Hutton and Jones 13)

Of the four Beatles, Harrison was the most devoted in following the path laid out in TM and Hinduism. In the second part of the interview, Harrison explained in greater detail his spirituality. Consistent with his beliefs, he noted Indian music's attraction for the youth of the day. Following the "Catholic trick," that is, "brainwashing" the young, he said that music, "the main interest of the younger people," could be used to draw them to the "truth": "In actual fact, do this sort of thing—but brainwash people with the truth—turn them all onto music and books at that age, then they'll live a better life. Then it's the next generation that does it more, and after that . . . so it doesn't matter if we see the perfection of the Golden Age or not. . . . With Pepper it's just that anybody who feels anybody wants to be in Pepper's Band is in it. Anybody who feels any identification. And this all gets back again to God." Jones prompted, "A lot of people, though, never realise what you're giving them?" "Well," offered Harrison, "lots of people do, but then there's always the other ones who write saying 'Why the fuck do you think you are doing that.' There's always that, you see, and it all gets back to the thing of the Maharishi and God" (Jones 16). This is a fascinating exchange in that it implicitly and explicitly reveals both

Harrison's countercultural bearing and the Beatles' status within the counterculture. One example, of course, is the topic—Harrison's advocacy of an Eastern philosophy. Another is Harrison's use of the word "fuck," conforming to the counterculture's use of scatological language as evidence of authenticity. Finally, the Beatles' status as leaders of the counterculture is implicit in Jones' question; as posed, the Beatles are understood to have so much to offer, if only people would listen.

The Beatles' sojourn to India in the spring of 1968, to study with the Maharishi, was cut short when it was alleged that he had propositioned Mia Farrow's sister, Prudence, also in attendance. Lennon and McCartney publicly disavowed their association with the Maharishi, including during an appearance on *The Tonight Show* in which McCartney ridiculed one of the more bizarre entertainments of the era, the Beach Boys' tour with the Maharishi: "On top of everything else, it was a flop" ("Are They More Popular" 18). Harrison continued as a devotee and patron of the International Society for Krishna Consciousness, while the other three to varying degrees remained interested in alternative faiths and philosophies. Their stances on recreational drug use and advocacy of Eastern religions and philosophies were important and necessary components of their leadership of the counterculture, and of their image as opponents of the establishment. For *Rolling Stone*, the views of the Beatles added weight to its claims on behalf of the counterculture.

Of the magazine's writers and editors, Wenner and Gleason were the most adamant in identifying the Beatles with the counterculture and in promoting through them the counterculture lifestyle over radical left politics. The accomplishments of the Beatles were often framed in terms of the goals and achievements of the counterculture. As noted earlier, Wenner assumed the Beatles were "one of us"; as such, they were an important part of Wenner's arsenal in his assault on the establishment. Gleason was equally prone to set the Beatles off against the establishment. Importantly, however, the establishment was not the only target of Wenner and Gleason: the radical left was also criticized. Wenner's uneasiness with activism has already been noted. Gleason, whose views were more developed than Wenner, nevertheless shared with Wenner a belief in the revolutionary possibilities of rock and roll.

In October 1968 a lengthy interview with Herbert Marcuse appeared in the *New York Times Magazine*. The following March, Gleason applauded Marcuse, often called the "father of the New Left," for endorsing a "non-doctrinaire" approach within the New Left, but also criticized him and his peers for failing to account for the revolutionary implications of rock and roll:

> [Quoting Plato] "The new style quietly insinuates itself into manners and customs ... and from there it issues a greater force ... goes on to attack laws and constitutions, displaying the utmost impudence, until it ends by overthrowing everything, both in public and in private."
>
> We are, at this point, still some distance from the end envisaged by Plato but we are on the road to it. .... Gilbert & Sullivan may have made a government tremble, but I am convinced that rock 'n' roll in its total manifestations will cause one to fall. .... If Professor Marcuse could write a couple of songs, now, that might do more than all his books. ("Perspectives: Songs Would Do More" 21)

Gleason was even more pointed in his critique of the methods of the New Left in the "Perspectives" column appearing in the "American Revolution 1969" issue published in April of that year. Espousing the countercultural antipathy to politics and radicalism, Gleason criticized the SDS and the rising militancy of the radicals:

> Politics has failed. .... No, the hippies and the Beatles and the Pop musicians present no Program for Improvement of the Society.

What they do is to present a program for improvement of the
young people of the world. You can't change the society until
you reach a state of grace. . . . But [the political radicals] have
the old approach. You can't make an omelet without breaking
eggs. True, man, true. But you better figure out how to make a
revolution without killing people or it won't work. We've had all
that. We really have. . . . It's all very well to talk about dying on
your feet being better than living on your knees. Just don't ask
me to do it. I'd rather be red than dead and I would also rather
be alive than inside.

Rock and roll, not politics, provided the only tenable option for
the youth culture, for the Beatles were not "just more popular than
Jesus," they were also "more potent" than the SDS. The Beatles and
Bob Dylan, Gleason's and Wenner's model countercultural and artistic ideals, had provided a fertile environment for peaceful revolutionary change:

What do you think Dylan is doing up there in Woodstock?
Counting his money? You don't resign from being an artist. Not
until you're dead. No. He and the Beatles started something
which is beyond politics, past the programs of the planners and
out there in McLuhanland changing the heads of the world.
     Out of it will come the programs. Out of it will come the
plans. When the time is right. ("Perspectives: Is There a Deathwish in U.S.?" 18)

A number of points should be made about the beliefs espoused
by Wenner and Gleason. First, in their aversion to radicalism they
are consistent with the views associated with the counterculture at
its peak. Second, their beliefs were not unanimously held at *Rolling
Stone*. Third, these beliefs are consistent with views publicly stated
by the Beatles. The first point has been demonstrated in the fore-

going discussion. The other two points, however, require further explanation.

With regard to the views of the staff at *Rolling Stone*, Wenner, as editor, exerted great influence on the direction and viewpoint the magazine manifested, and opposing views were allowed only within narrowly defined parameters, if at all. Nevertheless, there was a great deal of dissension among the staff over the editor and his mentor's (i.e., Gleason's) failure to embrace the program of the radical left. Gleason's piece was met with derision among the staff, and was just one of many incidents leading to efforts to have him (as well as Wenner) removed from the magazine, or at least to circumscribe his editorial freedom (Draper 127–28).

While the magazine (due to Wenner's reservations) approached the subject of politics only sporadically and hesitantly, political views nevertheless found their way into music criticism and news. Just as the Beatles had been held up as standard-bearers for the counter-culture, they were set against the Rolling Stones' ostensible radicalism. In a review of their new album, *Beggar's Banquet*, Jon Landau,[12] one of the magazine's most capable and influential critics, criticized McCartney for being out of step with the times, unlike the Stones:

> From the beginning they themselves have been exponents of emotional violence and it's hard to imagine any group more suited to voicing the feelings of discontent we all share in these most violent of times. Wherever they wind up themselves, they are writing songs of revolution because they are giving powerful expression to the feelings that are causing it. . . . There is no way they can separate themselves as human beings from what is going on. It isn't a question of feeling sorry for people in India, as Paul McCartney seems to think.[13] The point is that the things that keep those people in a state of near starvation are the same ones that may force John [i.e. Lennon] to take a drug rap, that

almost sent [Stones' guitarist] Brian Jones to jail, and which has
forced Elridge [sic] Cleaver into hiding. Sooner or later, something brings that home to each of us. (Landau, "Beggar's Banquet" 12)[14]

If Landau's political leanings were not clear enough, he applauded the Rolling Stones for being the "first band to say, 'Up
against the wall, motherfucker' and they said it with class" ("Beggar's Banquet" 11). Landau refers to the slogan that was often
chanted at policemen attempting to break up student and radical
demonstrations. Taken from a line in a poem by "beat-turned-
black-nationalist" Leroi Jones, the crudity was also the source for
the moniker of the Lower East Side Motherfuckers (Gitlin, *The Sixties* 239). Landau, critical of London Records for changing the cover
of the Rolling Stones' *Beggar's Banquet* album (initially a photograph
of a most unsavory and filthy lavatory), jokingly(?) comments, "The
next time New York's East Side revolutionary contingent wants to
shake somebody up . . . why don't they head up town to London
Records. I'm sure the President of London Records could use the
education." Landau is referring to the Motherfuckers, "tough hippies," and "postbeat, postbiker, would-be Hell's Angels with mani-
festoes," who had formed a chapter of the SDS. Employing street
theater and violence in the service of their "cultural revolution,"
the Motherfuckers, inspired by European anarchism and Frankfurt
School Marxism (the group included Marcuse's stepson), were contemptuous of "milky student politics." Many newer SDSers welcomed the Motherfuckers and their disposition toward direct action
(Gitlin, *The Sixties* 238–41). In 1968, for instance, the Motherfuckers
set piles of refuse aflame during the New York City garbage strike
and pelted firemen with stones (Caute 311–12).[15] While a description of the full extent of his views is beyond the scope of this work,
Landau clearly was more sympathetic to the increasingly activist
left than either Wenner or Gleason; as such, he found the Beatles'

leadership of the counterculture flaccid at best, and nominated instead the Rolling Stones, a band whose dark side seemed more in
tune with the times.[16]

With regard to the Beatles' views, one is struck by their similarity to that of the magazine's dominant published opinions. Recall Wenner's denouncement of the Chicago Yip-In: "Rock and roll
is the *only* way in which the vast but formless power of youth is
structured, the only way in which it can be defined or inspected"
(Wenner, "Musicians Reject" 22).[17] Rock and roll, for Wenner, was
the bridge to a new lifestyle, one based upon counterculture values.
As Harrison had remarked, music, "the main interest of the younger
people," could be used to draw them to the "truth." "[B]rainwash
people with the truth—turn them all onto music and books at that
age [i.e., youth], then they'll live a better life" (Jones 16). Recall also
Gleason's championing of the Beatles' "program" over that of SDS
("Perspectives: Is There a Deathwish in the U.S.?"). In Lennon's
first *Rolling Stone* interview, Jonathan Cott pressed him on Jean-Luc
Godard's criticism[18] of the Beatles' apoliticism. Lennon responded,
"There's no point in dropping out, because it's the same there and it's
got to change. But I think it all comes down to changing your head,
and sure, I know that's a cliché" (Cott, "Rolling Stone Interview"
14). Cliché or not, this was the maxim by which Lennon proceeded
throughout the peace campaign, and that he did not forsake even as
he flirted with American radicalism in the early-1970s.

Unwilling to follow the rabble led by intellectuals such as Fou-
cault, Sartre, Lacan, and Althusser into the streets, Lennon and
the other Beatles instead decried the violence. The remedy lay not
in changing leaders, but in "changing minds." This was the gist of
Harrison's previously noted pronouncements on religion. Lennon's
approach, however, was more inflammatory to the left, especially
after the release of the recording "Revolution," which contained
the lines "But when you talk about destruction / don't you know
that you can count me out" and "You tell me it's the institution /

204 ROLLING STONE, 1967–70

Well, you know, you better free your mind instead." *Black Dwarf*, a revolutionary socialist newspaper published in Britain, became openly critical of the Beatles' apoliticism. As Ian MacDonald notes in *Revolution in the Head*, this was a view shared by many among the New Left in Britain and the United States. Increasingly, New Left and counterculture editors and writers were coming to believe that the Beatles were more interested in protecting their fortunes than changing society (226–27).

In contrast, many believed the Rolling Stones to be radicals. A questionable assertion at best, it nevertheless points up the widely held view that rock music was itself a vehicle for change, even revolution. In 1968, after the Beatles rejected his overtures to appear in his new movie[19] (an offer the Rolling Stones accepted), Jean-Luc Godard expressed his consternation at the Beatles: "There are plenty of people in Britain with money and open minds. But alas, they don't use their minds, and they are usually corrupted by money. . . . Look at the Beatles, for instance" (Giuliano 372). An early critique of the Beatles, appearing in *Black Dwarf* in Autumn 1969, closed with the wish that the Beatles would "get so fucked-up with their money-making that they become as obscure as Cliff Richard." The next issue of the newspaper, which also promoted the Rolling Stones' radical status, contained "An Open Letter to John Lennon." The letter, written by John Hoyland, moved Lennon to respond with his own "A Very Open Letter to John Hoyland from John Lennon," and this was met by a response from the editors of *Black Dwarf*, responding collectively under the pseudonym "John Hoyland" (Wiener 81–83).

Rolling Stone published Hoyland's "Open Letter" and Lennon's response side by side in its May 3, 1969, issue. Hoyland's "Open Letter" indicates a program far from the lifestyle agenda advocated by either the counterculture or the Beatles:

Now [that Lennon had been busted for possession] do you see what was wrong with your record "Revolution"? That record was no more revolutionary than Mrs. Dale's Diary. In order to change the world we've got to understand what's wrong with the world. And then—destroy it. Ruthlessly. This is not cruelty or madness. It is one of the most passionate forms of love. Because what we're fighting is suffering, oppression, humiliation—the immense toll of unhappiness caused by capitalism. And any "love" which does not pit itself against these things is sloppy and irrelevant.

Hoyland compared the Beatles to the Rolling Stones:

> But recently your music has lost it [sic] bite, at a time when the music of the Stones has been getting stronger and stronger.
>
> Why? Because we're living in a world that is splitting down the middle. The split is between the rich and the poor, the powerful and the powerless. You can see it here, and in the jungles of Vietnam, and in the mountains of South America, and in the ghettos of the U.S. and the Universities all over the world. It's the great drama of the second half of the twentieth century—the battle for human dignity fought by the exploited and the underprivileged of the world. The Stones, helped along a bit by their experiences with the law, have understood this and they've understood that the life and the authenticity of their music—quite apart from their personal integrity—demanded that they take part in this drama—that they refuse to accept the system that's fucking up our lives. ("Revolution: The Dear John Letters" 22)

Hoyland patronized Lennon in his conclusion: "But learn from it, John. Look at the society we're living in, and ask yourself: why? And then—come and join us. Yours fraternally, John Hoyland."

Lennon was angered by the criticism, and his response took the New Left to task for its willingness to turn to violence and criticized the false dichotomy of Beatles versus Rolling Stones:

You're obviously on a destruction kick. I'll tell you what's wrong with it—People—so do you want to destroy them? Ruthlessly? Until you/we change your/our heads—there's no chance. Tell me of one successful revolution. Who fucked up communism— christianity [sic]—capitalism—buddhism [sic], etc? Sick heads, and nothing else. Do you think all the enemy wear capitalist badges so that you can shoot them? It's a bit naïve, John. You seem to think it's just a class war. . . . Look man, I was/am not against you. Instead of splitting hairs about the Beatles and the Stones—think a little bigger—look at the world we're living in, John, and ask yourself: why? And then—come and join us. Love, John Lennon P.S.: You smash it—and I'll build around it. ("Revolution: The Dear John Letters" 22)

The dialogue between Lennon and Hoyland embodies many of the tensions that accompanied the increased influence of the New Left as the decade came to a close. Always tenuous, connections between the left and the counterculture snapped with the escalation in Vietnam. Many young people, apprehensive that the countercultural apathy to politics was self-defeating, turned to the activist left to speak for them.

The halcyon days of the Summer of Love were a distant memory, but Wenner maintained his stand against the radicals and, much to the chagrin of many of his writers and editors, refused to allow *Rolling Stone* to be incorporated by the New Left. In May 1968, as previously noted, Wenner, in his criticism of the proposed Yip protest at the Democratic Convention in Chicago, had already let the left know where he and his magazine stood. Rock and roll was the solution, not politics or violence. In his critique of the Yippies he had written: "But what they [i.e., the Yippies] do not understand is that as surely as the Beatles, Bob Dylan, the Grateful Dead and scores of other rock and roll people have changed the face of popular music, become the de facto spokesman of youth, as surely as all that has happened, they have also brought with them new ideas, new approaches, new means and new goals" (Wenner, "Musicians Reject" 22). By the end of the decade, however, his ideas and goals, and those of the Beatles, seemed to many to be out of touch with the increasingly radicalized and fragmented youth movement. The Beatles, their unity largely a myth in 1969, stayed out of the political fray. Lennon, as noted above, would forsake the counterculture ideal for activist politics, but that was only hinted at in 1969.

The Beatles' image was employed by *Rolling Stone* to validate the counterculture program espoused by Jann Wenner, and to increase circulation, ultimately broadening the publication's audience. Wenner's placement of the Beatles at the vanguard of the assault on "straight" society is important to our analysis of the Beatles' image in a number of ways. First, with regard to the band's artistry and status as an engine of progress, and their role in the legitimization of rock and roll as art, the magazine was largely amplifying sentiments present in the mainstream press.[20] Second, putting forward the Beatles as counterculture leaders was, again, to amplify an opinion current in contemporary mainstream media. Third, in light of the growing militancy of the antiwar movement, it is noteworthy that this underground publication and the mainstream press presented such similar views on the Beatles. For the mainstream press, the countercultural values embedded in the Beatles' image presented a "safe" alternative to the growing militancy of the student radicals. For the magazine, political apathy walked hand in hand with commerce. True, Wenner, like most Americans, rejected the overt politicism (and violence) of the antiwar movement and of those publications pressing the radical agenda, but many among the magazine's staff attributed this rejection to Wenner's avarice, and believed Wenner to be pursuing commercial interests at the expense of advocacy. One staff member, Michael Lydon, recalled of Wenner: "He didn't want it to be an underground newspaper. He wanted to meet the Beatles. He wanted to do something that would put him on a par with the Beatles" (Anson 69). Speaking to this point years later, writer John Burks recalled, "Jann had a rule of thumb. . . . When in doubt, put the Beatles on the cover" (Anson 172). The magazine's staff may have preferred more political coverage and advocacy but, Wenner's aversion to politics aside, the Beatles sold.

In placing the Beatles at the vanguard of the counterculture, Wenner facilitated the publication's circulation among a much wider audience (concurrently giving his countercultural program greater dissemination in the U.S. and Britain). There are numerous examples of Wenner using the Beatles to increase circulation: The first issue's cover had a picture of Lennon on the set of *How I Won the War*. Later, the *Two Virgins* cover placed the magazine firmly within American popular culture. And, in 1970, following a series of financial miscues, a two-part interview with John Lennon (in which Lennon describes the disintegration of the band), perhaps Wenner's greatest journalistic coup, allowed the magazine to become profitable again (Anson 120–23). By 1971 *Rolling Stone*, the first issue of which had sold only 6,000 copies (on an initial press run of 40,000), had a circulation of 250,000.[21] Wenner's utilization of the Beatles clearly was a contributing factor to the magazine's increased success and circulation beyond its initial audience of committed counterculturalists.

An interesting dynamic was set up by Wenner's insistence that his magazine remain essentially apolitical and in his determination to use rock stars, especially the Beatles, to further his countercultural claims: though championing a counterculture lifestyle (one that rejected the values of middle-class society, notably consumerism), his magazine was becoming increasingly commercial. Record companies that had shied away from underground papers because of their use of scatological language and antiestablishment bearings found a willing partner in Jann Wenner; while the magazine's counterculture stance was to be tolerated, its apoliticism was to be exploited. Evidence of the magazine's commercialization is to be found in its changing content: Wenner increased the magazine's emphasis on music coverage after securing advertising from various record companies (Anson 172). And, much to the chagrin of the more politically active on the magazine's staff, the counterculture was easily exploited by corporate America. The Beatles' marketability and widespread acceptance by "straight" society granted the counterculture ideal an efficacy and currency that transcended committed counterculture advocates and fostered a wider audience among the country's young. Identification with the counterculture, whether committed or casual, was commonly manifested through consumer products such as clothes or music. As Anson notes: "The average nineteen-year-old *Rolling Stone* reader had more discretionary income for leisure-time activity than his parents. Every year, he . . . spent $600 on record albums, another $300 on stereo equipment. Roper found '*Rolling Stone* . . . comes out on top . . . delivers more musicians, together with more young people who are heavily into music than any other media anywhere—a total potential market of more than one million'" (Anson 218). The counterculture culture was commodity-based— one could purchase one's way into the counterculture. In a sense, one could buy rebellion. Clearly, this marriage of countercultural advocacy and mass marketing is at the center of the magazine's success.

Gramsci, as earlier noted, theorized the intellectual, the stratum or strata of individuals within a social group that "give it homogeneity and an awareness of its own function" within the economic, social, and political fields (*SPN* 5). *Rolling Stone* amplified certain perceptions of the Beatles already current in the mainstream press, including the band's superiority to other bands, the exceptional artistry of their albums, the band's function in the legitimizing of rock and roll as an art form, and the notion that they were an engine for artistic and societal progress. It also publicized and promoted the Beatles' adherence to countercultural values, and promoted the band as countercultural ideals. *Rolling Stone* helped to define and solidify within American consciousness the Beatles' status as counterculture leaders. Ultimately exhibiting their general disdain for politics (one they shared with many among the counterculture), the Beatles rejected direct political involvement in the issues of the time and so lost credibility among the student radicals. Wenner's nomination of the band to a leadership role within the youth culture—in effect, to fill the function of Gramscian intellectuals—was rejected by both the Beatles and the radicals. Nevertheless, the ground the Beatles occupied, the area of struggle between the dominant culture and the counterculture, was also the location for assimilation of much of the counterculture's program into the "compromise equilibrium"[22] of hegemony. While the Beatles rejected explicit leadership of a political movement (as did most of the rock elite), they clearly led in the realm of lifestyle, as the mainstream press acknowledged and as Wenner championed. The terrain the Beatles inhabited was the area of resistance and incorporation. The compromise manifested itself in, among other things, the commodification of the counterculture. It remains in the loosening of many societal restrictions on self-expression.

In the wake of the Ohio National Guard's killing of four student protestors at Kent State University in May 1970, the *Rolling Stone* staff mutinied and drew up a manifesto that would have, in essence, wrested editorial control of the magazine from its founder and thus moved politics to the foreground. Wenner was able to maintain control only after exhorting his cadre to "Get Back, Get Back, Get Back to where they once belonged." In quoting the Beatles' song, Draper notes, Wenner was drawing the line: politics were only a secondary concern; *Rolling Stone* was first, and foremost, about music and culture (Draper 131). Numerous resignations and firings followed. Even as the cultural revolutionaries were being brushed aside by the more politically motivated, the society aspired to in the pages of *Rolling Stone* remained a Beatle-inspired Eden of peace, love, communalism, free sex, recreational drug use—qualities embodied in the Beatles' image and the things of counterculture dreams.

The Beatles reached the pinnacle of their influence within the counterculture at its acme, from 1966 to mid-1968. Their popular decline coincided with the waning of the counterculture, as the youth movement become more radicalized with the intensification of hostilities in Vietnam. It also coincided with the protracted demise of the band, a period during which they each pursued other interests and—at least for Harrison and Lennon—only grudgingly contributed to Beatles projects. Now a fascinating document of the last days of the Beatles, at the time *Let It Be* was a singular failure. The film was the product of too many masters, so to speak, and the final result fails to capture either the Beatles' or director Michael Lindsay-Hogg's vision. Once intended to show the Beatles in the process of creating an album and presenting their music in concert, ultimately the film was about the disintegration of the 1960s' single most influential cultural agents. The film record of the so-called *Get Back* sessions was such a personal and professional disaster that the Beatles, all but broken up yet not wanting *Let It Be* to be their swan song, reconvened in Abbey Road Studios with producer George Martin to make the album *Abbey Road*.

The film contains hints of what might have been. Michael Lindsay-Hogg later commented, "There was material in that film which was the most accurate anywhere about the break-up, showing the kind of ennui they felt. But, because they were the stars as well as the producers, they didn't want that material to be scrutinized by the public" (Carr 161). Nevertheless, incidents in the disintegration are put on full view. McCartney and Harrison have a row over Harrison's failure to get the sound McCartney wants from the guitar, with Harrison finally declaring that he "won't play at all," if

McCartney prefers; the discomfort caused to McCartney, Harrison, and Starr by Yoko Ono's presence is palpable. In the end, however, the film fails fully to document the breakup and attendant tension. Nor does it satisfy as a chronicle of the band's creative process, the scenes too haphazardly edited to offer any insight into the musical genius of the Beatles. Rather, what is presented are snippets of dialogue, jamming, and squabbling.

There are some fine moments in the film. The final rooftop concert is exhilarating and shows that, in spite of the sad state of their affairs, the Beatles were still a great rock and roll combo. Other moments centering on the music, such as the group's performance of "Two of Us," stand up quite well even by the standards of today's music videos. These moments are too few and far between, however, and fans, critics, and the Beatles themselves roundly flayed the film. *Rolling Stone* called it "a bad movie," and continued that it was a "crashing bore" that could have been better "if only there had been a director" (Goodwin 52). The *New York Times* reviewer lamented that the film was "none too artfully made," though it "provides a revealing close-up of the world's most famous quartet" (Thompson, "Film: Beatles Together" 11). Following the breakup of the Beatles, a bitter Lennon commented to Wenner:

> That film was set up by Paul for Paul. That's one of the main reasons the Beatles ended. 'Cause—I can't speak for George, but I pretty damn well know—we got fed up of being sidemen for Paul. After Brian died, that's what happened, began to happen to us. The camera work was set up to show Paul and not to show anybody else. And that's how I felt about it. And on top of that, the people that cut it as "Paul is God" and we're just lyin' around there. That's what I felt. And I knew there were some shots of Yoko, and me, that had been just chopped out of the film for no other reason than the people were oriented towards Engelbert Humperdinck. I felt sick. (Wenner, *Lennon Remembers* 49–51)

Lennon was all too ready to lay the blame at McCartney's feet following the breakup, though in reality, he (Lennon) had all but ceased
acting as a Beatle, missing numerous recording and editing sessions.
None of the Beatles, in fact, come off very well in this film.

The *Let It Be* album, like the film, was roundly panned by the
critics. *Time* called the album "one of their worst," due to Phil
Spector's over lush production ("Spector" 64). Longtime producer
George Martin's involvement in the project was sporadic, and in
the end none of the Beatles could face the hours of recorded material. Spector, one of the top producers of the 1960s, was brought
in to clean up what Lennon later called the "shittiest load of badly
recorded shit with a lousy feeling to it ever" (Wenner, *Lennon Remembers* 120).

Happily, the Beatles were able to bring themselves together for
one more album. *Abbey Road* (1969) was recorded after though released before *Let It Be*. George Martin agreed to produce the Beatles
one more time, provided the members of the band allowed him to
produce as in the early days, and that they kept their bickering to a
minimum. The result showed that the Beatles could still come together to produce well-crafted music. Side one was designed to cater
to Lennon's taste; it is a collection of rock and roll songs in the best
tradition, including Lennon's "Come Together," Harrison's "Something," McCartney's blistering vocals on "Oh! Darling," and Lennon's "I Want You." Side two allowed Martin and McCartney to experiment. Conceived as a mini-opera, it runs like a continuous piece
of music, each song segueing into the next. Highlights include the
opening number, Harrison's acoustic "Here Comes the Sun," Lennon's "Sun King"/"Mean Mr. Mustard," and, finally, "The End."
The latter features a rousing finale in which McCartney, Harrison,
and Lennon trade guitar leads; it also contains the only drum solo
Starr ever played on a Beatles album. The album was a popular
success, sitting at the top of the *Billboard* album charts for eleven
weeks (Whitburn, *Top 40 Albums* 29). *Time* called it the Beatles'

best album since *Sgt. Pepper's Lonely Hearts Club Band*, displaying a "cheerful coherence . . . and a sense of wholeness clearly contrived as a revel in musical pleasure" ("The Beatles: Cheerful Coherence" 57). *Rolling Stone* had two reviews of the album. Ed Ward, critical of the Beatles' preoccupation with electronics and the studio since the release of *Revolver* (1966), complained, "They've been shucking us a lot recently, and it's a shame because they don't have to. Surely they must have enough talent and intelligence to do better than this. Or do they?"(Ward 33). John Mendelsohn's review, consistent with mainstream reception of the album, was more generous: "To my mind, they're equalable, but still unsurpassed" (Mendelsohn 32). Largely a positive experience in the making, *Abbey Road* was the last album recorded by the Beatles. In April 1970 Paul McCartney left the Beatles; in December he brought suit to dissolve the band, and the Beatles, "unsurpassed," were no more.

SIX

"Beautiful People"
The Beatles' Idealized Past

THIS BOOK BEGAN WITH THE DEATH of John Lennon. As we have seen, the Beatles' image embodied, reflected, and sometimes was a catalyst for, much of the change that occurred during the 1960s. Small wonder, then, that Lennon's death unleashed such a torrent of comment both celebrating and condemning the accomplishments of that decade. The airwaves and newsstands were inundated with news of the event and assessments of Lennon's and the Beatles' impact on society. The media saturation was such that the *New York Times'* Elizabeth Flynn commented, "Almost more ruthless than Lennon's death was the press coverage." She criticized the single-mindedness of the news media in covering the story, pushing all other matters to the sidelines. Flynn, who was unsure whether she would file the stacks of news items littering her desk under "Lennon" or "media," was also critical of her colleagues for relying so heavily upon Lennon's Beatle past in eulogizing him. Criticizing as "lazy" the many writers who quoted Beatles lyrics in commenting on the event, she continued, "What it comes down to in the long run is: Lennon is dead and the era is dead. But the era died when the Beatles broke up. . . . Need we quote the scriptures of the Beatles infinitely?" (Flynn K29).

While the "era died when the Beatles broke up," in fact the cultural divide that had marked the period remained, and the response to Lennon's death encapsulated and highlighted lingering

hostility. In the wake of Lennon's murder, old animosities perco-
lated to the top as pundits on the left and right attempted to define the legacy of the 1960s. Undoubtedly, of the Beatles, Lennon
had most provoked the political and social conservatives, particularly through his dalliance with radical politics in the early 1970s.
In September 1971, Lennon and Yoko Ono moved their headquarters to New York, and briefly joined forces with radicals Jerry Rubin and Abbie Hoffman. Rubin and Hoffman, the founders of the
Yippies (Youth International Party), had been tried as members of
the "Chicago Seven" for their part in the disruptions of the 1968
Democratic National Convention in Chicago. They were among
the five convicted of inciting to riot, though those convictions were
thrown out on appeal. Far from humbled by the experience, Rubin
and Hoffman continued to protest against the war in Vietnam, organizing various events and protests, and further provoking the authorities. As a result, when Lennon fell in with them, he became
the target of the Nixon administration, which feared Lennon would
become involved in leading the antiwar movement. The full force of
the federal government was brought to bear to prevent Lennon's obtaining United States residency. Only after a prolonged battle in the
nation's courts did he finally (in September 1975) win the right to
stay in the country.[1] Thus, Lennon had a long history at odds with
American conservatives.

The reaction to Lennon's death must be understood within the
context of a culture war being waged in the United States. The
growing prosperity of the 1950s and 1960s had many effects upon
the culture of the United States, not the least of which was the appearance of a new class of people educated at the country's colleges
and universities and promoting a political and cultural agenda quite
different from that of the white lower middle class. William C. Berman, in *America's Right Turn: From Nixon to Bush* (1994), places this
new class of young professionals within the context of the American
political landscape of the 1970s: "Representing the 'progressive'

middle class, this cohort . . . generally opposed the Vietnam War, favored the decriminalization of marijuana, appeared sympathetic to environmental and consumer causes, and supported civil rights for black Americans and greater equality for women" (Berman 9). This new class emerged from the youth culture of the 1960s, and its values remained at odds with those of the socially conservative white working class. The repercussions for American politics were vast, most notably in the alienation from the Democratic Party of many socially conservative (and largely working-class) northeastern Democrats, a constituency that had been essential to the party's success since Franklin Roosevelt's New Deal. Conservative Republicans were quick to seize the opportunity provided by this break in Democratic ranks, and a strategy evolved from Nixon's victory in 1968 by which northern Catholic blue-collar voters would align themselves with discontented white southerners in the sunbelt, and a new Republican majority would be created by stressing traditional social and moral values, rejecting the counterculture, and renouncing big government programs, especially those tied to race (Berman 9–10). By late 1980, with the election of Ronald Reagan to the Presidency of the United States, it appeared that the strategy had worked.

The conservative victory was more than political, however. In *Culture Wars: The Struggle to Define America* (1991), James Davison Hunter attributes to the electoral process the symbolic value of allowing citizens to "embrace or reject certain symbols of national life." He continues, "[I]n the final analysis, candidates . . . run principally on the basis of the symbols of collective life with which they identify." In fact, over time, candidates become symbols of community ideals: "In this light, elections can be seen as rituals regularly enacted through which ordinary people select the ideals of their life together—ultimately, the ideals of what America is and should be" (272–73). Nowhere is the validity of Hunter's assertion more readily demonstrated than in the 1980 presidential election. Ronald

Reagan, governor of California from 1967 to 1975 and a vocal opponent of the New Left and counterculture,[2] emerged as the Republican nomination for president. He aligned himself with cultural conservatives, both Republican and Democrat. President Jimmy Carter remained the banner carrier for liberal and progressive values. For voters, the lines in the culture war were clearly drawn.

Unfortunately for Carter and the Democratic Party, by the mid-1970s the coalition of blacks, women, Jews, organized labor, and environmentalists—which had undergirded progressive policies pursued by the federal government during the 1960s—was badly fragmented, and the constituent parts, far from unified, were often at odds with one another. As Berman (42–43) notes, this Democratic coalition was unable to offer a program with which a majority of voters could identify. Faced with the singular purpose symbolized by Ronald Reagan and the conservative Republican platform, and a cacophonous chorus from the Democrats, voters selected Ronald Reagan over Carter in a landslide, ushering in twelve years of Republican and conservative domination of the executive and judicial branches of government.

Thus, in early December 1980, with Reagan's inauguration just over a month away, it must have seemed to many of those who had "stormed the barricades" during the 1960s that their world was, metaphorically speaking, coming to an end. Certainly, their opponents viewed Reagan's ascendancy as an opportunity to vindicate socially conservative values, and as a rejection of 1960s-era liberalism. Emblematic of the conservative critique, Terry Eastland (now the publisher of the conservative publication *The Weekly Standard*), writing in *Commentary* in June 1981, offered this indictment: "If the liberalism of the 60's has a definite legacy, it is found in the far more liberalized and hedonistic lives many Americans, including many older Americans, and indeed many political conservatives, now lead." Equally significant, there had been a change in "ethical *thinking*," with moral education lacking the "virtues of courage, temperance, prudence" (Eastland 43). As far as many social conservatives were concerned, the public mourning of Lennon was not to go unchallenged. Dorothy Rabinowitz, also writing in *Commentary*, criticized television coverage of the silent vigil held for Lennon in Central Park, condemning the "spate of unabashedly reverent reflections on their own youthfulness expressed by the mourners, reflections broadcast with a confidence suggesting that the world at large was no less preoccupied with the subject than they were themselves" (Rabinowitz 60).

Rabinowitz's critique could have been applied to much of the mainstream media. *People* opened its portrait of the artist, "In Praise of John Lennon: The Liverpool Lad as Musician, Husband, Father and Man," by noting, "As a voice of change in music and society, John Lennon never backed away from risk, in his work or in his life" ("In Praise" 27). The magazine's assessment reflected the tone of much of the comment in the mainstream press. Lennon was presented as encompassing the best of the 1960s generation as a man, as a father, as a husband, and as an artist. Where his failings were noted, he yet remained a sympathetic figure. Yes, he had strayed: There was the so-called "lost weekend" of the mid-1970s[3] and the concurrent affair with May Pang. There was his admitted abuse of women, as well as his well-known experimentation with recreational and addictive drugs. Nevertheless, all was forgiven, for he had come back to true love with Yoko (and son Sean), and the joys of househusbandry. The great tragedy for many was that, with his first album in five years on the record shelves (*Double Fantasy*), and his resumption of a public life, Lennon was poised to take up the mantle of the semi-dormant peace movement and reinvigorate his lately moribund social activism.[4] Even those without a political or philosophical axe to grind were critical of the ubiquity of this narrative and the "end of an era" stance taken by so many commentators. Harry Stein, in his article "Oh, Grow Up!" appearing in *Esquire* (April 1981), while presenting a fond recollection of Lennon and the

Beatles, bemoaned the mainstream-press insistence on characterizing Lennon's death as the "end of our youth" (Stein 18).

Commentators on the left tried to draw something positive from the tragedy. In doing so they touched on the very things that infuriated conservatives, including Lennon's opposition to the Vietnam conflict and his involvement in the peace movement. An editorial in *The Nation* noted, without the hyperbole which tainted so much of the mainstream's coverage, that Lennon "opened up rock and roll for politics, and in an innocent, impulsive way, he worked for peace. Young people loved him for that and the music. Not so young now, they are behaving as though a President had been killed. An unacknowledged President who stood for peace." It continued, "it would be a far better remembrance of John Lennon to work for the peace movement he believed in than to long nostalgically for the decade he symbolized" ("Lennon Has a Legacy" 657). Todd Gitlin, once the president of the Students for a Democratic Society, countered the right's less than charitable remarks concerning the death and mourning in an essay appearing in *The Center Magazine*: "In the week after he was assassinated, some mourners were certain that their sixties, holding on through a long illness, had finally died. For others, keeping silence in the cold in Central Park and around the world, a big question mark hovered. Could it be that this vast longing for peace, and lightness, and a solidarity that is not based on anyone's misery, that this force of, yes, love which had once seemingly come out of nowhere and turned so many lives upside down, could it be in some crazy way that its time, which had once come, could come again?" (Gitlin, "Lennon Legacy" 4). Even for a sixties radical, a member of the New Left that had lamented the Beatles' failure to take a leading role in its efforts against the establishment, "love"—so much a part of the worldview of the counterculture at its apex—remained precious. For many, the Beatles represented an ideal, a focal point for their memories and a catalyst for so many of the experiences of their youth. For others, however, they were emblematic of a culture that had lost its moral compass. The Beatles' image had meaning for both advocates and critics of the social transformation of the 1960s, and continued to resonate with the public at the time of Lennon's murder in 1980. A quarter century after his death, and nearly four decades after the breakup of the band, the image continues to capture the imagination of the American public.

The Beatles, of course, have remained very public figures. McCartney followed in the footsteps of Cliff Richard and George Martin when knighted in 1997. His publishing interests have made him one of the richest men in the world, even though he does not own the rights to his own Beatles music. He has continued to play to packed coliseums and stadiums throughout the world. Always the "cute" Beatle, in his sixties he remains "safe": In February, 2005, the National Football League contracted with McCartney to play the Super Bowl halftime show; the League was not about to allow another "wardrobe malfunction"[5] to sully its reputation and undermine its status as a family entertainment.

McCartney retained his commitment to an alternative lifestyle—on at least one occasion with disastrous consequences. Always a proponent of the legalization of marijuana, he was incarcerated in Japan for a short time in 1980 after being arrested for bringing the substance into the country at the start of a tour by his band, Wings. Lucky to be released without the ordeal of a trial, he continued to enjoy the plant's calming effects, and reportedly swore off marijuana only after the birth of his daughter, Beatrice Milly, in 2003.

Generally, McCartney's advocacy of countercultural values, while often newsworthy, has been measured. While perhaps less dedicated to publicly promoting drug use, McCartney has nevertheless demonstrated his countercultural sensibilities numerous times. He and wife Linda McCartney supported People for the Ethical Treatment of Animals (PETA), the largest animal rights organization in the world. Additionally, Linda introduced her own line of vegetarian meals, which continue to be sold after her death in 1998. Remarried in 2002, McCartney and wife Heather Mills became vocal opponents of the use of landmines, and participated in numerous other causes before their separation in 2006. He has also turned his attention to his hometown, Liverpool, where he opened the Liverpool Institute for Performing Arts in 1996.

In addition to the causes McCartney has taken up, he has also become iconic of the freedom and sense of community that permeated the counterculture. He closed the Live Aid show in 1985 with "Let It Be," and twenty years later opened the Live 8 concert in London, playing "Sgt. Pepper's Lonely Hearts Club Band" ("It was twenty years ago today . . .") with U2 singer Bono, and closed the program that night, leading the day's performers and the Hyde Park audience in a rendition of "Hey Jude." In 2003, he and his band played in Moscow; the DVD that followed, *Paul McCartney Live in Red Square*, captured his show and reminiscences by Russians who had developed their own counterculture in the 1960s, and for whom the Beatles had become the supreme model.

McCartney has continued his musical evolution and, as in the Beatles, his solo career has been marked by experimentation: In the 1980s, he collaborated with Michael Jackson, then Elvis Costello. In the 1990s, he teamed with Carl Davis in composing the generally well-received *Liverpool Oratorio*; he also released two albums of ambient music recorded with Mark Glover, of the UK band Killing Joke, under the name "the Fireman." In 2005, McCartney released *Twin Freaks*, a double album of remixes by one of England's premier DJs, remixers, and producers, the Freelance Hellraiser.

Like McCartney, Starr and Harrison continued to pursue lives imbued with the countercultural values of their youth. Starr, whose All Starr Band composed of rock luminaries continues to draw crowds, has continued to record. Starr released *Ringo Rama* in 2003 and *Choose Love* in 2005. Both musically harken back to the heyday of British psychedelia. Starr has never strayed far from the "flower power" of the 1960s, and is as likely to flash a peace sign today as he was during the Summer of Love. Harrison, as discussed, was out-spoken in promoting countercultural values as a Beatle. In the years after the group disbanded, Harrison remained committed to the values he had held in the 1960s. He became an adherent of the Hare Krishna tradition and, in 1973, donated a mansion to the International Society for Krishna Consciousness that continues to house the Society's headquarters for the United Kingdom. He continued to be associated with the Society throughout his life.

In the 1960s, Harrison played an instrumental role in popularizing non-Western music among Western youth after studying sitar with Indian sitar virtuoso, Ravi Shankar. The two struck up a lifelong friendship. In 1971, Shankar brought the plight of flood-ravaged Bangladesh to Harrison's attention. Harrison organized a charity benefit concert at New York's Madison Square Garden that brought together numerous rock luminaries, including Harrison, Starr, the reclusive Bob Dylan, Eric Clapton, Badfinger, Billy Preston, and Leon Russell, for two performances. Importantly, Harrison pioneered the whole idea of rock concert as fund-raiser, and the Concert for Bangladesh was a forerunner of the Live Aid (1985), Farm Aid (held annually since 1985), and Live 8 (2005) concerts. Harrison's effort initially lost money due to mismanagement and expenses, though the triple-album box set and feature film and video have brought $15,000,000 to the United Nations Children's Emergency Fund (UNICEF) over the years (UNICEF). It was rereleased in 2005 on CD and DVD. Proceeds still go to UNICEF.

Harrison battled lung cancer throughout the 1990s before finally succumbing to the illness that had metastasized to his brain, in 2001. Upon his death, his family released the following statement: "He left this world as he lived in it, conscious of God, fearless of death and at peace, surrounded by family and friends. He often said, 'Everything else can wait, but the search of God cannot wait, and love one another.'" His commitment to the most basic countercultural ideal remained: "He died with one thought in mind—love one another," said friend Gavin De Becker, at whose Los Angeles home Harrison died ("Beatle George Harrison Dies"). Harrison's image as the spiritual Beatle helped fuel the whole new age movement and he remained an icon for anti-materialism for an entire generation. His final album *Brainwashed*, released posthumously, showed that Harrison hadn't strayed far from his Beatle self; he still cautioned of the dangers of living in the aspiritual material world.

The Beatles continue to be a commercial force. In 2005, the Festival for Beatles Fans, a yearly gathering of fans, scholars, old Beatlehands, and other interested parties, celebrated its twenty-ninth year. A cottage industry has arisen around the Beatles, with hundreds of books, movies, recordings and various ephemera available on the market. *Beatles 1*, a collection of the Beatles' number one hits released in 2000, is well positioned to become the best-selling album of all time. Fans can take Beatle walking tours of New York, London, and Liverpool. Nearly four decades after the fact, the Beatles remain an amazing success story, or, as Derek Taylor put it, "the twentieth century's greatest romance."[6] But what of the image?

I write with the experience of teaching a course on the culture of rock music. Today's college students, born a decade and more after the breakup of the band, are fascinated by the phenomenon of the Beatles. Many of my female students will admit that they and their girlfriends had a "crush" on the band while in high school or junior high. When I show *A Hard Day's Night*, or footage from the *Sullivan* programs, the students' attention is rapt, just like mine. For my students, there is a sense that the music of the 1960s, as opposed to much of the current output of the music industry, had "something to say," that it mattered.

Today, rock and roll music has become a device in commercials advertising everything from Cadillacs to credit cards. The recordings of the Who, Led Zeppelin, the Rolling Stones, Eric Clapton, and many more have all been employed by advertisers attempting to exploit the rebellious connotations of the music for their own profit.

The Beatles' music has remained beyond commercial exploitation of this type. Of course, Michael Jackson and Capitol Records[7] licensed the Beatles' "Revolution" to Nike for a commercial in 1987. The surviving Beatles brought suit against Nike and Capitol, but admittedly had very little power to stop use of the recording. The fans would have none of it, however, and public outcry culminated in Nike dropping the campaign. Since then, there have been only minor efforts to employ Beatles' music in advertising. "Beatlepeople" abound, and Beatles fans continue to champion their heroes. But why? What is the connection that continues to be guarded so tenaciously? I offer the following concluding remarks about the image and its continued popularity.

The Beatles' success signaled the shift to a market catering to youth and an increasingly youth-obsessed culture. Their image evolved to account for this success; it also evolved to reflect more clearly the values of the Beatles. At first, the Beatles were introduced to America according to a model with a pedigree—their image conformed to requirements of the star-making machine first perfected in Hollywood and transferred to the music industry. In 1963, the teen idol reigned supreme, and so the Beatles were marketed. Their image, a result of the processes of standardization and pseudo-individualization befitting a product of the culture industries, was designed to elicit identification from its intended audience, and so promoted the band members' ordinariness and working-class backgrounds. At the same time, the Beatles were differentiated from other teen idols, primarily through their "Britishness," revealed in their jargon and speech, and their appearance, notably their long hair. As described in chapter 2, the American myth of success had been integrated into the Hollywood star-making apparatus and had become a standardized part of the promotion of the star long before the arrival of the Beatles. The band's image was crafted to fit this model: all from modest backgrounds, these four working-class lads made it out of the tough port city of Liverpool by pursuing their shared dream of becoming rock and roll musicians, and through sheer will and hard work (and a little luck) achieved success beyond their wildest dreams. Their story validated a positive reading of the myth.

The Beatles' vaunted humor quickly differentiated them from their competition. Never before had the public witnessed such casual, if good-natured, disrespect and irreverence. From the start, a certain amount of cheekiness was expected from the band. This irreverence, so important to the early image, allowed them a bit of leeway when they transgressed the boundaries; Beatle banter made good press. It also opened up a space for the evolution of the image. They could be critical of the establishment without seeming dangerous. Constant prodding by the press eventually drew the band into dialogue on the great issues of the time, including racism and the conflict in Vietnam. Perhaps no event demonstrated more fully the loosening of the restrictions on the speech of youth-oriented entertainers and their fans than did Lennon's declaration that the Beatles were more popular than Jesus Christ—which, while met with a good deal of antagonism in some quarters, was more apt to be forgiven as youthful indiscretion, or accepted as essentially true. For the Beatles, the event liberated the group to project a more authentic image of themselves, one more consistent with the evolving self-image of much of its audience.

Once touring ended, the Beatles took on even greater importance for the counterculture and those adapting aspects of that lifestyle to their own: They became the most visible proponents of countercultural values, "beautiful people" advocating a new consciousness based in Eastern meditative philosophies, expansive notions of love, the exploration of alternative lifestyles, and the liberal use of drugs. At the same time, their commercial dominance guaranteed that their views would be widely distributed and discussed. In the wake of *Sgt. Pepper's Lonely Hearts Club Band*, the youth audience witnessed the legitimization of their culture's art and, thereby, aspects of their culture, as establishment intellectuals declared the importance of the Beatles as artists and as a cultural force. Important to the evolution of the Beatles' image and its continued resonance with audiences was the resoluteness with which they maintained their countercultural values, even as those values fell out of favor with an increasingly radicalized youth culture. Lennon's dialogue with the editors of London's revolutionary socialist newspaper, *Black Dwarf*, in 1969 (discussed in chapter 5), captures perfectly the chasm that was widening between committed lifestyle counterculturalists and the New Left radicals attempting to force political change.

An important factor in the Beatles' continued success and influence throughout the 1960s was their ability to mature with their audience. Appearing first in early 1964, bringing cheer to the young people of a nation still mourning a fallen president, they were introduced as young, clean-cut, "safe" teen idols singing catchy boy-loves-girl songs to adolescent females. Just three years later, they were leaders of the counterculture and being celebrated as artists of the first order. This evolution—this maturation—was made possible by, among other things, the self-sufficiency of the band, particularly the ability of Lennon and McCartney to write commercially and critically successful songs. Certainly, the pair's mastery of the ballad provided inroads into the marketplace and the realm of art. McCartney quickly graduated from writing songs like "Thank You Girl" to "Yesterday," the most covered song in history, before expanding his artistic palette even further with "Eleanor Rigby," and its string octet, and the complexity of the albums that followed. Lennon, prodded forward by Dylan, quickly came to treat his songwriting as an act of self-revelation, and his role as that of the artist. As the Beatles matured and their music grew in complexity, Lennon's and McCartney's (and Harrison's) abilities as composers allowed them to retain a close relationship with their audience, which was also maturing: The Beatles introduced new ideas at the same time that their core audience of baby boomers was primed to explore those ideas as they entered young adulthood, attended college, found jobs, and for the first time, perhaps, considered their place in the scheme of things.[8] The Beatles' perceived artistic competence was an important part of their continued appeal for an audience whose members were themselves undergoing the intellectual journey that accompanies the passage into adulthood. The band's establishment of rock music as art among establishment critics and recognized cultural authorities was an essential part of the self-definition of the youth culture—particularly the counterculture as displayed in the pages of Rolling Stone.

As described in chapter 4, within the Beatles' image artistry walked hand in hand with opposition. The image developed first as an affirmation of the American myth of success, the notion that the United States is a land of limitless opportunity and social mobility. The veracity of the myth has always been at issue, however. As noted by Weiss (1969), the myth is a "two-edged sword," on one hand encouraging complacency within a system perceived to be just, on the other standing as a marker of "what ought to be" and encouraging reform (Weiss 7). These two readings evince radically different ideological positions. The affirmative reading is based around notions of the rewards due those living by the ethical maxims of "industry, frugality, and prudence," as exemplified in early-twentieth-century media representations of industrialists such as John D. Rockefeller, J. P. Morgan, and Henry Ford, self-made men whose success resulted from right living encapsulated in the maxims of the Protestant work ethic (Weiss 5). The paradigm of the self-made man was integrated into the Hollywood star machine and was central to the creation of the star.

An oppositional reading finds within the myth of success the very means of its refutation, for the myth can be viewed as a baseline against which social realities can be measured. In fact, the Beatles' early image, the one most perfectly modeled after the dominant, ideology-affirming model, and the one most controlled by Capitol, quickly gave way to one incorporating more "authentic" qualities consistent with the Beatles' perceptions of themselves and, then, one imbued with the countercultural values that they came to hold from the middle of the decade. The latter embodied a critique of the social values of an establishment viewed as alienating, stifling, exploitive, and voracious in its appetite for profit and power. The counterculture questioned the very premise that one should even strive to be "self-made"; rather, the effort was "to be." Specifically, the effort was to achieve an authentic self beyond the machinations of straight society and the establishment.

The new, post-touring image that debuted in late 1966 was a declaration by the Beatles of their status as "beautiful people" and of their membership in the counterculture. Suddenly, the affable, clean-cut, cheeky "Fab Four" of the Beatles' early image was eclipsed by a more authentic version that incorporated their opposition to the establishment and its institutions. The "new" Beatles released "Penny Lane"/"Strawberry Fields Forever" in February 1967; *Sgt. Pepper's Lonely Hearts Club Band* came next, then their performance of "All You Need Is Love" before a global television audience, followed by the film *Magical Mystery Tour*. All reflected countercultural preoccupations. The Beatles, as "beautiful people," envisioned a hippie utopia in which the traditional institutions of control, such as the state and church, would be altered to foster the intellectual and spiritual development of the individual. The Beatles criticized a society they viewed as antithetical to the individual reaching their full potential, and which alienated people from one another. The Beatles' countercultural values were displayed in their long locks and facial hair, the clothes they wore, their promotion of experimentation with alternative lifestyles and drug use, and their exploration of alternative belief systems to the Judeo-Christian tradition. Their counterculture credentials were also on display in their abortive attempt to create in Apple Corps a "kind of western communism."[9] The Beatles' image could entertain both readings of the American myth of success: the positive celebration of America as a land of opportunity, so central to the Beatles' early image, as well as a progressive critique of a society viewed as alienating and stultifying to individual expression and development.

While the Beatles' image evolved to incorporate the countercultural values held by the band, the band's oppositional status was based around an ideal of youthful rebellion; while enjoying apparently universal appeal, their image was receptive to an oppositional, or "us versus them," interpretation from the start. Recall the reaction of one young fan in February, 1964, who was attracted by the Beatles' "toughness": "They're tough. . . . Tough is like when you don't conform." Further, while the mania of the Beatles' early success was tolerated by many adults as just a harmless expression of youth, the reaction of young female fans to any appearance by the band can be viewed as a first protest against the strictures of a male-dominated culture by many of those who joined the women's movement later in the decade, as did Ehrenreich, Hess, and Jacobs (1992).

To a large extent, the "rebellion" inherent in the Beatles' image was voiced in terms of feelings and ideals. The image held symbolic value that extended across a wide spectrum of American life. An examination of the symbolism of the Yellow Submarine is an informative case in point. Initially a novelty sung by Ringo Starr and released in August 1966, by the end of the year the "Yellow Submarine" was picked up by student activists as a symbol of unity (as discussed in chapter 3). Later, after release of the *Yellow Submarine* film, it even became a symbol for so-called "submarine churches" in the United States,[10] as noted by William O'Neill in *Coming Apart: An Informal History of America in the 1960s* (1971). One church leader commented, "In the Beatles' movie the submarine was the place where they loved each other in a groovy way and got strength to do battle with the Blue Meanies. It also shows that a Church has to have flexibility and maneuverability" (O'Neill 317)—not unlike the Beatles' image. Another glimpse into the capacity of the image to encompass both unifying and oppositional qualities is found in an October 1969 incident in which Capitol policemen dragged a man out of the U.S. House of Representatives after he had unfurled a banner that read "Beatle Power," described in small print as a "fun loving movement toward world peace" ("Banner Unfurled" 10). The Beatles' image might signal protest for some, but it did so while affirming the joy of being alive and promoting a sense of unity.

With the Beatles' self-assertion of a more "real" and adult image in early 1967, the opposition manifested within the image held the promise of a life unencumbered by the banalities of an adult workaday existence, one based around idyllic notions of community and universal love. Even when called upon to comment or take a stand on issues of importance to the young, the Beatles did so from a detached position—advocating ideals, as a child might, but lacking a program for practical implementation. This, of course, was the source of their falling out with the New Left, displayed in the "Dear John Letters" episode (1969). As Tom Hayden, one of the founders of the SDS, later said, "I was in confrontations. I wanted those people [the Beatles and other musicians] to join the confrontation" (The Beatles Revolution). The Beatles, committed counterculturalists, were unable to shed their apathy to politics, and remained outside of the political fray. Lennon would take up radical politics, but only for a short time in the early 1970s (a move that he later called a mistake).

Their countercultural aversion to politics aside, it is clearly the case that the Beatles simply were not up to leading a revolution. Not sharing the viewpoint of the radicals, they possessed neither the will nor the energy necessary to such an undertaking. Even before abstaining from the political process as a hippie, Lennon, a Labor supporter, often told journalist Ray Coleman that he would have to vote Conservative if he did participate, because, after all, "you've got to protect your money" (Coleman 232). Hardly a ringing endorsement for the overthrow of western capitalism. Harrison, of course, had made his views crystal clear on the 1966 recording, "Taxman," a song that criticized the huge portion of money being taken out of the Beatles' till by England's tax code. Harrison was always the most aware of the Beatles' finances and was trusted to keep the others informed (Barrow 53). McCartney, too, aggressively pursued acceptance within the establishment, using his romance with Jane Asher as an introduction into London's upper crust. It is difficult to imagine the Beatles (or any of the pop aristocracy, for that matter) looking for the complete dismantling of the system they had striven so hard to master. Just as importantly, by the end of 1968 the band was beginning to come undone. Only with the greatest effort were they able to reunite in the studio for recording. Their private time was spent away from "the Beatles," in pursuit of their own interests and lives away from the band. Rumors circulated with greater frequency and credibility that the band was splitting up.

In this atmosphere, two television broadcasts from 1970 capture the vast appeal that the band still enjoyed. In March, amid rumors of the band's breakup, Ed Sullivan presented *The Beatles Songbook*, a program intended to highlight the music of the band through interpretations by respected (mostly) performers from across the performing arts. Included was a performance, to the accompaniment of the Beatles' recording of "Lucy in the Sky with Diamonds," by Edward Villella, the principal male dancer for the New York City Ballet. Torch singer Peggy Lee sang "Maxwell's Silver Hammer," and jazz legend Duke Ellington performed a medley including "She Loves You," "All My Loving," "Eleanor Rigby," "She's Leaving Home," and "Norwegian Wood." Pop singer Dionne Warwick sang "We Can Work It Out" and joined Lee for a duet on "Yesterday," accompanied by footage of McCartney's performance of the song on the *Ed Sullivan Show* in 1965. The highlight was the somewhat disturbing spectacle of Steve Lawrence and Eydie Gorme performing "Can't Buy Me Love," complete with Sinatra-esque revisions of the lyrics: "I'll buy you a diamond ring my love like the one Dick bought for Liz[11] / I'll buy you anything my love as long as you ain't his" (*Ed Sullivan: Beatle Songbook*).

Far away from this showbiz tribute was that of Nam June Paik. In August 1970, just months after McCartney's April announcement that he was suing to end the Beatles, WGBH-TV (Boston's public broadcasting company) teamed with Paik, the "father of video art," to produce the four-hour long "Video Commune: Beatles from Beginning to End—An Experiment for Television," which utilized one of his inventions, a video synthesizer. Paik, an artist associated with the Fluxus[12] movement, combined live mixes of videotapes and camera images with the music of the Beatles. Consistent with his past "happenings,"[13] he also invited people off the street to take part in the creation of this new television art. Pictures mixed live from completed videotapes and camera images were shown to the accompaniment of Beatles music. The program invited the viewer to "do your own thing and treat it (the visual and aural display) like electronic wallpaper or like a light show" (Paik). These two radically different broadcasts indicate the wide appeal the band still enjoyed—for much of the country located between Ed Sullivan's middle America and Paik's avant-garde coterie, the Beatles remained of interest and continued to be important.

Because the Beatles' image never took on the aura of radicalism, and because it encapsulated a countercultural ideal, it retained a nostalgic connection to youth, even for those who were radicalized at the end of the 1960s. In any event, one should not overestimate the appeal of the radicals. Despite the growing popularity of the New Left as the decade came to an end, most students and young people were not radicalized. Rather than advocate a complete restructuring of society, many of those sympathetic to aspects of the New Left program opted instead to abide by a widely accepted code of ethics, defined by Whalen and Flacks (1989) to include avoidance of complicity with the "war machine" by eschewing of employment within the defense industry or multinational corporations, and organizing one's life so that it not be "part of the problem," including declining employment with environmental polluters and firms that "rip people off." Many also resolved not to cooperate with the draft (13). For these people, the Beatles' absence at the barricades was less likely to be viewed as a failure on their part. Further, as Todd Gitlin's comments on Lennon's death, discussed above, demonstrate, at least anecdotally, even New Left activists who had once criticized the Beatles' political inertia could look back fondly, and hopefully, on the ideal embodied in the Beatles' image and zeitgeist of the times.

For many observers, the failure of a revolution to emerge out of the pop world undoubtedly demonstrates the victory of the system. The New Left failed in its efforts to force a revolution, and much of its support evaporated with the U.S. withdrawal from Vietnam in early 1973. In starkest terms, for these critics the culture industries theorized by Horkheimer and Adorno produced an audience incapable of questioning the machinations of those industries or those of the interests which they serve. They produced a mass consciousness manipulated to remove the possibility of critical thinking. The audience was, claimed Adorno, "forcibly retarded" (Adorno, "On the Fetish Character" 41). The culture industries occupy and mollify, creating a complacent audience lacking the mental faculties to challenge the authoritarian system under which it toils. Adorno, though writing into the 1960s, never altered this view of the culture industries in any substantial way. Others have countered his position, considering it pedantic and unsustainable given the oppositional content of much of the culture of the 1960s and that which followed. Nevertheless, it is impossible to deny that the mass media was far more inclined to filter the issues of the day through pop musicians viewed as a safe alternative than to give voice to the student radicals. And these pop musicians tended to approach society's ills as the product of a false consciousness: If one wanted to change society, one had to change minds first. The radicals required something more direct—and more of a threat to the stability embraced by the establishment. As a result, as noted by Gitlin (1980), they were framed by the media in such a way as to discredit their efforts. The love-laden and apolitical priorities of the Beatles were far more palatable to the powers that be, and for that reason were far more likely to receive a mass hearing.

Such a narrow understanding of revolution, however, obfuscates the revolution in consciousness inaugurated by the Beatles. They did not attempt to overturn the system, but they did envision something more benign. That is, the Beatles and their contemporaries, while not wishing to overthrow the capitalist project, nevertheless intended that it be more responsive to human needs, whether of a functional nature (food, shelter), or something less tangible, such as spiritual and intellectual development. The Beatles' image encapsulated this effort.

In 1995, with the broadcast of the *Anthology* series on ABC, Harrison, McCartney, and Starr once again reinvented the Beatles. Much as they had in 1967, the Beatles revealed a new image. The *Anthology*, not simply an appeal to nostalgia, was an attempt to "set the record straight." It is tempting, perhaps, to view the results as a self-serving sanitization of the Beatles' story. Gone is the strife within the band, and tales of infighting, drug excess, and neuroses, which were publicized in numerous books, magazine articles, and television interviews, particularly after Lennon's death. Missing, too, is the well-documented hostility between the remaining Beatles and Yoko Ono, whom onetime Beatle confidant Tony Bramwell referred to as "the artist of mass destruction" in his 2005 memoir of life with the band, *Magical Mystery Tours* (Bramwell 171). For some commentators the omissions are too many, and the documentary tends to be viewed by them as crassly commercial at the expense of candor.[14] Yet, at worst, the Beatles' sins are sins of omission. The story they choose to tell is no more fantastic than what the record reveals. Their commercial achievements and cultural impact were widely attested to in the 1960s, and are no less so at the dawn of the twenty-first century.

To view the *Anthology* (or its companion book) as mere self-promotion or nostalgia is, perhaps, to miss its most significant aspect: As in the 1960s, the Beatles, their art, and their image, remain above all else life-affirming. The image the Beatles proposed in this last great joint effort harkened back to the halcyon days of 1967 and the Summer of Love. McCartney, still one of the "beautiful people," offered a fitting coda to the story: "I'm really glad that most of the songs dealt with love, peace, understanding. . . . It's all very 'All You Need is Love' or John's 'Give Peace a Chance.' There was a good spirit behind it all, which I'm very proud of. Anyway . . . It were a grand thing, The Beatles."[15]

Yes, it were.

NOTES

PREFACE

1. Ledbetter, Les. "John Lennon of Beatles is Killed; Suspect Held in Shooting at Dakota." *New York Times* 9 December 1980: B7; in another story on B7, "Crowds of Lennon Fans Gather Quickly at the Dakota and Hospital," the total was put at one thousand mourners at the two locations.

2. For our purposes, "Beatlemania" refers to the extreme hysterical reaction of the Beatles' young female fans prompted by any appearance of the band. It is primarily a feature of the touring years, especially from late 1963 to 1966, though the reaction, on a smaller scale, continued to accompany any public appearance by band members throughout their careers, both as Beatles and solo artists.

1. "THE TWENTIETH CENTURY'S GREATEST ROMANCE": IMAGINING THE BEATLES

1. We are concerned here with the image's resonance for an essentially white audience. As Nelson George notes in his history of music and black culture, *The Death of Rhythm and Blues* (1988), by 1965 rock and roll had become white music made for a white audience. There were blacks that listened to the Beatles and other rock and roll acts, but just as rock and roll music had become essential to the youth culture of whites, soul music had become integral to black youth culture (George 106–8).

2. Dyer, in defining the source materials for the image (60–63), notes the importance of film in development of the film star image. I have substituted "work product" for this category, because the Beatles' career, and therefore image, encompassed work in sound recording, on film and video, and various other pursuits, all of which contributed to the evolving image. Christine Gledhill,

in her introduction to *Stardom: Industry of Desire* (1991), a collection growing out of Dyer's pioneering work, defines the star, a mechanism of identification for the audience, as "an intertextual construct produced across a range
of media and cultural practices" (Gledhill xiv–xv).

3. Of the four, only Starr was actually working class. Lennon, Harrison, and
McCartney came from modest but middle-class backgrounds, though they
clearly identified with the working class and posed a northerner's critique of
the London establishment's dominance of British society.

4. The approach was popularized in works such as *Elements of Semiology*
(1967), *S/Z* (1970), and *Mythologies* (1972), which offered analyses of subjects ranging from literature to fashion.

5. In 1923, the "Frankfurt School" was formed at the newly founded Institute
for Social Research in Frankfurt, Germany. Theodor Adorno, Leo Lowen-
thal, Friedrich Pollack, Mark Horkheimer, and Herbert Marcuse, were
among the Marxist intellectuals gathered at the Institute. They, with affili-
ated intellectuals including Walter Benjamin, developed "critical theory"
as a powerful critique of Western capitalist societies. The Frankfurt School
formed in response to the general failure of revolutionary movements in Europe and the United States. Escaping Nazi Germany in the early 1930s, the
members of the School migrated to Great Britain and the United States,
where they witnessed the full extent of the rise of mass culture in film, radio, music, television, and advertisement. Their critique of capitalism and
mass culture continued into the 1960s; *One-Dimensional Man*, published
in 1964, propelled its author, Herbert Marcuse, into the vanguard of New
Left radicalism.

6. In June 2005, forty-one years after the murders, a Philadelphia, Mississippi,
jury convicted an eighth Klansman, Edgar Ray Killen, of three counts of
manslaughter for his leadership role in the crimes.

7. *Beatles Anthology*, vol. 8 (VHS), sleeve notes.

2. "LADIES AND GENTLEMEN, THE BEATLES!":
INTRODUCING THE IMAGE

1. EP: Extended play vinyl records containing more songs than a single but
fewer than an album, typically four or more tracks, which are played, like
singles, at 45 revolutions per minute (rpm).

2. Acker Bilk, the trad jazz clarinetist, had success with "Stranger On the

Shore," which reached number one on the *Billboard* singles charts in May, 1962 (Whitburn, *Billboard's Top 10* 77). Laurie London's "He's Got the Whole World in His Hands" reached number one in 1958 (Spizer, *Beatles' Story, Part I* 5–8).

3. The offending incident involved a joke about the meaning of "W.C." An English woman, planning a trip, had written her prospective host and queried as to whether or not her lodgings would have a W.C. ("water closet," or toilet). Far from fluent in English, the host eventually, and wrongly, determined that "w.c." meant "wayside chapel" and responded that they do indeed have a w.c., but that it was likely to be quite crowded on the two days a week that it was open. The NBC censors cut the joke from the show. The following night, Paar went on stage and, criticizing the censors' decision, left the show (McNeil 853).

4. Christine Keeler, along with Mandy Rice-Davies, figured in a sex scandal involving a British cabinet minister, the Conservative Secretary of State for War, John Profumo. Profumo ultimately resigned in disgrace. Further, public hostility toward Prime Minister Harold MacMillan, arising out of his failure to remove Profumo from the cabinet in a timely fashion, was a factor in the Prime Minister's resignation. The scandal riveted British attention during the summer and fall of 1963.

5. Two other items, both by Clive Barnes, appeared in the *New York Times* in December 1963. One noted the appearance of "long-haired youths" who have "created a cult of clothes, haircuts and conversation, and are responsible for a craze of girlish screaming that Frank Sinatra might have envied." These youths were the patrons of Liverpool's Cavern Club, which is notable, for "from its depths emerged the Beatles" ("Liverpool Cellars" 34). The other item detailed the production, in London, of a ballet inspired by the music of the Beatles ("Teen-Age Craze" 41).

6. Before Starr, drummers, even when not obscured by the star, were still little more than sidemen: imagine D. J. Fontana, Presley's drummer when he appeared on the Sullivan show in September 1956, or Jerry Allison from Buddy Holly's and the Crickets on the same show in December 1957 (Bryant). Starr transcended the sideman status and enjoyed equal status to his bandmates, to that point unheard-of in rock and roll.

7. See also Ray Coleman, *Lennon*. 1984. New York: McGraw-Hill, 1986, 522. Norman further notes that even "Elvis Presley, and his scandalous torso, in 1957, did not attract so big a response" (*Shout* 218).

8. Teddy boys were a youth subculture that developed in the United Kingdom during the 1950s. "Teds" sported Edwardian style clothes and listened to rock and roll music. They were often associated with juvenile delinquency.

9. *The Deputy*, a 1963 play alleging that Pope Pius and the German clergy had betrayed European Jewry, caused a great deal of controversy, leading the Vatican to release volumes of documents exonerating the Church. The play had just begun a nine month run at Broadway's Brooks Atkinson Theatre at the time of this letter ("Rolf Hochhuth"). The play's German author, Rolf Hochhuth (b. 1931), would stoke further controversy with *Soldiers* (1967), which implicated Winston Churchill in the firebombing of civilians during World War II.

10. At this time, as noted in the *Life* article, the film was to be a documentary entitled *Beatlemania*. The film became *A Hard Day's Night*.

11. In 1954, British linguist Alan Strode Campbell Ross coined the terms "U" and "non-U" to distinguish between "U" (i.e., upper class) and all other dialects ("non-U"). The terms reflected growing anxiety over the impact that working-class culture was having on British culture following World War II.

12. In another item, the *New York Times* reported just how helpful the Beatles had become: "According to Barclay's Bank Review, the Liverpool singing group has become an 'invisible' export and made a significant contribution to Britain's balance of payments. The value of exported Beatle records last year came to about $7 million. As the Beatles reputation grew, The Review said, royalties flowed into Britain. The group's foreign tours also funneled some receipts home, 'adding to Britain's gold and foreign reserves'" ("Random Notes From All Over" 11). The Beatles' contribution to the British economy was an important factor in the bestowal upon them of the title Members of the Order of the British Empire, in 1965.

13. Numerous histories detailing the development of rock and roll music are available. Charlie Gillett's *The Sound of the City: The Rise of Rock and Roll* (New York: Outerbridge & Dienstfrey, 1970), now into a second edition (1996), remains one of the best books on the topic. Paul Friedlander's *Rock and Roll: A Social History* (Boulder: Westview Press, 1996) is an informative study, as is James Miller's *Flowers in the Dustbin: The Rise of Rock and Roll, 1947–1977* (New York: Fireside, 1999). *The Rolling Stone History of Rock and Roll* (New York: Random House, 1992), edited by Anthony DeCurtis, with James Henke and Holly George-Warren, continues the work of editor James Miller's first edition, and contains numerous chapters discussing the

history and rock and roll, penned by some of the most influential rock critics of the last three decades.

14. Berry was convicted under the Mann Act of transporting a minor over state
lines for sexual purposes, and served two years in prison. The minor in question was an underage girl he had met in Mexico and brought to his St. Louis
club to work as a hatcheck girl. Berry ran afoul of the St. Louis authorities
and was charged under the act when she was arrested for prostitution.

15. In 1959, at the urging of ASCAP (American Society of Composers, Authors
and Publishers), Congress announced it would hold hearings on "payola,"
the practice of giving money and gifts to disk jockeys in exchange for playing a record. ASCAP charged that Broadcast Music Incorporated (BMI)
was using payola to ensure radio play for BMI artists, who included most of
the black and southern artists popularizing rock and roll, rhythm and blues,
and country and western music. The scandal effectively ended the career of
disk jockey Alan Freed.

16. Jon Fitzgerald notes that relationships figure in more than four in five Lennon-McCartney songs from 1964–66 (Fitzgerald, "Lennon-McCartney . . ."
57).

17. Eliot Tiegel. "British Beatles Hottest Capitol Singles Ever." *Billboard* 18
January 1964: 1.

18. "I Want to Hold Your Hand"/"I Saw Her Standing There" was released
earlier than initially planned when deejays started spinning pressings of the
current British single, "I Want to Hold Your Hand"/"This Boy" (Spizer,
Beatles' Story, Pt. I 29–30).

19. A top ten hit for Pat Boone in 1956, here McCartney delivered the song as a
shouter, complete with Little Richard–esque whoops and screams.

20. With little fanfare or promotion, Capitol rereleased these songs in March
1965 on *The Early Beatles*, after Vee-Jay's rights to its Beatles masters reverted
back to Capitol in October 1964.

21. Of those works speaking directly of the impact of Brill Building pop and
Tin Pan Alley upon the Beatles, see Timothy Scheurer, "The Beatles, the
Brill Building, and the Persistence of Tin Pan Alley in the Age of Rock."
Popular Music and Society vol. 20 no. 4 (1996): 89–102; Jon Fitzgerald,
"When the Brill Building Met Lennon-McCartney: Continuity and Change
in the Early Evolution of the Mainstream Pop Song." *Popular Music and Society* vol. 19 no. 11 (1995): 59–77. For more general discussions of the Beatles'
musical influences and attributes, see Wilfrid Meller's seminal work, *Twi-
light of the Gods: The Music of the Beatles*. New York: Schirmer, 1973; and

Terence O'Grady's *The Beatles: A Musical Evolution*. Boston: Twayne, 1983. Walter Everett's work, *The Beatles as Musicians* (New York: Oxford University Press), published in two volumes in 1999 and 2001, is a landmark of scholarship about the Beatles' music.

22. For instance, Michael Caine was the son of a fish-market porter, Sean Connery was born to a charwoman and truck driver in Edinburgh, Scotland, and Peter O'Toole, born in Ireland but raised in Leeds, was the son of a bookie. And, of course, there were the Beatles and the numerous northern bands that found success in their wake.

23. Gay Talese, *The Kingdom and the Power*, 231.

3. "PREPARING OUR TEENAGERS FOR RIOT AND ULTIMATE REVOLUTION": THE TOURING YEARS, 1964–66

1. The "angry young men" were a group of English writers in the 1950s that focused on the alienating effects of the class system. Taking flight with John Osborne's play *Look Back in Anger* (1956), the movement included Kingsley Amis (*Lucky Jim*, 1953), John Braine (*Room at the Top*, 1957), Alan Sillitoe (*The Loneliness of the Long Distance Runner*, 1959), and Shelagh Delaney (*A Taste of Honey*, 1957), whose works were brought to the screen as social realism was taken up within the British film industry in the late 1950s and early 1960s.

2. "Kitchen sink films," so called because much of the action takes place in the cramped kitchens of the characters' flats, included Jack Clayton's *Room at the Top* (1959), Reisz's *Saturday Night and Sunday Morning* (1960), and Anderson's *The Sporting Life* (1963).

3. See "Police Hide Beatles from 2,500 Fans." *Plain Dealer* 15 September 1964: 1. See also "Beatles Gone; Malady Lingers." *Plain Dealer* 17 September 1964: 1. The day following the Beatles' departure from Cleveland, the Beatles and Cleveland law enforcement officers blamed each other for the near riot. It was reported by the *Plain Dealer* that Starr called the Cleveland police "stupid." The story continued, "The Beatles manager, Derek Taylor [Taylor, in fact, was personal assistant to Beatles manager Brian Epstein], accused the police of being lax in keeping back the crowds." The police accused Lennon of "almost starting a riot by making faces at Deputy Inspector Carl C. Bare [i.e., the officer who stopped the show]." A number of policemen even accused the Beatles of being "unwashed" and "smelly."

4. The Order of the British Empire, founded by George V in 1917, includes five

classes, of which Member, or M.B.E., is the lowest. The others, from highest to lowest, are Knight Grand Cross, Knight Commander, Commander, and Officer.

5. See "Irked by Award to Beatles, Canadian returns Medal," *New York Times* 15 June 1965; "12-Medal Man Reacts Sharply to the Beatles," *New York Times* 17 June 1965; "Two British Heroes Protest Award of Honors to Beatles," *New York Times* 16 June 1965. It should be noted that criticism of individual awards is common following the announcement of the annual honors list.

In November, 1969, Lennon returned his M.B.E. to Buckingham Palace to protest "Britain's involvement in the Nigeria–Biafra thing, against our support of America in Vietnam, and against 'Cold Turkey' slipping down the charts." See "Lennon Returns MBE," *Variety* 26 November 1969: 2.

6. *Yellow Submarine* (1968) completed the Beatles' contract with United Artists.

7. For an excellent discussion of the development and impact of the Independent Group, see Anne Massey, "The Independent Group: Towards a Redefinition," *Burlington Magazine*, April 1987, 232–42.

8. For an interesting account of the art school and its relationship to class and popular music in Great Britain in the 1960s and 1970s, see Simon Frith and Howard Horne's *Art Into Pop* (London: Methuen, 1987).

9. United Artists' earnings exceeded those for 1964 (the year of *A Hard Day's Night's* release), boosted by the Beatles' *Help!* and the James Bond film *Goldfinger*, as well as the comedies *How to Murder Your Wife* and *What's New Pussycat* ("United Artists Sets" 65).

10. See also Crowther's analysis of *Help!* in relation to other "absurd" comedies, including *What's New Pussycat* and *Those Magnificent Men in Their Flying Machines*, all of which debuted in the summer of 1965, "Pop Go The Beatles," *New York Times*, 29 August 1965: 7.

11. See also Philip Norman, *Shout!*, page 253: "The U.S. authorities . . . obtained a New York court order freezing $1 million in concert proceeds while 'clarification' was sought."

12. Solomon & Co. was the underwriter for the offering.

13. See Mitchell Axelrod's *Beatletoons: The Real Story Behind the Cartoon Beatles* (Pickens, SC: Wynn Publishing, 1999) for an entertaining and thorough description of the show's production and promotion.

14. For a description of the Egyptian rock and roll scene, see Osgood Carruthers. "Rock 'n' Roll Cuts Swath in Egypt," *New York Times* 23 June 1957, late edition: 24. Harrison Salisbury's discussion of the Soviet Bloc's

liberalizing atmosphere following the death of Stalin can be found in "Diversity in East Europe Replaces Stalinist Rigidity," *New York Times* 21 October 1957, late edition: 1. The rock and roll record craze and burgeoning youth culture of the Soviet Union is further described in Salisbury's "Presley Records a Craze in Soviet," *New York Times* 3 February 1957, late edition: 4, as well as in "The News of the Week in Review: State of Soviet," in the *New York Times* 17 January 1960, late edition: E1. News of the hapless East German youths is to be found in "Leipzig Presley Fans Jailed," *New York Times* 3 November 1959, late edition: 19, and "Poll Shocks Reds in East Germany," *New York Times* 29 March 1959, late edition: 29.

15. See also *The Beatles Anthology*, vol. 6. Nearly thirty years later, McCartney recalled that the Beatles had politely turned down the invitation, as it was the band's "day off."

16. See also "Comment on Jesus Spurs a Radio Ban Against the Beatles," *New York Times* 5 August 1966, in which a slightly shorter version of Lennon's statement appears.

17. See also "Stock in Beatles Songs is Cheaper in London," *New York Times* 11 August 1966: 35. The *Times* reported that stock in Northern Songs, Ltd., the company started in February 1965, dropped precipitously in value, from $1.64 to $1.26, as a result of the furor caused by Lennon's remarks. The *Times* quoted Robert Putnam, a *Daily Express* columnist, who wrote: "It seems a nerve for Americans to hold up shocked hands at the Beatles when, week in, week out, America is exporting to us a subculture that makes the Beatles seem like four stern churchwardens."

18. Wrote Cleave of Lennon's voracious appetite for media, "John reads a great deal, particularly about history and religion. He takes an enthusiastic rather than an informed interest in these subjects. . . . He reads all the daily national newspapers published in Great Britain. He watches all television news coverage" ("Old Beatles" 32).

19. For a longer and somewhat different account of Lennon's apology, see Ray Coleman, *Lennon*, 283–84.

20. The Beatles. Neil Aspinall interview. *The Beatles Anthology*. San Francisco: Chronicle Books, 2000. 225.

21. *The Early Beatles* was essentially a collection of recordings first released on Vee-Jay's *Introducing the Beatles*. Vee-Jay's rights to these masters reverted back to Capitol in October 1964. The Capitol release, on March 22, 1965, came two years after release of the recordings on the Beatles' first British album, *Please Please Me*. *The Early Beatles* was viewed as a replacement album

by Capitol, not an album of new Beatles material, and hence was not the focus for a major promotional campaign (Spizer, *Beatles' Story, Pt. II* 72).

22. Numerous commentators, and Lennon himself, have noted Lennon's depression during this period. A product of his mental exhaustion following two years of continuous touring, it manifested itself in what Lennon later called his "fat Elvis" period.

23. The tallies for number one singles and albums continued to mount (*Billboard* singles and album charts):

"Single A-side"/Album	Release Date	Top Chart Position
"I Feel Fine"	November 23, 1964	1
Beatles '65	December 15, 1964	1
"Eight Days a Week"	February 15, 1965	1
*The Early Beatles	March 22, 1965	43
"Ticket to Ride"	April 16, 1965	1
Beatles VI	June 14, 1965	1
"Help!"	July 19, 1965	1
Help!	August 13, 1965	1
"Yesterday"	September 13, 1965	1
"We Can Work It Out"	December 6, 1965	1
Rubber Soul	December 6, 1965	1
"Nowhere Man"	February 21, 1966	3
"Paperback Writer"	May 30, 1966	1
"Yesterday" . . . And Today	June 20, 1966	1
"Eleanor Rigby"/ "Yellow Submarine"	August 8, 1966	11 and 2, respectively
Revolver	August 8, 1966	1

*The Early Beatles was viewed as a replacement for Vee-Jay's *Introducing the Beatles*, not an album of new Beatles material warranting a large promotional campaign.

24. While a professor of psychology at Harvard, Timothy Leary, with his colleague, Richard Alpert, had conducted early experiments with LSD and other mind-altering drugs. Uneasy about the experiments, sometimes carried out with students, Harvard dismissed Leary and Alpert from the university in 1963. Leary continued his experiments, urging people to "Tune in, turn on, and drop out," and helping to fuel the psychopharmacological experimentation that was a foundation for the counterculture.

25. To create the tape loops, the erase head was removed from the tape recorder,

and the tape was saturated by repeatedly recording over the same finite length of tape. As an example, the elephant-like trumpeting opening the song is, in fact, a recording of a distorted guitar repeatedly played into a loop (Lewisohn, *Complete* 216).

26. Lennon and McCartney differed as to the song's origins. Lennon, though acknowledging that McCartney had the first verse and structure developed before introducing it to him, claimed much of the remaining lyrics as his own (Sheff 118–19). McCartney, however, claimed otherwise: "I'd put it down 80–20 to me" (Miles 283).

27. The song reportedly evolved from an acid trip Lennon shared with members of the Byrds while in Los Angeles in August 1965. The son of American actor Henry Fonda (and Jane's brother), Peter, the future star of *Easy Rider*, showed up and proceeded to describe a near-death experience he had had, telling Lennon, "I know what it's like to be dead." Lennon, fearing a "bad trip," had him thrown out (Ian MacDonald 169).

4. "THE MOOD OF THE SIXTIES": THE BEATLES AS ARTISTS, 1966–68

1. See "Beatles Personal Letters." *16* March 1965: 50; "The Girls Who Invade the Beatles Privacy!" *Tiger Beat* December 1965; and "Beatles: What They Really Say About U.S. Teens!" *Tiger Beat* January 1966.

2. The famous piccolo trumpet solo, inspired by McCartney's viewing of a broadcast of Bach's *Brandenburg Concerto*, was played by the New Philharmonia's Dave Mason.

3. The company was founded in 1962 by Brian Epstein and his brother Clive to manage Epstein's burgeoning entertainment interests (notably the Beatles' tours and appearances) as well as the merchandising of the band.

4. This is likely a reference to Swedish auteur Ingmar Bergman's 1957 film *Wild Strawberries*.

5. For a detailed discussion of the art school–pop music connection, see Simon Frith and Howard Horne, Art *Into Pop* (New York: Methuen & Co., 1987).

6. Peter Blake, too, was an admirer of Carroll's novels, and would explore the work of the author more fully in 1970–71, when he made a series of watercolors to illustrate a new edition of *Through the Looking Glass*.

7. Following two centuries of administration by the British East India Company, the British Crown ruled India from the mid-nineteenth century until India won independence in 1947.

8. Two influential centers in the production of electronic music arose, one in Paris and the other in Cologne. In Paris the interest was primarily in *musique concrète*, a form composed largely of altered and rearranged natural sounds. The Cologne school, led by Karlheinz Stockhausen, was concerned with "pure" electronic music created solely through the use of pure frequencies (Griffiths, *Modern Music* 147–48). McCartney, at the time the Beatle most aware of contemporary artistic currents, was influenced by the work of Stockhausen.

9. For an interesting memoir of the making of the film, see Tony Barrow's *The Making of the Beatles' Magical Mystery Tour*. London: Omnibus, 1999.

10. Bob Neaverson provides a detailed and informative analysis of the film and its countercultural underpinnings in his excellent book, *The Beatles Movies* (London: Cassell, 1997).

11. "Trance films" take the structure of a journey through the dream world of the central character. Deren's *Meshes in the Afternoon* and Anger's *Fireworks* are influential examples of the form. For an informative discussion of avant-garde and experimental film, and of Deren's and Anger's works as examples of trance film, see P. Adams Sitney's landmark history of American avant-garde film, *Visionary Film: The American Avant-Garde* (Oxford: Oxford University Press, 2002).

12. Lennon and Yoko Ono pursued an ambitious program of experimental filmmaking in the late 1960s and early 1970s, but the Beatles, as a group, would not repeat the exercise.

13. McCartney's brainchild, this experimental label was to have specialized in spoken-word albums by the likes of Charles Bukowski, Ken Weaver, Charles Olson, and Richard Brautigan, though little progress was made in bringing this dream to fruition (DiLello 133).

14. As defined by Bürger, the historical avant-garde "negate those determinations that are essential to autonomous art: the disjunction of art and the praxis of life, individual production, and individual reception as distinct from the former. The avant-garde intends the abolition of autonomous art by which it means that art is to be integrated into the praxis of life" (Bürger 53–54).

15. For Bürger, the neo-avant-garde "institutionalizes the *avant-garde as art* and thus negates genuinely avant-gardiste intentions. . . . It is the status of their products, not the consciousness artists have of their activity, that defines the social effect of works. Neo-avant-gardiste art is autonomous art in the full sense of the term, which means that it negates the avant-gardiste intention of returning art to the praxis of life" (Bürger 58). Bürger's central

point, as noted by Russell Berman, is that the historical avant-garde consti-
tuted itself as a "rejection of the aesthetic of autonomy that had attained
a privileged . . . status in the bourgeois culture of the nineteenth century"
(Berman 49).

16. See, for instance, Edera, 87–88; Stephenson, 91; Bowman, 174; Hieronimus, 311–30.

5. "BEATLEPEOPLE": *ROLLING STONE*, 1967–70

1. See Jann Wenner, review of *The Beatles: The Authorized Biography*, by Hunter
Davies, *Rolling Stone*, 26 October 1968, 17; "Beatle people" was first coined
by American fanzines in reference to Beatlemaniacs. It was something of a
joke to the members of the band – McCartney termed it "low-level journal-
ese" in a 1965 interview with *Playboy*'s Jean Shepherd ("Playboy Interview:
The Beatles," *Playboy*, February 1965, 57).

2. Our focus is on the years 1967 through 1970, a period in which the magazine—
the first issue of which appeared in November 1967—was clearly an underground publication (Atkin 188). *Rolling Stone* presents a fascinating window into the youth culture of the 1960s. In total, for the period 1967–70,
there were eighty-three items concerned specifically with the Beatles; seventeen additional items about Harrison; fifty-three about Lennon; ten related
to McCartney; and ten pertaining to Starr. In addition to an analysis of these
173 pieces is an extensive examination of other items written by Jann Wenner,
Ralph Gleason, and numerous *Rolling Stone* writers and editors.

3. *The American Heritage Dictionary*, office edition, based on New 2nd College
Edition. Boston: Houghton Mifflin Company, 1983; Dell, 1987. 160.

4. See also Robert Draper. *Rolling Stone Magazine: The Uncensored History*
(New York: Doubleday, 1990), 121.

5. Anson, 105ff; see also Draper, 33–34.

6. The New Left increasingly viewed Wenner as a capitalist "shuck," particularly after his denouncement of the Yip-In. See Draper, 131–32.

7. For an interesting discussion of the tensions between the California camps,
see Derek Taylor. *It Was Twenty Years Ago Today* (New York: Fireside, 1987),
73–83. The Monterey Pop Festival (June 1967) was almost scuttled by dis-
trust between the two West Coast music meccas. These tensions sprang
full force in negotiations between the San Francisco music establishment
and that of Los Angeles, and animosity remained even after the event had
been successfully completed. Recalled the Jefferson Airplane's Paul Kantner:

"Monterey was totally ruined by Los Angeles interests in terms of money, though money wasn't what everyone was there for. Being there was just a huge brotherhood of people" (76).

8. Buci-Glucksmann, Christine. "Hegemony and Consent: A Political Strategy." *Approaches to Gramsci*. Ed. Anne Showstack Sassoon. London: Writers and Readers Publishing Cooperative Society, Ltd., 1982: 116–26.

9. An ounce of marijuana.

10. John Lennon, "The Rolling Stone Interview: John Lennon, Part One. The Working Class Hero," interview by Jann Wenner, *Rolling Stone*, 7 January 1971: 32+; "The Rolling Stone Interview: John Lennon, Part Two. Life with the Lions," interview by Jann Wenner, *Rolling Stone*, 4 February 1971: 36+.

11. See Patricia Coffin, "The Beatles," *Look* 9 January 1968: [Quoting Harrison] "Yoga and discipline, that's the way to get high" (41); "Preacher of Peace: Marashi Mahesh Yogi," *New York Times* 22 January 1968: "'Transcendental meditation is good for everyone,' according to Paul McCartney. . . . 'Since meeting His Holiness, I feel great,' said Ringo Starr . . ."(24).

12. Landau's talents extended beyond criticism. He later became Bruce Springsteen's manager and producer.

13. This is a reference to a statement made by McCartney to the London music publication *New Musical Express*. He told the interviewer: "Starvation in India doesn't worry me one bit. Not one iota. It doesn't, man. And it doesn't worry you . . . if you're honest. You just pose. You don't even know it exists. You've only seen the Oxfam ads. You can't pretend to me that an Oxfam ad can reach down into the depths of your soul and actually make you feel for those people any more, for instance, than you feel about getting a new car. If it comes to a toss-up, you'd get a new car . . . and don't say you wouldn't because that's the scene, with you and with most people" (quoted in Gleason, "The Beatles Tell It" 16).

14. Further indicative of Landau's pique at the inaction of the counterculture and its most visible proponents, in the same review Landau favorably compared the Rolling Stones to the MC5, a rock band managed by John Sinclair, a leader of the White Panther Party—an organization whose manifesto exhibited all of the excesses of the counterculture: "Fuck God in the ass. Fuck your woman until she can't stand up. . . . Our program of rock and roll, dope, and fucking in the streets is a program of total freedom for everyone" (Caute 312–13).

15. Compare to Gitlin, who notes only that the Motherfuckers carried garbage

to the "upper-class mausoleum" of then-new Lincoln Center, the realization of which had "uprooted the inconveniently located poor and kept art sealed away from 'the people'" (Gitlin, *The Sixties* 239).

16. The full ramifications of this dark side were fully realized, at least symbolically, at the music festival held at northern California's Altamont Raceway in December 1969, when the West Coast's answer to the Woodstock Festival (August 1969) turned into a nightmarish journey through a drug-addled and increasingly menacing counterculture and, at least symbolically, put a final end to the "peace and love" orientation of the counterculture. Headlined by the Rolling Stones, the concert was to have included performances by the Flying Burrito Brothers, Santana, the Jefferson Airplane, and the Grateful Dead. The Hell's Angels acted as security for the show and, as the day wore on, the Angels, fueled by alcohol and drugs, turned on the crowd and the musicians, at one point knocking the Airplane's singer, Marty Balin, unconscious. Alarmed by the Angel's behavior, the Dead refused to play. By the time the Stones hit the stage that evening, the crowd was awash in "bad trips" and violence. Four people were killed, most famously Meredith Hunter, whose murder by an Angel was captured on camera in Albert and David Maysles' brilliant documentary of the Stones tour and the Altamont festival, *Gimme Shelter*.

17. See also Draper, 121.

18. In 1968, in an interview with London's *International Times* (September 6, 1968), Godard was critical of the Beatles' failure to join the revolutionary left. Lennon was less than amused: "Oh yeah, right, he said we should do something. Now that's sour grapes from a man who couldn't get us to be in his film [i.e., *One Plus One*; the Rolling Stones appeared, instead], and I don't expect it from people like that. Dear Mr. Godard, just because we didn't want to be in the film with you, it doesn't mean to say that we aren't doing any more than you. We should do whatever we're all doing" (Cott, "The Rolling Stone Interview" 14). Lennon was equally blunt in his lyrics to "Revolution," which were dismissive of the Euro-Maoists (including Godard) at the vanguard of European radicalism, warning: "But if you go carryin' pictures of Chairman Mao / You ain't gonna make it with anyone anyhow" (The Beatles, "Revolution").

19. *One Plus One* (also known as *Sympathy for the Devil*).

20. See Porterfield, Christopher, and Jesse Birnbaum. "The Messengers." *Time* 22 September 1967: 60–68. See also Kroll, Jack. "It's Getting Better . . ." Review of the sound recording *Sgt. Pepper's Lonely Hearts Club Band*, by

the Beatles. *Newsweek* 26 June 1967, 70; Rorem, Ned. "The Music of the Beatles." *The New York Review of Books* 18 January 1968, 23–27; Coffin, Patricia. "The Beatles." *Look* 9 January 1968, 32.

21. Sandra Wenner, "Rolling Stone," *American Mass Market Magazines*, eds. Alan Nourie and Barbara Nourie (New York: Greenwood Press, 1990), 442.

22. Gramsci, *Selections from the Prison Notebooks* 161.

6. "BEAUTIFUL PEOPLE": THE BEATLES' IDEALIZED PAST

1. For an excellent discussion of this period in Lennon's life, see Jon Wiener's, *Come Together: John Lennon in His Time*. 1984. Chicago: University of Illinois Press, 1991. The efforts to deport Lennon are captured in his *Gimme Some Truth: The John Lennon FBI Files* (Los Angeles: University of California Press, 1999).

2. In the 1966 California governor's race, Reagan defeated incumbent Pat Brown in a landslide, promising to "clean up the mess at Berkeley." Viewed as a hotbed of student protest and opposition to the Vietnam conflict, and the birthplace of the Free Speech Movement, which Reagan believed to be infiltrated by communists, the campus had become the focus of conservative criticism of its liberal faculty and administration, and of its disruptive student body. As governor, Reagan worked closely with the FBI to infiltrate and curb student activism and bring the University of California campus to heel.

3. In late 1973, Lennon separated from Ono and went on an eighteen-month drinking binge in Los Angeles with friends such as Bobby Keyes, Harry Nilsson, and Keith Moon. At Ono's instigation, he also had an affair with May Pang, Ono's secretary.

4. *Newsweek*'s Barbara Graustark, in "An Ex-Beatle Starting Over," noted that, on the day of his death, Lennon and Ono had decided to fly to San Francisco the following weekend and march with Asian workers demonstrating for wage equality (46).

5. During the halftime show of the previous Super Bowl, a "wardrobe malfunction" had revealed singer Janet Jackson's breast to a shocked audience. The public furor over that offending incident and others in the MTV-produced extravaganza led the NFL to opt for McCartney and a safe, family-friendly halftime show.

6. *Beatles Anthology*, vol. 8 (VHS), sleeve notes.

7. In 1985, Michael Jackson outbid Paul McCartney to acquire the publishing rights for the Northern Songs catalog. He and Capitol, which owns the

performance rights to the Beatles' recordings, licensed use of "Revolution" for the campaign.

8. The Beatles, because of the very public nature of their maturation, sometimes opened themselves to ridicule. Just a month after joining other leading figures from the British arts and entertainment world in a full-page advertisement in the *London Times* calling laws against marijuana "immoral in principle and unworkable in practice," the Beatles announced that they had sworn off drug use and were, instead, devoting their energies to Transcendental Meditation, as espoused by the Maharishi Mahesh Yogi. The Beatles' public advocacy of TM lasted only eight months, but countless individuals had followed their example. William F. Buckley, writing in the conservative *National Review*, lamented: "The truly extraordinary feature of our time isn't the faithlessness of the Western people, it is their utter, total ignorance of the Christian religion. . . . The Beatles know more about carburetors than they know about Christianity, which is why they, like so many others, make such asses of themselves in pursuit of Mr. Gaga Yogi" (Buckley 259).

9. While the Beatles' plans for Apple Corps were never realized, the more communal, idealistic vision they introduced into the corporate world was taken up successfully by other companies, including Ben and Jerry's, Apple Computer, and Google.

10. See Fiske, Edward B. "Yellow Submarine is Symbol of Youth Churches," *New York Times*, 20 April 1970: 23.

11. The stormy relationship of actors Richard Burton and Elizabeth Taylor was the stuff of the tabloids and entertainment press, thus accounting for Lawrence's shared joke with the audience. In 1968 Burton gave Taylor (then his wife) a monstrous 33.19-carat diamond. Later he gave her a 69-carat diamond, the so-called Taylor-Burton diamond.

12. The Fluxus movement, started by George Macunias in the early 1960s, proposed a blending of artistic media and often invited the participation of audience members in the creative process. The movement, like Pop Art, challenged the high art–low art dichotomy. Artists associated with Fluxus include, among others, Paik, who studied with John Cage and Karlheinz Stockhausen, La Monte Young, Joseph Beuys, and Yoko Ono.

13. Allan Kaprow coined the term "happening" in the late 1950s to refer to a performance, often multidisciplinary, for which essential elements have been predetermined but in which the audience is frequently involved. Many trace the form's development to the pioneering work of John Cage (a teacher of Kaprow's) at Black Mountain College in the early 1950s. A popular form in

the 1960s, happenings were organized by, among others, Claes Oldenburg and Robert Rauschenberg. Yoko Ono, alone and later with Lennon, frequently organized happenings.

14. See, for instance, James M. Decker's "Baby, You're a Rich Man: The Beatles, Ideology, and the Cultural Moment," in *Reading the Beatles*, eds. Kenneth Womack and Todd F. Davis (New York: SUNY Press, 2006), 183–95. Decker provides a trenchant analysis of the market strategy employed in promotion of the *Anthology* and *Beatles 1*. Rightly attributing the commercial success of these products to a well-crafted campaign of "cross-valorization," the notion that one's symbolic value might be exploited to enhance one's commercial value, and vice versa (as we have seen, a process clearly in evidence throughout the Beatles' career), Decker nevertheless, I think, underestimates the symbolic values extraneous to the market or reference to it that continue to hold meaning for the audience.

15. See *The Beatles Anthology*, episode 8; see also, The Beatles, *The Beatles Anthology*, 357.

BIBLIOGRAPHY

Adler, Renata. "Beatles, Comic Strip Style." *New York Times*. 17 November 1968, late ed., sec. 2: 1+.

Adorno, Theodor. "On Popular Music." 1941. In *On Record: Rock, Pop, and the Written Word*, Frith, Simon, and Andrew Goodwin, eds. London: Routledge, 1990. 301–14.

Adorno, Theodor W. "On the Fetish Character in Music and the Regression of Listening." 1938. In *The Culture Industry*, edited by J. M. Bernstein, 26–52. London: Routledge, 1991.

Adorno, Theodor, and Max Horkheimer. *Dialectic of Enlightenment*. 1944. London: Verso, 1979.

Ahlstrom, Sydney E. "The Radical Turn in Theology and Ethics: Why It Occurred in the 1960s." In *Religion in American History: Interpretive Essays*. John M. Mulder and John F. Wilson, eds. Englewood Cliffs, NJ: Prentice-Hall, 1978. 445–56.

Alden, Robert. "Wild-Eyed Mobs Pursue Beatles." *New York Times* 13 February 1964, late ed.: 26.

Allsop, Kenneth. "Pop Goes Young Woodley." *Class*. Richard Mabey, ed. London: Anthony Blond Ltd., 1967. 127–71.

The American Heritage Dictionary, office edition, based on New 2nd College Edition. Boston: Houghton Mifflin Company, 1983; Dell, 1987.

Anson, Robert Sam. *Gone Crazy and Back Again: The Rise and Fall of the Rolling Stone Generation*. Garden City: Doubleday & Company, Inc., 1981.

"Are They More Popular Than Maharishi Now?" *Rolling Stone* 22 June 1968: 18.

Armes, Roy. *A Critical History of British Cinema*. New York: Oxford University Press, 1978.

Arnold, Martin. "4 Beatles and How They Grew: Moneywise." *New York Times* 17 February 1964, late ed.: 1+.

Atkin, David J. "From Counterculture to Over-the-Counter Culture: An Analysis of *Rolling Stone*'s Coverage of the New Left in the United States from 1967–1975." In *Studies in Newspaper and Periodical History, 1995 Annual*. Michael Harris and Tom O'Malley, eds. Westport, Connecticut: Greenwood Press, 1995. 185–98.

Axelrod, Mitchell. *Beatletoons: The Real Story Behind the Cartoon Beatles*. Pickens, SC: Wynn Publishing, 1999.

Barnes, Clive. "Teen-Age Craze Inspires Ballet," *New York Times* 19 December 1963, late ed.: 41.

———. "Liverpool Cellar Clubs Rock to Beat Groups." *New York Times* 26 December 1963, late ed.: 34.

"Bards of Pop." *Newsweek* 21 March 1966: 102.

Barrow, Tony. *John, Paul, George, Ringo & Me*. New York: Thunder's Mouth Press, 2005.

"Beatle George Harrison Dies." Cable News Network (CNN). December 1, 2001. Accessed August 26, 2005. http://archives.cnn.com/2001/SHOWBIZ/Music/11/30/harrison.obit/.

"Beatlemania." *Newsweek* 18 November 1963: 104.

"Beatlemania and the Fast Buck." *Christian Century* 24 February 1965: 230.

The Beatles. *The Beatles Anthology*, eight episodes. 1995. Produced by Chips Chipperfield; directed by Geoff Wonfor. Apple Corps, Ltd., 2003. DVD.

———. *The Beatles Anthology*. San Francisco: Chronicle Books, 2000.

"Beatles are 'Helpful,' Prince Philip Thinks." *New York Times* 26 February 1964, late ed.: 5.

"Beatles Are Booed At Manila Airport." *New York Times* 6 July 1966, late ed.: 39.

"The Beatles Beat a Retreat From Fans in Cleveland." *New York Times* 16 August 1966, late ed.: 35.

"The Beatles: Cheerful Coherence." Review of the sound recording *Abbey Road*, by the Beatles. *Time* 3 October 1969: 57.

"Beatles Depart for Britain as 4,000 Admirers Scream." *New York Times* 22 February 1964, late ed.: 18.

"Beatles Fans Fight Police At New Zealand Concert." *New York Times* 24 June 1964, late ed.: 20.

"Beatles' Film and Music Company." *London Times* 16 May 1968: 7h.

The Beatles: The First U.S. Visit. Directors Albert Maysles and David Maysles. Videocassette. MPI. 1991.

"Beatles Gambling Lives in Las Vegas." *New York Times* 21 August 1964, late ed.: 15.

"Beatles Gone; Malady Lingers." *Plain Dealer* 17 September 1964: 1.

"Beatles Greeted by Riot At Paris Sports Palace." *New York Times* 21 June 1965, late ed.: 17.

"Beatles Manager Here to Quell Storm Over Remark on Jesus." *New York Times* 6 August 1966, late ed.: 13.

"Beatles May Do Free Concert Tour In U.S.A." *Rolling Stone* 7 December 1968: 1.

"Beatles on Coast for Tour of U.S.; 9,000 at Airport." *New York Times* 19 August 1964, late ed.: 28.

The Beatles. "Playboy Interview: The Beatles." By Jean Shepherd. *Playboy* February 1965: 51+.

"Beatles reply to TV film critics." *London Times* 28 December 1967: 2c.

The Beatles' Revolution. Television Broadcast. American Broadcasting Company. November 17, 2000.

"Beatles' Set Hot B.O. Pace for UA; Ad Campaign Now Aimed at Adults." *Variety* 26 August 1964: 4.

"Beatles Signed for Film." *New York Times* 18 February 1964, late ed.: 28.

"Beatles to Get $150,000 For Kansas City Program." *New York Times* 24 August 1964, late ed.: 22.

"Beatles to Shun U.S. Because of Tax Rift." *New York Times* 5 January 1965, late ed.: 24.

"Beatles' TV Spec Draws Critical Rap; Loses Ratings, But Will Turn Profit." *Variety* 10 January 1968: 1+.

Beniger, James R. *The Control Revolution.* Cambridge, Massachusetts: Harvard University Press, 1986.

Berman, Russell A. *Modern Culture and Critical Theory.* Madison: University of Wisconsin Press, 1989.

Berman, William C. *America's Turn to the Right: From Nixon to Bush.* Baltimore: The Johns Hopkins University Press, 1994.

Bernstein, Lewis G. Letter. *New York Times* 8 March 1964, late ed., sec. 6: 4.

Best, Steven. "The Commodification of Reality and the Reality of Commodification: Jean Baudrillard and Post-Modernism." In *Current Perspectives in Social Theory* 9. John Wilson, ed. Greenwich, Conn.: JAI Press, 1989. 23–51.

Best, Steven, and Douglas Kellner. *Postmodern Theory: Critical Interrogations.* New York: The Guilford Press, 1991.

"Beware, the Red Beatles." *Newsweek* 15 February 1965: 89A.

Blue-Chip Beatles." *Newsweek* 4 October 1965: 82.

Bowman, David. 1972. "Scenarios for the Revolution in Pepperland." *Journal of Popular Film* 1.3: 173–84.

Box Office Report. http://www.boxofficereport.com/database/1969.shtml. Accessed 12 June 2005.

Braden, William. *Age of Aquarius: Technology and the Cultural Revolution.* Chicago: Quadrangle Books, 1970.

Bramwell, Tony, with Rosemary Kingsland. *Magical Mystery Tours: My Life with the Beatles.* New York: Thomas Dunne Books, 2005.

Brauer, Ralph. "Iconic Modes: The Beatles." 1978. In *The Age of Rock.* Timothy E. Scheurer, ed. Bowling Green, OH: Bowling Green University Popular Press, 1989. 151–59.

"Britons Given Chance To Buy Beatle Stock." *New York Times* 13 February 1965, late ed.: 9.

Brookhiser, Richard. "John Lennon, RIP." *National Review* 31 December 1980: 1555.

Brown, Peter, and Steven Gaines. *The Love You Make.* New York: McGraw-Hill, 1983.

Bryant, John. "Thirteen Reasons to Give Ringo Some Respect." World Wide Web. http://web2.airmail.net/gshultz/bryant.html. Accessed 19 June 2005.

Buci-Glucksmann, Christine. "Hegemony and Consent: A Political Strategy." In *Approaches to Gramsci.* Anne Showstack Sassoon, ed. London: Writers and Readers Publishing Cooperative Society, Ltd., 1982. 116–26.

Buckley, Thomas. "Beatles Prepare for Their Debut." *New York Times* 9 February 1964, late ed.: 70.

Buckley, William F. "The Beatles and the Guru." *National Review* 12 March 1968: 259.

Bürger, Peter. *Theory of the Avant-Garde.* Minneapolis: University of Minnesota Press, 1984.

Buxton, David. "Rock Music, the Star System, and the Rise of Consumerism." In *On Record: Rock, Pop and the Written Word.* Simon Frith and Andrew Goodwin, eds. New York: Pantheon, 1990. 427–40.

"Buying the Beatles." *Time* 19 February 1965: 94.

Caine, Michael. *What's It All About?: An Autobiography.* New York: Ballantine Books, 1994.

Cameron, Gail. "A Disaster? Well, Not Exactly: There Stood the Beatles as the Smoke Lifted." *Life* 28 August 1964: 58A–60+.

————. "Yeah-Yeah-Yeah! Beatlemania Becomes a Part of U.S. History." *Life* 21 February 1964: 34–34B.

Carlson, Walter. "Advertising: Beatles to Sing Tunes for Toys." *New York Times* 1 June 1965, late ed.: 58.

Carr, Roy. *Beatles at the Movies*. New York: Harper Perennial, 1996.

Carrighan, Sally. Letter. *New York Times* 19 April 1964, late ed., sec. 6: 48.

Caute, David. *The Year of the Barricades: A Journey Through 1968*. New York: Harper & Row, 1988.

CBS News Special: Inside Pop—The Rock Revolution. Orig. broadcast April 25, 1967. Columbia Broadcasting System. Museum of Television and Radio, New York. Video holdings accessed June 22, 2004.

Chaikin, Alan. Letter. *New York Times* 8 March 1964, late ed., sec. 6: 4.

Chapman, Emerson. "Visit From the Beetorusu Gives Tokyo Police Hard Day's Night." *New York Times* 1 July 1966, late ed.: 38.

Christgau, Robert. "Secular Music." *Esquire* December 1967: 283–86.

Clark, Alfred E. "2,000 Beatle Fans Storm Box Office Here." *New York Times* 1 May 1966, late ed.: 80.

Cleave, Maureen. "How does a Beatle live? John Lennon lives like this." 1966. In *The Lennon Companion: Twenty-Five Years of Comment*. Elizabeth Thomson and David Gutman, eds. New York: Schirmer Books, 1987. 71–75.

————. "Old Beatles—A Study in Paradox." *New York Times Magazine* 3 July 1966: 10–11+.

"Cleveland to Bar Beatles And the Like in Public Hall." *New York Times* 4 November 1964, late ed.: 46.

Cmiel, Kenneth. "The Politics of Civility." In *The Sixties: From Memory to History*. David Farber, ed. Chapel Hill: University of North Carolina Press, 1994. 263–90.

Coffin, Patricia. "The Beatles." *Look* 9 January 1968: 37+.

Coleman, Ray. *Lennon*. 1984. New York: McGraw-Hill, 1986.

"Comment on Jesus Spurs a Radio Ban Against the Beatles." *New York Times* 5 August 1966, late ed.: 20.

"Convent Yields on Presley." *New York Times* 16 April 1957, late ed.: 30.

Cook, David A. *A History of Narrative Film*. 2nd ed. New York: W. W. Norton, 1990.

Corliss, Richard. "A Beatle Metaphysic." *Commonweal* 12 May 1967: 234–36.

Cott, Jonathan. "Two Virgins." Review of *Two Virgins*, by John Lennon and Yoko Ono. *Rolling Stone* 1 March 1969: 20.

———. "The Rolling Stone Interview: John Lennon." *Rolling Stone* 23 November 1968: 11–14.

———. "We Thought People Would Understand—Paul." *Rolling Stone* 10 October 1968: 22.

Crawdaddy! #11. September/October 1967.

"Critics Scorn Beatle Film But Audience Enjoys Itself." *New York Times* 29 July 1965, late ed.: 19.

Crowther, Bosley. "Screen: The Four Beatles in 'A Hard Day's Night.'" Review of the motion picture *A Hard Day's Night. New York Times* 12 August 1964, late ed.: 41.

———. "Prides of Liverpool." *New York Times* 16 August 1964, late ed., sec. 2: 1.

———. "Screen: Beatles Star in 'Help!,' Film of the Absurd." Review of motion picture *Help! New York Times* 24 August 1965, late ed.: 25.

———. "Pop Go The Beatles." *New York Times* 29 August 1965, late ed., sec. 2: 1.

———. "The Other Cheek To the Beatles." *New York Times* 12 September 1965, late ed., sec. 2: 1.

Dallos, Robert E. "Beatles Strike Serious Note in Press Talk." *New York Times* 23 August 1966, late ed.: 30.

Davies, Hunter. *The Beatles.* 1968. Revised. New York: McGraw-Hill, 1978.

"Death of a Beatle." *Newsweek* 22 December 1980: 31–36.

"Death threat after Beatles incident." *London Times* 11 July 1966: 9.

"Debris Is Hurled At Baetle [sic] Concert." *New York Times* 20 August 1966, late ed.: 11.

Dempsey, David. "Why the Girls Scream, Weep, Flip." *New York Times* 23 February 1964, late ed., sec. 6: 15+.

Deren, Maya. "Cinematography: The Creative Use of Reality." In *Film Theory and Readings.* Gerald Mast and Marshall Cohen, eds. 3rd ed. London: Oxford University Press, 1985.

Draper, Robert. *Rolling Stone Magazine: The Uncensored History.* New York: Doubleday, 1990.

Dyer, Richard. *Stars.* 1980. New ed., with a supplementary chapter by Paul McDonald. London: British Film Institute, 1998.

Eastland, Terry. "In Defense of Religious America." *Commentary* June 1981: 39–45.

Ebert, Roger. "Cinema: *Two Virgins* and *Number Five*, by Yoko Ono and John Lennon." *Rolling Stone* 21 December 1968: 15+.

Edelstein, Andrew J. *The Pop Sixties*. New York: World Almanac Publications.

Edera, Bruno. *Full Length Animated Feature Films*. John Halas, ed. New York: Hastings House, 1977.

The Ed Sullivan Show. Originally broadcast February 9, 1964. Columbia Broadcasting System. Museum of Television and Radio, New York. Video holdings accessed June 22, 2004.

The Ed Sullivan Show: The Beatles Songbook. Originally broadcast March 1, 1970. Columbia Broadcasting System. Museum of Television and Radio, New York. Video holdings accessed June 22, 2004.

"Eggs Shower the Beatles." *New York Times* 28 June 1964, late ed.: 59.

"Eggs Thrown at Beatles." *New York Times* 29 June 1964, late ed.: 32.

Ehrenreich, Barbara, Elizabeth Hess, and Gloria Jacobs. "Beatlemania: Girls Just Want To Have Fun." In *The Adoring Audience: Fan Culture and Popular Media*. Lisa A. Lewis, ed. New York: Routledge, 1992. 84–106.

"Elvis—A Different Kind of Idol." *Life* 27 August 1956: 101–9.

Emery, Michael, and Edwin Emery. *The Press in America: An Interpretive History of the Mass Media*. 6th ed. Englewood Cliffs, NJ: Prentice Hall, 1988.

Entman, Robert M. "Framing: Toward Clarification of a Fractured Paradigm." *Journal of Communication* 43.4 (1993): 51–58.

Epstein, Brian. *A Cellarful of Noise*. 1964. New York: Pocket Books, 1998.

"Fab? Chaos." *Time* 5 January 1968: 60–61.

Faggen, Gil. "Beatles: Plague or Boon for Radio?" *Billboard* 10 October 1964: 16, 24.

Field, Richard S. *Richard Hamilton: Image and Process, 1952–82*. Stuttgart: Edition Hansjörg Mayer, 1983.

Fiske, Edward B. "Yellow Submarine is Symbol of Youth Churches." *New York Times* 20 April 1970: 23.

Fitzgerald, Jon. "Lennon-McCartney and the Early British Invasion, 1964–1966." In *The Beatles, Popular Music and Society: A Thousand Voices*. Ian Inglis, ed. New York: St. Martin's Press, 2000. 53–85.

———. "Songwriters in the U. S. Top Forty, 1963–1966." *Popular Music and Society* vol. 21 no. 4 (1997): 85–110.

"Flashes: Mystery Tour Making Local Stops Soon." *Rolling Stone* 6 April 1968: 4.

Flynn, Elizabeth. "A Legacy of Words, Words, Words." *New York Times* 11 January 1981: K29.

"4,000 Hail Beatles Arrival in Miami." *New York Times* 13 February 1964, late ed.: 16.

Frith, Simon, and Howard Horne. *Art into Pop*. New York: Methuen, 1987.

Frith, Simon, and Andrew Goodwin, eds. *On Record: Rock, Pop and the Written Word*. New York: Pantheon, 1990.

Frontani, Michael. *The Beatles as Sign: Their Transformation from Moptops to Gramscian Intellectuals*. Ph.D. diss., Ohio University, 1998.

Gardner, Paul. "3,000 Fans Greet British Beatles." *New York Times* 8 February 1964, late ed.: 25+.

———. "The British Boys: High-Brows and No-Brows." *New York Times* 9 February 1964, late ed., sec. 2: 19.

George, Nelson. *The Death of Rhythm and Blues*. New York: Plume, 1988.

"George, Paul, Ringo, and John." *Newsweek*. 24 February 1964: 54–57.

Gillain, Anne. "The Script of Delinquency: François Truffaut's *Les 400 coups* (1959)." In *French Film: Texts and Contexts*. Susan Hayward and Ginette Vincendeau, eds. London: Routledge, 1990. 187–99.

Gilroy, Harry. Review of *In His Own Write*, by John Lennon. *New York Times* 24 April 1964, late ed.: 31.

Gitlin, Todd. *The Whole World is Watching: Mass Media in the Making and Unmaking of the New Left*. Berkeley: University of California Press, 1980.

———. "The Lennon Legacy." *The Center Magazine* May/June 1981: 2–4.

———. *The Sixties: Years of Hope, Days of Rage*. New York: Bantam Books, 1987.

Giuliano, Geoffrey. *Blackbird: The Life and Times of Paul McCartney*. New York: Plume, 1992.

———. *The Lost Beatles Interviews*. New York: Plume, 1996.

Gleason, Ralph J. "The Beatles Tell It To The Activists." *Jazz & Pop* November 1968: 16.

———. "Perspectives: The British Group Syndrome." *Rolling Stone* 20 January 1968: 10.

———. "Perspectives: Changing With Moneychangers." *Rolling Stone* 24 February 1968: 9.

———. "Perspectives: Is There A Deathwish In U.S.?" *Rolling Stone* 5 April 1969: 18.

———. "Perspective: Songs Would Do More Than Books." *Rolling Stone* 1 March 1969: 21.

Gledhill, Christine. *Stardom: Industry of Desire*. London: Routledge, 1991.

Glessing, Robert J. *The Underground Press in America*. Bloomington: Indiana University Press, 1970.

Goldman, Peter. "My Crazy Weeks with the Beatles." Lasse Bengtssen, *The Beatles Page*. 2000. http://home.swipnet.se/~w-29168/BeatMore.htm. Accessed 19 June 2005.

Goldstein, Richard. "The Beatles: Inspired Groovers." Review of the sound recording *The Beatles*, by the Beatles. *New York Times* 8 December 1968, late ed., sec. 2: 33+.

————. "We Still Need the Beatles, but . . .". Review of the sound recording *Sgt. Pepper's Lonely Hearts Club Band*, by the Beatles. *New York Times* 18 June 1967, late ed., sec. 4: 24.

Goodwin, Michael. "Let It Be." Review of the motion picture *Let It Be* (United Artists). *Rolling Stone* 25 June 1970: 52.

Goulart, Ron. *Great American Comic Books*. Lincolnwood, Ill.: Publications International, Ltd., 2001.

Gould, Jack. "Elvis Presley." *New York Times* 16 September 1956, late ed.: X13.

————. "TV: It's the Beatles (Yeah, Yeah, Yeah)." *New York Times* 4 January 1964, late ed.: 47.

————. "TV: The Beatles and Their Audience." *New York Times* 10 February 1964, late ed.: 53.

Gramsci, Antonio. *Selections from the Prison Notebooks*. Trans. and eds., Quintin Hoare and Geoffrey Nowell-Smith. New York: International Publishers, 1972.

Graustark, Barbara. "An Ex-Beatle Starting Over." *Newsweek* 22 December 1980: 45–46.

Green, Timothy. "Here Come Those Beatles: Four Screaming Mopheads Break Up England." Photographed for *Life* by Terence Spencer. *Life* 31 January 1964: 24–31.

————. "They Crown Their Country with a Bowl-Shaped Hairdo." *Life* 31 January 1964: 30.

Griffiths, Paul. *Modern Music: A Concise History*. Revised. New York: Thames and Hudson, 1994.

————. "Music." In *The Cambridge Guide to the Arts in Britain*, vol. 9. Boris Ford, ed. Cambridge: Cambridge University Press, 1988.

Gross, Leonard. "John Lennon: Beatle On His Own." *Look* 13 December 1966: 58+.

Grossberg, Lawrence. *We Gotta Get Out of This Place: Popular Conservatism and Postmodern Culture*. New York: Routledge, 1992.

Guralnick, Peter. *Last Train to Memphis: The Rise of Elvis Presley*. New York: Little Brown, 1994.

Haberman, Clyde. "Silent Tribute to Lennon's Memory Is Observed Throughout the World." *New York Times* 15 December 1980: A1, B8.

Hall, Stuart. "The Rediscovery of 'Ideology': Return of the Repressed in Media Studies." 1982. In *Culture, Society and the Media*. Michael Gurevitch, Tony Bennett, James Curran, and Janet Woollacott, eds. London: Routledge, 1988. 56–90.

Hamilton, Richard. *Collected Words, 1953–1982*. New York: Thames and Hudson, 1983.

———. *Richard Hamilton*. London: Tate Gallery Publications Department, 1970.

Harry, Bill. *Beatlemania: An Illustrated Filmography*. London: Virgin, 1984.

Hayward, Susan. *French National Cinema*. London: Routledge, 1993.

Hayward, Susan, and Ginette Vincendeau, eds. *French Film: Texts and Contexts*. London: Routledge, 1990.

Hebdige, Dick. *Subculture: The Meaning of Style*. New York: Routledge, 1979.

Hieronimus, Robert. *Inside the Yellow Submarine: The Making of the Beatles' Animated Classic*. Iola, WI: Krause, 2002.

The Hollywood Palace. Originally broadcast February 8, 1964. American Broadcasting Company. Museum of Television and Radio, New York. Video holdings accessed June 22, 2004.

———. Originally broadcast February 25, 1967. American Broadcasting Company. Museum of Television and Radio, New York. Video holdings accessed June 22, 2004.

———. Originally broadcast March 30, 1968. American Broadcasting Company. Museum of Television and Radio, New York. Video holdings accessed June 22, 2004.

"Home Says Safety of Britain Requires an Atom Deterrent." *New York Times* 16 February 1964, late ed.: 3.

"Hometown Honors Presley." *New York Times* 27 September 1956, late edition: 42.

Hudson, Winthrop S. *Religion in America*. 3rd ed. New York: Charles Scribner's Sons, 1981.

Hunter, James Davison. *Culture Wars: The Struggle to Define America*. New York: Basic Books, 1991.

Hutton, Jack, and Nick Jones. "The Rolling Stone Interview: Ringo and George." *Rolling Stone* 10 February 1968: 12–13.

Huyssens, Andreas. *After the Great Divide*. Bloomington: Indiana University Press, 1986.

"I Wanna Hold Your Stock." *Newsweek* 1 March 1965: 70–71.

"In Praise of John Lennon: The Liverpool Lad as Musician, Husband, Father and Man." *People* 22 December 1980: 26–36.

Inglis, Ian. "Conformity, Status and Innovation: The Accumulation and Utilization of Idiosyncrasy Credits in the Career of the Beatles." *Popular Music and Society* 19 (1995): 41–74.

"Irked by Award to Beatles, Canadian Returns Medal." *New York Times* 15 June 1965, late ed.: 15.

"Israel Bars Beatles." *New York Times* 18 March 1964, late ed.: 47.

"Is Beatlemania Dead?" *Time* 2 September 1966: 38–39.

"It Happened in 1968: The Best of 1968." *Rolling Stone* 1 February 1969: 15+.

The Jack Paar Program. Originally broadcast January 3, 1964. National Broadcasting Corporation. Museum of Television and Radio, New York. Video holdings accessed June 22, 2004.

"Jakarta to Burn Beatle Music." *New York Times* 9 August 1965, late ed.: 8.

"John & Yoko's Christmas Gifts." *Rolling Stone* 21 January 1970: 6.

Jones, Nick. "The Rolling Stone Interview: George Harrison." *Rolling Stone* 24 February 1968: 16.

"Just the Usual Din As Beatles Open Tour in Chicago." *New York Times* 13 August 1966, late ed.: 10.

Kael, Pauline. "Metamorphosis of the Beatles." Review of the motion picture *Yellow Submarine* (United Artists). 1968. *The Lennon Companion*. Elizabeth Thomson and David Gutman, eds. New York: Schirmer Books, 1987. 134–37.

Kane, Larry. *Ticket to Ride*. Philadelphia: Running Press, 2003.

Kellner, Douglas. "Boundaries and Borderlines: Reflections on Jean Baudrillard and Critical Theory." In *Current Perspectives in Social Theory* 9. John Wilson, ed. Greenwich, CT: JAI Press, 1989. 5–22.

Kittleson, Barry. "Beatles Giving Trade a Solid Bite." *Billboard* 25 January 1964: 4, 8.

Kroll, Jack. "Beatles vs. Stones." *Newsweek* 1 January 1968: 62–63.

———. "It's Getting Better . . .". Review of the sound recording *Sgt. Pepper's Lonely Hearts Club Band*, by the Beatles. *Newsweek* 26 June 1967: 70.

Landau, Jon. "Stones." *Rolling Stone* 10 February 1968: 18+.

———. "Beggar's Banquet." Review of *Beggar's Banquet*, by The Rolling Stones. *Rolling Stone* 4 January 1969: 10–13.

Laufer, Charles. "The Beatles: Why They are Equal!" *Tiger Beat* April 1966: 8.

"The Last Day in the Life." *Time* 22 December 1980: 18–24.

Leapman, Michael. "Wave of grief over John Lennon's murder." *London Times* 10 December 1980: 1.

Ledbetter, Les. "John Lennon of Beatles is Killed; Suspect Held in Shooting at Dakota." *New York Times* 9 December 1980: B7.

"Lennon Has A Legacy." *Nation* 20 December 1980: 657.

"Lennon of Beatles Sorry for Making Remark on Jesus." *New York Times* 12 August 1966, late ed.: 38.

"Lennon Returns MBE." *Variety* 26 November 1969: 2.

Leo, John. "Educators Urged to Heed Beatles." *New York Times* 25 July 1967, late ed.: 29.

Lewis, Anthony. "Queen's Honors List Includes the Beatles." *New York Times* 12 June 1965, late ed.: 1+.

Lewis, Frederick. "Britons Succumb to 'Beatlemania.'" *New York Times Magazine* 1 December 1963: 124–26.

Lewisohn, Mark. *The Complete Beatles Chronicle*. New York: Harmony Books, 1992.

Lippard, Lucy, ed. *Pop Art*. London: Thames and Hudson, 1966.

Lipsitz, George. "Who'll Stop the Rain?" In *The Sixties: From Memory to History*. David Farber, ed. Chapel Hill: University of North Carolina Press, 1994. 206–34.

Lobenthal, Joel. *Radical Rags: Fashions of the Sixties*. New York: Abbeville Press, 1990.

"Love Letters to the Stars!" *Tiger Beat* April 1966: 40–41.

Macdonald, Dwight. "Masscult and Midcult." *Partisan Review*, vol. 27, no. 2 (Spring 1960): 214–33.

MacDonald, Ian. *Revolution in the Head: The Beatles' Records and the Sixties*. New York: Henry Holt, 1994.

Maher, Jack. "Beatles Bug as They Control the Air." *Billboard* 29 February 1964: 1, 8.

———. "Beatlemania Revisited: Nobody Loves the Beatles 'Cept Mother, Capitol, Etc." *Billboard* 14 March 1964: 3.

"The Mannerist Phase." Review of the sound recording *The Beatles*, by the Beatles. *Time* 6 December 1968: 53.

Marcuse, Herbert. "Marcuse Defines His New Left Line." Interview with

Jean-Louis Ferrier, Jacques Boetsch, and François Giroud. Trans. Helen Weaver. *New York Times Magazine* 27 October 1968: 29+.

Martin, George (with Jeremy Hormsby). *All You Need is Ears*. New York: St. Martin's Press, 1979.

Martin, George, and William Pearson. *With A Little Help From My Friends: The Making of Sgt. Pepper*. New York: Little, Brown and Company, 1994.

Massey, Anne. "The Independent Group: Towards a Redefinition." *Burlington Magazine* April 1987: 232–42.

McFadden, Robert D. "Legions of Lennon Admirers to Join in Tributes Today." *New York Times* 14 December 1980: 43.

McNeil, Alex. *Total Television*. 4th ed. New York: Penguin Books, 1996.

Mendelsohn, John. Review of the sound recording *Abbey Road*, by the Beatles. *Rolling Stone* 15 November 1969: 32.

Miles, Barry. *Paul McCartney: Many Years from Now*. New York: Henry Holt and Company, 1997.

Miller, Edwin. "Bit by the Beatles." *Seventeen* March 1964: 82–83.

—————. "On the Scene with the Beatles." *Seventeen* August 1965: 230–31+.

—————. "What Are the Beatles Really Like?" 1964. *Seventeen Interviews: Film Stars and Superstars*. London: The MacMillan Company/Collier-Macmillan Ltd., 1970. 168–79.

Miller, Jim. "The Beach Boys." In *The Rolling Stone Illustrated History of Rock & Roll* (updated and revised). Anthony DeCurtis and James Henke, eds. New York: Random House, 1992. 193–98.

"Mix-Master to the Beatles." *Time* 16 June 1967: 67.

Montgomery, Paul L. "Teen-Age Siege of Delmonico's, Beatles' Fortress, Ends 2d Day." *New York Times* 30 August 1964, late ed.: 95.

—————. "The Beatles Bring Shea to a Wild Pitch of Hysteria." *New York Times* 24 August 1966, late ed.: 40.

Moore, Allan F. *The Beatles: Sgt. Pepper's Lonely Hearts Club Band*. New York: Cambridge University Press, 1997.

Morphet, Richard. "Richard Hamilton: The Longer View." *Richard Hamilton*. London: Tate Gallery Publications, 1992: 11–26.

National Record News: Special Beatles Issue. New York: Capitol Records publicity department, December 1963.

Neaverson, Bob. *The Beatles Movies*. London: Cassell, 1997.

Negus, Keith. "Popular Music: Between Celebration and Despair." In *Questioning the Media*, 2nd ed. John Downing and Annabelle Sreberny-Mohammadi, eds. London: Sage, 379–92.

"The New Madness." *Time* 15 November 1963: 64.

Norman, Philip. *Shout!: The Beatles in Their Generation*. New York: Fireside, 1981.

————. *The Stones*. 1984. London: Penguin Books Ltd., 1993.

"Ohio Girls Rush Beatles and Police Interrupt Show." *New York Times* 16 September 1964, late ed.: 36.

"100,000 Welcome Beatles Home." *London Times* 11 July 1964, final ed.: 8.

O'Neill, William L. *Coming Apart: An Informal History of America in the 1960s*. Chicago: Quadrangle Books, 1971.

Osmundsen, John. "4 Beatles and How They Grew: Peoplewise." *New York Times* 17 February 1964, late ed.: 1+.

O'Sullivan, Tim, John Hartley, Danny Saunders, Martin Montgomery, and John Fiske. *Key Concepts in Communication and Cultural Studies*. 2nd ed. London: Routledge, 1994.

"Other Noises, Other Notes." *Time* 3 March 1967: 63.

Paik, Nam June. *Video Commune: Beatles from Beginning to End—A Television Experiment*. Originally broadcast August 8, 1970. WGBH. Museum of Television and Radio, New York. Video holdings accessed June 22, 2004.

Passman, Arnold. *The Deejays*. New York: Macmillan, 1971.

Patterson, James T. *Grand Expectations: The United States, 1945–1974*, vol. 10 of *The Oxford History of the United States*. C. Vann Woodward, ed. New York: Oxford University Press, 1996.

"Paul McCartney Predicts Breakup of Beatles Soon." *New York Times* 23 January 1967, late ed.: 29.

The Paul McCartney World Tour Book. London: Emap Metro, 1989.

Phillips, McCandlish. "4 Beatles and How They Grew: Publicitywise." *New York Times* 17 February 1964, late ed.: 1+.

————. "Concentration of Squealing Teen-Agers Noted at Hotel." *New York Times* 29 August 1964, late ed.: 9.

Phillips, Tom. "Beatles' 'Sgt. Pepper': The Album as Art Form." Review of the sound recording *Sgt. Pepper's Lonely Hearts Club Band*, by the Beatles. *Village Voice* 22 June 1967: 15.

Poirier, Richard. "Learning from the Beatles." 1967. In *The Beatles Reader*, Collector's Edition. Charles P. Neises, ed. Ann Arbor: Popular Culture, Ink., 1991. 107–28.

"Police Halt Beatles' Show to Avoid Riot in Australia." *New York Times* 13 June 1964, late ed.: 14.

"Police Hide Beatles from 2,500 Fans." *Plain Dealer* 15 September 1964: 1.

Pollack, Lynn. Letter. *New York Times* 15 March 1964, late ed., sec. 6: 12.

"Pope Warns Youth on Wild Outbursts over Entertainment." *New York Times* 5 July 1965, late ed.: 2.

Porterfield, Christopher, and Jesse Birnbaum. "The Messengers." *Time* 22 September 1967: 60+.

"Preacher of Peace: Maharishi Mahesh Yogi." *New York Times* 22 January 1968, late ed.: 24.

"Presley Receives a City Polio Shot." *New York Times* 29 October 1956, late ed.: 33.

Rabinowitz, Dorothy. "John Lennon's Mourners." *Commentary* February 1981: 58–61.

"Random Notes From All Over: Golden Beatles." *New York Times* 2 March 1964, late ed.: 11.

Reusch, Mrs. Victor M. Letter. *New York Times* 5 April 1964, late ed., sec. 6: 10.

"Revolution: The Dear John Letters." *Rolling Stone* 3 May 1969: 22.

"The Rock is Solid." *Time* 4 November 1957: 48, 50.

"Rolf Hochhuth." Internet Broadway Database. 2004. League of American Theatres and Producers, Inc., New York. 22 December 2004. http://www.ibdb.com.

Rorem, Ned. "The Music of the Beatles." *The New York Review of Books* 18 January 1968: 23–27.

Saal, Hubert. "Double Beatle." Review of the sound recording *The Beatles*, by the Beatles. *Newsweek* 9 December 1968: 109.

Scheurer, Timothy E. "The Beatles, the Brill Building, and the Persistence of Tin Pan Alley in the Age of Rock." *Popular Music and Society* vol. 20 no. 4 (1996): 89–102.

Schmidt, Dana Adams. "John, Paul, Ringo and George, M.B.E." *New York Times* 27 October 1965, late ed.: 49.

Schumach, Murray. "Teen-Agers (Mostly Female) and Police Greet Beatles." *New York Times* 14 August 1965, late ed.: 11.

———. "Shrieks of 55,000 Accompany Beatles." *New York Times* 16 August 1965, late ed.: 29+.

"Script." *The Beatles in A Hard Day's Night: The Complete Uncut Movie.* CD-ROM. Irvington, NY: Voyager, 1993.

"Sgt. Pepper." Review of the sound recording *Sgt. Pepper's Lonely Hearts Club Band*, by the Beatles. *New Yorker* 24 June 1967: 22–23.

Shabecoff, Philip. "Beatles Winning in East Germany." *New York Times* 17 April 1966, late ed.: 64.

Sharnik, John. "The War of the Generations." *House and Garden* October 1956: 40–41.

Shaw, Greg. "The Teen Idols." In *The Rolling Stone Illustrated History of Rock and Roll* (updated and revised). Anthony DeCurtis and James Henke, eds. New York: Random House, 1992. 107–12.

Sheff, David. *The Complete Playboy Interviews with John Lennon and Yoko Ono.* G. Barry Golson, ed. New York: Putnam, 1981.

Shepard, Richard F. "Stokowski Talks Something Called Beatles." *New York Times* 15 February 1964, late ed.: 13.

Shepherd, Jean. "Playboy Interview: The Beatles." *Playboy* February 1965: 51–52+.

Sitney, P. Adams. *Visionary Film: The American Avant-Garde, 1943–2000.* 3rd ed. Oxford: Oxford University Press, 2002.

Sloane, Leonard. "Advertising: Yellow Submarine Art Is the Thing Today." *New York Times* 24 August 1969, late ed., sec. 3: 15.

"Spector of the Beatles." Review of the sound recording *Let It Be*, by the Beatles. *Time* 18 May 1970: 64.

"Spellman in Plea to Save U.S. Youth." *New York Times* 1 October 1956: 22.

Spitz, Bob. *The Beatles: The Biography.* New York: Little Brown, 2005.

Spizer, Bruce. *The Beatles' Story on Capitol Records: Part One, The Singles.* New Orleans: 498 Productions, 2000.

———. *The Beatles' Story on Capitol Records: Part Two, The Albums.* New Orleans: 498 Productions, 2000.

Stein, Harry. "Oh, Grow Up!" *Esquire* April 1981: 16–18.

Stephenson, Ralf. *The Animated Film.* London: The Tantivy Press, 1973.

"Stock in Beatles Songs is Cheaper in London." *New York Times* 11 August 1966, late ed.: 35.

Storey, John. *An Introductory Guide to Cultural Theory and Popular Culture.* Athens: The University Press of Georgia, 1993.

Strongin, Theodore. "Musicologically . . ." *New York Times* 10 February 1964, late ed.: 53.

Sullivan, Leo. "Director of 'Help!' Sets Beatles Ablaze." *Washington Post* 13 August 1965: D11.

Sullivan, Mark. "More Popular than Jesus: The Beatles and the Religious Far Right." *Popular Music* 6 (1987): 313–27.

Talese, Gay. "Beatles and Fans Meet Social Set." *New York Times* 21 September 1964, late ed.: 44.

——. *The Kingdom and the Power*. New York: New American Library, 1966.

Taylor, A. J. W. "Beatlemania—The Adulation and Exuberance of Some Adolescents." 1966. In *Sociology and Everyday Life*. Marcello Truzzi, ed. Englewood Cliffs, NJ: Prentice-Hall, 1968. 161–70.

Taylor, Derek. *It Was Twenty Years Ago Today*. New York: Fireside, 1987.

"Theology: Toward a Hidden God." *Time* 8 April 1966: 82–87.

Thomson, Elizabeth, and David Gutman, eds. *The Lennon Companion: Twenty-Five Years of Comment*. New York: Schirmer Books, 1987.

Thompson, Howard. "Film: Beatles Together." *New York Times* 29 May 1970, late ed.: 11.

Thompson, Thomas. "The New Far-Out Beatles." *Life* 16 June 1967: 100–2+.

Tiegel, Eliot. "British Beatles Hottest Capitol Singles Ever." *Billboard* 18 January 1964: 1+.

Trumbull, Robert. "Tokyo Is Girding for the Beatles." *New York Times* 22 May 1966, late ed.: 12.

Trynka, Paul, editor. *The Beatles: Ten Years That Shook the World*. New York: Dorling Kindersley, 2004.

"12-Medal Man Reacts Sharply to the Beatles." *New York Times* 17 June 1965, late ed.: 3.

"Two British Heroes Protest Award of Honors to Beatles." *New York Times* 16 June 1965, late ed.: 13.

"250,000 Australians Jam Beatles' Route." *New York Times* 15 June 1964, late ed.: 35.

"2 U.S. Students Held in Spain." *New York Times* 6 July 1965, late ed.: 5.

"The Unbarbershopped Quartet." *Time* 21 February 1964: 46–47.

UNICEF. "The History." Accessed August 26, 2005. http://www.unicefusa. org/site/apps/s/content.asp?c=duLRI8OoH&b=27736&ct=127304.

"United Artists Sets Profit Mark." *New York Times* 2 December 1965, late ed.: 65.

"U.S. and British Taxes Vie to Shear Beatles." *New York Times* 3 January 1965, late ed.: 84.

"Usual Sound and Fury Confront The Beatles at London Airport." *New York Times* 23 February 1964, late ed.: 87.

Vaizey, Marina. *Peter Blake*. Chicago: Academy Chicago Publishers, 1986.

"Vatican Accepts Lennon's Apology." *New York Times* 14 August 1966, late ed.: 13.

Wachtel, Paul L. *The Poverty of Affluence: A Psychological Portrait of the American Way of Life.* Philadelphia: New Society Publishers, 1989.

Ward, Ed. Review of the sound recording *Abbey Road*, by the Beatles. *Rolling Stone* 15 November 1969: 32–33.

Watts, Stephen. "The Beatles' 'Hard Day's Night.'" *New York Times* 26 April 1964, late ed., sec. 2: 13.

———. "'Knack' for Talent." *New York Times* 29 November 1964, late ed., sec. 2: 1+.

Weiss, Richard. *The American Myth of Success: From Horatio Alger to Norman Vincent Peale.* 1969. Chicago: University of Illinois Press, 1988.

Wenner, Jann. Review of *The Beatles: The Authorized Biography*, by Hunter Davies. *Rolling Stone* 26 October 1968, 17–18.

———. "The Beatles." Review of the sound recording *The Beatles*, by the Beatles. *Rolling Stone* 21 December 1968: 10–13.

———. *Lennon Remembers.* 1973. New York: Fawcett Popular Library/ Rolling Stone Press, 1981.

———. "Musicians Reject New Political Exploiters." *Rolling Stone* 11 May 1968: 1+.

———. "Rock and Roll Music." *Rolling Stone* 14 December 1967: 16.

———. "The Rolling Stone Interview: John Lennon, Part One. The Working Class Hero." *Rolling Stone* 7 January 1971: 32+.

———. "The Rolling Stone Interview: John Lennon, Part Two. Life with the Lions." *Rolling Stone* 4 February 1971: 36+.

———. "Rolling Stones Comeback: Beggar's Banquet." *Rolling Stone* 10 August 1968: 1+.

Wenner, Sandra. "Rolling Stone." In *American Mass Market Magazines.* Alan Nourie and Barbara Nourie, eds. New York: Greenwood Press, 1990. 442–44.

Westcott, Jimmy. "An Overdue Confession." *Seventeen* September 1966: 14.

Whalen, Jack, and Richard Flacks. *Beyond the Barricades: The Sixties Generation Grows Up.* Philadelphia: Temple University Press, 1989.

"What He Meant Was . . ." Editorial. *New York Times* 16 Aug 1966, late ed.: 38.

"What the Beatles Have Done to Hair." *Look* 29 December 1964: 58–59.

Whitburn, Joel. *Billboard Book of Top 40 Albums.* 3rd ed. New York: Billboard Books, 1995.

———. *Joel Whitburn's Billboard Top 10 Charts.* Menomonee Falls, WI: Record Research Inc., 1998.

————. *Joel Whitburn's Top Pop Singles, 1955–1996*. 8th edition. Menomonee Falls, WI: Record Research Inc., 1997.

Wiener, Jon. *Come Together: John Lennon in His Time*. 1984. Chicago: University of Illinois Press, 1991.

————. *Gimme Some Truth: The John Lennon FBI Files*. Berkeley: University of California Press, 1999.

Wolfe, Tom. *The Kandy-Colored Tangerine-Flake Streamline Baby*. New York: Farrar, Straus and Giroux, 1965.

Wuthnow, Robert. "Old Fissures and New Fractures in American Religious Life." In *Religion and American Culture: A Reader*. David G. Hackett, ed. New York: Routledge, 1995. 369–82.

"Yeah, Yeah, Yeah." *Newsweek* 17 February 1964: 88.

Yorke, Ritchie. "A Private Talk with John." *Rolling Stone* 7 February 1970: 22–23.

Yule, Andrew. *Richard Lester and the Beatles*. New York: Primus Paperback, 1995.

Zeitlin, Kim. Letter. *New York Times* 19 April 1964, late ed., sec. 6: 46, 48.

INDEX

Abbey Road (album), 213–14; reviews of, 214

"Act Naturally," 117

Adorno, Theodor: and culture industries, 9, 28, 234, 238n5; and *Dialectic of Enlightenment*, 9; on popular music, 9–10; referenced in *New York Times* regarding Beatles, 35–36

Allison, Jerry, 239n6

"All I've Got to Do," 53

"All My Loving," 31, 53, 232

"All You Need Is Love" (broadcast), 148, 229

"All You Need Is Love"/"Baby, You're a Rich Man," 139

Alpert, Richard, 245n24

America, postwar culture: and baby boomers, 9; and consumerism, 9, 10; and 1960s, 12–13; and religion, 14–15, 101–5; and teenage threat, 46–47

American Bandstand, and reaction to "new look" Beatles, 134

American myth of success, definition of, 7, 58–59, 228

American Myth of Success, The, 58

American Tour with Ed Rudy, The, 57–58

Anderson, Lindsey, 73–74

"And I Love Her," 81

"And I Love Her"/"If I Fell," 78

"And Your Bird Can Sing," 117, 118

Anger, Kenneth: and *Fireworks* (1947), 164, 165; and trance films, 247n11

"angry young men," 242n1

"Anna (Go to Him)," 55

Apple Corps, 166–67; as oppositional apparatus, 166–69

Arnold, Martin, 64

articulation: Grossberg on, 6; Negus on, 6

art school, and British pop stars, 136–37, 243n8, 246n5

"Ask Me Why," 55

"Aunt Jessie's Dream," 164–65

avant-garde, defined, 167–69, 247n14, 247n15

"Baby It's You," 55

"Baby's in Black," 113, 114

"Bad Boy," 114

Barnes, Clive, 239n5